THE MODERN HISTORY OF CEYLON

The Praeger Asia-Africa Series

THE PRAEGER ASIA-AFRICA SERIES
Editor : Bernard Lewis

Other volumes in the series :

THE MODERN HISTORY OF JAPAN
W. G. Beasley

A MODERN HISTORY OF THE SUDAN
P. M. Holt

A MODERN HISTORY OF SOVIET GEORGIA
D. M. Lang

THE MODERN HISTORY OF SOMALILAND
I. M. Lewis

THE MODERN HISTORY OF CEYLON
E. F. C. Ludowyk

THE MODERN HISTORY OF LEBANON
K. S. Salibi

THE MODERN HISTORY OF SOVIET CENTRAL ASIA
Geoffrey Wheeler

THE MODERN HISTORY
OF
CEYLON

E. F. C. LUDOWYK

FREDERICK A. PRAEGER, *Publishers*

NEW YORK · WASHINGTON

BOOKS THAT MATTER
Published in the United States of America in 1966
by Frederick A. Praeger, Inc., Publishers
111 Fourth Avenue, New York, N.Y. 10003

Library of Congress Catalog Card Number: 66-18910

Printed in Great Britain

CONTENTS

20,680

CONTENTS

ILLLUSTRATIONS

(between pages 148 and 149)

ACKNOWLEDGEMENTS

Ina Bandy: Plates 1, 3, 5; D. C. L. Amarasinghe: Plate 2; *The Times of Ceylon*: Plates 4, 8, 10, 25, 26, 27, 28, 29; William Daniell, R. A.: Plate 6; Ceylon Tea Centre: Plates 7, 12, 13, 16, 17, 18, 20; *Daily Graphic*: Plate 11; Edith Ludowyk: Plates 19, 21, 22, 23, 30; Ananda Coomaraswamy: Plate 24; Lionel Wendt: Plate 31.

PREFACE

In his study of monetary experience in Ceylon between the years 1825 and 1957, Professor Gunasekera made the comment that 'the period from the rise of coffee to the present day possesses an essential unity in that the basic economic structure remains unchanged'. I have ventured to use his image, and to extend it, as a clue to the history of Ceylon since 1796, when the British occupation of the Maritime Provinces previously held by the Dutch brought the whole country much more definitely than ever before into that process of political, economic and social interrelationships which is the subject matter of modern history.

I am aware of the danger of attempting to overload the vehicle of an image. What I have tried to do with it is only to transport the reader easily over a period of history which may otherwise seem needlessly complicated. I have not intended to supply a neat teleological device which fits everything into its ordered place, for the history of no country can be contained in any simplified formula.

My obligations to the work of many scholars who have helped me are considerable. I should like to acknowledge first of all the interest and helpful criticism provided me by Professor Bernard Lewis, the General Editor of this series, whose careful reading of my manuscript together with numerous suggestions made a difference to this book.

Like all others who have worked on this subject I owe a great deal to the pioneer studies of Dr Garrett Mendis. I owe a great deal, too, to the more recent work of younger colleagues in the University of Ceylon. I wish to acknowledge in particular the kindness of K. M. de Silva, H. A. de S. Gunasekera, S. Rajaratnam, I. H. Vanden Driesen and A. J. Wilson for allowing me to quote from their work. I am indebted to many others for their work into the history of Ceylon – to Yasmin Gunaratne, B. Hewavi-tarne, Kumari Jayawardena, V. Kanapathy and U. C. Wickre-meratne whose studies I have quoted from. I wish to acknowledge the kindness of H. E. Newnham, C.M.G., who placed at my disposal valuable information relating to the Ceylon Civil Service and the British colonial administration. I owe a similar debt to Professor W. T. Stace for his communications on the riots in Ceylon and the Governorship of Sir John Anderson. I am grateful to H. A. J. Hulugalle for permission to quote from *The Life and Times of D. R. Wijewardene* and *British Governors of Ceylon;* to Leonard Woolf for permission to quote from *Growing*. I am specially grateful to H. A. I. Goonetilleke of the University of Ceylon and S. Weeraperuma, Assistant at the National Central Library, for checking many references and providing me with help in tracing them.

I owe a very special debt of gratitude to Vere de Mel and to Bernard Soysa, who gave me the benefit of their special knowledge and followed every stage of my work with interest and criticism. I regret that ill-health prevented the latter from reading the last chapter of the book. They are not of course responsible for the conclusions I drew from the material they placed at my disposal.

For illustrations to the book I am indebted to the following whose readiness to meet my demands I gratefully acknowledge: Lionel Amarasinghe, Madame Ina Bandy, The Ceylon Tea Centre, Mrs Ananda Coomaraswamy for the photograph of her late husband, Dr Paul Feldman, Harold Peiris, Tori de Souza and *The Times of Ceylon*, and lastly my wife.

June 1965.

LIST OF ABBREVIATIONS

AR	Administration Report.
CO	Colonial Office Archives in the Public Record Office. CO 54 contains dispatches from the Governors of Ceylon.
CHJ	*Ceylon Historical Journal.*
CJHSS	*Ceylon Journal of Historical and Social Studies.*
DLCC	Debates in the Legislative Council of Ceylon.
DSCC	Debates in the State Council of Ceylon.
HRD	House of Representatives – Debates.
PPHC	Parliamentary Papers, House of Commons.
SP	Sessional Paper.
UCR	*University of Ceylon Review.*

CHAPTER 1

A FAVOURED AREA

On 19 February 1815, Robert Brownrigg, the Governor of the
Crown Colony of His Britannic Majesty's possessions in Ceylon,
realized an ambition cherished by himself ever since he had taken
up his governorship. He was able to announce that the king of
Kandy (the mountainous region of the central highlands) had
been captured by British forces advancing into his territories.
Brownrigg had been expressly warned by the Secretary of State,
Bathurst, who was repeating the wishes of the Prince Regent
himself, against any operations against the king of Kandy,[1] but he
had decided to disobey these instructions.

The scene at the dinner table when the news was announced has
been described by Marshall, who was sitting beside Brownrigg:

> The report of the capture of the king reached General Brownrigg
> on the 19th [of February], while he was at dinner with a small party of
> officers. The intelligence being highly gratifying, and in many respects
> of the utmost importance, his Excellency became greatly affected. He
> stood up at table, and, while the tears rolled down his cheeks, shook
> hands with everyone present, and thanked them for their exertions in
> furtherance of an object which seemed to be nearly accomplished, and
> which had been vainly attempted for nearly three centuries by three
> European powers in succession – the conquest of the kingdom of
> Kandy.[2]

Brownrigg's emotion was understandable. More than three
European powers in the past three centuries had cast envious eyes
on the favoured area of Ceylon. And long before their time Indian
and Asian peoples had been drawn to it by legends of its wealth in
gems, its fertile plains and its position in the Indian Ocean. Its
ancient Sanskrit name was Lanka, with the epithet *Sri* preceding
it, to suggest everything which was happy and blessed. It was the

terra felix of Indian waters; in Arab story it lay next to the Paradise Adam vacated. The island had now come completely under British control. More than 'success beyond his wildest expectations'[3] which attended Brownrigg's disobedience went into his flood of tears.

He had nothing to fear except the uncertainty of chance which attends all human calculations. He had protected himself from the displeasure of his superiors by proceeding strictly according to the letter of Bathurst's dispatches: he was not to make war on the king of Kandy, but he was allowed to defend the British possessions, in case they were attacked. He had the help, advice and personal support of the king's late First *Adigar* (minister and general) who had given up his allegiance to his late lord and master; he had the assurance that the general on the opposing side, Molligoda, would not engage in any combat with the British forces; he had great superiority in men and equipment – against the Kandyan forces he had trained veterans from the Peninsular War. Finally he had the trump card of an excellent *casus belli* –his forces had moved only when British territory was 'invaded' by the Kandyans. Of course there was the fear of treachery on the part of the Sinhalese, the reason often enough adduced for the ill-success of campaigns against them. But having left the smallest margin to chance or error Brownrigg could reasonably expect to succeed where his predecessors – Portuguese, Dutch and British – had failed.

In actual fact the success of his arms in this Second Kandyan War in which hardly any fighting took place, had been guaranteed by three hundred years of history. Brownrigg could scarcely be certain of this; nor, had he pondered on its possibility, could he have reckoned it of great weight in the scale of military considerations. None the less the Kandyan kingdom against which his troops marched out of Colombo on 9 December 1814 was ripe for shaking. It was the last of the fruit on the tree of the much older realm which, forced into decay by pressures from the warring kingdoms of South India, had contrived to keep this branch intact only because of its geographical isolation from regions already in the power of first the Portuguese and then the Dutch.

But the very isolation of the Kandyan kingdom, nearly three hundred and fifty years old in 1815, was a danger too. As a Dutch

Governor of Ceylon put it, it was 'netted like a fish' in an area hemmed in by Western European naval powers. Gradually the net would close and the fish would lie gasping on the bank. The Second Kandyan War was an incident in the process in which king and country moved to the inescapable end which had been determined by three hundred years of foreign rule in the Maritime Provinces and the internal dissensions of a feudal court. Marshall, who recalled the scene at Brownrigg's dinner table that afternoon, correctly estimated its significance when he quoted a later Englishman, Knighton, writing on it: 'from this day we may date the extinction of Ceylonese independence, an independence which had continued without any material interruption for 2,357 years'.

The independent kingdom of Ceylon had, according to the tradition of its chronicles, been 'established' on the very day on which the Buddha finally passed away from this earth and attained Nirvana. This date – 483 BC – on which Vijaya, a refugee Aryan prince from Central India, is supposed to have landed in Ceylon, would give the kingdom he set up on the North Central plain of the island over two millennia of existence before its last fragments were broken up.

As little is known of pre-Vijayan Ceylon as is known of the land Vijaya's followers colonized. To both the Indian and the Ceylonese of average education Lanka (the Sanskritic name of the island) was the kingdom ruled over by the demon king Ravana, whose rape of Sita from her husband Rama led to a war which resembled that fought over Helen by Greeks and Trojans. If its events had been historical the description of Ceylon by the monkey god Hanuman, sent by Rama to reconnoitre Ravana's kingdom, would have been an extremely valuable record of the island, possessing more than canonical authority as its compiler was a god.

But the Lanka of the *Ramayana* may not have been Ceylon at all, though the name is certainly one of those by which the island was known. There were others too: Tambapanni; Taprobane of the Greeks; Sarandib of the Arabs; Ceylon of the Europeans – all of them evidence of the familiarity of voyagers from all over the world with the island. As for the demons and devils supposed to have been its ancient inhabitants, they were transfigured in later Buddhist legends, some of them surviving even now as recipients of propitiatory rites. They may still be believed in, but much

3

rather as uncomfortable presences in the world of today than as the oldest inhabitants of Ceylon.

Who originally lived in and possessed Ceylon should be of little consequence now. Surely the Sinhalese and the Tamils, who have been in the island for two millennia and more, can afford to disregard any claims against them for wrongful possession. Even those who followed them to the island in comparatively recent times should not have to trouble themselves with questions of archaeology and anthropology. What seems to matter most to both Sinhalese and Tamils, the largest groups in the island, is the legendary cluster of stories which could validate the claims of either to having been first on the spot, whether as conquerors or immigrants. Some Sinhalese affect to regard the Tamils as interlopers from the Indian mainland, whereas in truth if the Sinhalese were, as is most probable, first on the island, they were just as much immigrants there as the Tamils were. For the Sinhalese the legend provides the story of a tribe miraculously descended from the union of a lion and a princess. Their son not only killed the primal father, but espoused his sister. Their children were the Sinhalese: the people of the lion race, who, banished for their misconduct from the Indian mainland, fared over the seas and set up a kingdom in Ceylon. Buddhist legend gave this migration of a totemistic tribe a special significance, and endowed it with the qualities of divine election.

The Sinhalese, according to their legendary history, are therefore as much a chosen people as the Jews, the Japanese, the English, and all other self-conscious groups who have read history with an eye to their significant role in it. In the Sinhalese legend, when the Buddha lay dying in the grove of the twin *sal* trees, he foresaw that the Sinhalese prince, Vijaya, would arrive in Ceylon. He therefore entrusted the people and the island they were to inhabit to the special protection of Sakka, king of the gods, for there the religion of the Buddha would be established and flourish. On the day on which the exiled prince landed on the shores of Ceylon, the Buddha attained his *Mahaparinibbana* – his final and utter passing away.

The Tamils, who must have followed hard on the heels of the Sinhalese in their incursions into Ceylon, have their own legendary stories of their arrival in the north of the island. They

4

pushed back the Sinhalese from positions the latter had held for some time. According to the Pali chronicle, the *Mahavamsa*, Tamil chieftains or kings ruled over the northern kingdom in ancient times. The chronicle glorifies the exploits of the Sinhalese national hero and patriot who liberated the old Sinhalese kingdom from the Tamil yoke. On the side of the Sinhalese warrior king, Dutu Gemunu, were ten champions each possessed of super-human strength, the story of whose prowess forms one chapter of the chronicle. Each of these paladins was as strong as ten elephants. It is scarcely to be wondered at that Dutu Gemunu had to triumph. He slew his Tamil rival, Elara, but paid him in death all the honours due to a soldier and a king. The spot on which the Tamil king was cremated was to be venerated for all time: no music was to be played there and all persons, even kings, had to pass by on foot.

The broad pattern of the history of the ancient Sinhalese kingdom resembles that of various Indian kingdoms which once flourished and then declined. The first capital of the ancient kingdom was Anuradhapura in the north-central plain. In the south were chieftains who either owed allegiance to the king at Anuradhapura, or in periods of unrest could have ignored his authority. It was southwards that the Anuradhapura king had to flee if South Indian pressure on his kingdom proved too strong for him. Though this in its essentials seems to repeat the confused story of the rise and fall of South Indian kingdoms, yet it differs in one specific particular from it. Ceylon was an island, the religion of which was not the Hinduism which gradually absorbed Buddhism once pre-eminent in the north and centre of India, but a development of the Buddha's teaching which survived more or less intact as an integrated institutionalized religion. This difference from the South Indian kingdoms must always be borne in mind.

Politically, economically and socially, there was little to distinguish the history of the Sinhalese kingdom from that of the South Indian kingdoms. As a record it seems to the layman tortuous and as unrewardingly insusceptible to understanding except as a story of dynastic power politics, the clues of which might be available to the research worker alone. It is not an absence of material which disheartens the common reader, but the magnitude of work yet to be done on these materials, sorting them out, making them accessible, and giving them some shape which could be readily comprehensible. One loses one's direction in a luxuriant jungle of king warring against king; being assassinated by a rival claimant to the throne; the decline of the power of one ruler and the emergence of that of another; of feuds between clans – all of which leave an impression of a see-saw between benevolent despotism and anarchy. In addition, between the rival Buddhist sects of the Mahayanists and the ultimately victorious Hinayanists of the *Mahavihara* (or great monastery at Anuradhapura), a bitter struggle was waged involving kings and counsellors, and adding another complication to a period of strife. The history of Ceylon, as it is recorded in the Pali chronicle of the *Mahavamsa*, was intended, as the concluding verse of each chapter indicates, for the serene joy and contemplation of the pious. That serene joy should have been provided by the contemplation of struggles such as these seems at first sight paradoxical, yet what a prophylactic it must have been, stressing through the illusion and suffering which made up the story of human life the necessity of removing oneself from involvement in it.

Throughout this long period of history the island of Ceylon was often united under a king who could subdue its various petty chieftains; more often than not it found itself drawn into the wars of the South Indian kingdoms, either in self-defence, or in alliance with one or other of these warring princes. Or some disaffected prince or noble from Ceylon crossed into the mainland in the hope of recruiting support there for his dynastic claims. The balance of forces on the Indian mainland often influenced the turn of events in Ceylon, yet – it has to be repeated – the Sinhalese and their culture, strongly influenced though they may have been by the Indian, were things apart from it. Ceylon's connection with India always tended to express itself in ambivalent terms. Its culture was an Indian culture, yet it resisted 'Indianization' with a vehemence which makes one think of Ceylon in the first millennium of its recorded history as typically a Sinhalese national state. Though it owed to India practically everything which distinguished it as a cultural entity, yet it had a specifically Sinhalese character which was distinct from the Indian. In almost every single branch of human activity it was derivative from the Indian, but yet it was not Indian, but something else, and some-

6

thing else which was conscious of itself as Sinhalese. Its very stock was of Indian origin. Geologically it was an extension of the Indian mainland. Its religion, its social structure, its political institutions, its language, its agricultural economy all came from India. Its connections with India were never repudiated, yet the Sinhalese was something other than the Indian, and this otherness was often categorically asserted as being the intrinsic quality of Sinhalese culture.

In the attitude of the Sinhalese to the Indian culture from which he derives may perhaps be seen the ambivalence associated with the relationship of son to father. The strong ties which bind the two peoples are too easily overlooked in the hostility with which the separateness and the right of Ceylon to develop in its own way are asserted. It may be, too, that the small size of the island, and the unconscious fear of being overwhelmed by an enormous and powerful parent turned this assertiveness into a necessary defence mechanism. In the course of the history of Ceylon salvation has always come from India: the Buddha, Mahinda (who is credited with having brought Buddhism to Ceylon), Buddhaghosa (the fifth century AD Pali commentator), and everything suggested by the names of these three figures in religion and culture, were Indian. Likewise throughout the history of these times the foe too came from India and had to be resisted. The pattern is repeated in our own times. Ceylon's independence of British political suzerainty was the by-product of the struggle waged against the British by the Indian in India. Still today the greatest fear that stalks the mind of the nationalist Sinhalese is of the Indian – the disfranchised Indian labourer on the plantations; the wealthy Indian trader; the millions of Indians in South India not far away.

The old Sinhalese kingdom established itself because of the successful solution of the problem of irrigating the northern plain of Ceylon. The kingdoms the Sinhalese built up were feudal structures, based on village communities producing sufficient for their needs. At the head of the social hierarchy was the cultivator of land which he held in return for services owed to his overlord. The kingdom failed because internecine warfare, the attacks of South Indian invaders and the losses suffered by the bureaucracy

7

responsible for the maintenance of the irrigation system were disasters too heavy for the economy to bear. The ancient kingdom split up into a number of smaller units; was for a brief interval united once more; then fell away again at the time European naval powers entered Indian waters; in the hills the Kandyan kingdom continued the old in an attenuated form, until pressure from the commercial nations of Europe finished off the feudal economy and cleared the way for a new one.

Changes marked the course of these years, but they took place within a more or less fixed framework. This makes the great achievements of the Sinhalese culture, separated though they may be by hundreds of years, blossoms of the same branch. The three ancient capitals – Anuradhapura, Sigiriya and Polonnaruva – are moments in the single continuous process with the difference which a particular place made to the modification in Ceylon of the Indian tradition. Sigiriya flourished for a short interval of time during the zenith of Anuradhapura. Polonnaruva belongs to an age when Anuradhapura was declining and Sigiriya was obscured. It was the last capital of the Sinhalese kingdom of Lanka – the whole of the island of Ceylon. The kings of the smaller kingdoms which succeeded it, like those of Dambadeniya, Kotte or Kandy, were, with one notable exception, never kings of Lanka in the old sense.

When Marco Polo at the end of the thirteenth century touched at Ceylon on his voyage back from the court of the Great Khan to his native Venice, the capital of the Sinhalese kingdom was Yapahuva, still farther south than Polonnaruva. The island had been invaded by a king from Malaya who had been defeated, but his son remained to contest his father's rights. In addition, the Pandyan king from South India had taken a hand in the rivalries between the Sinhalese and Malayan claimants to the throne. Marco Polo refers to a Sendemain who was king of the island (or rather that part of it where his ships had called). This is likely to have been the Malayan Chandrabhanu.

In 1505 when the caravels of the Portuguese found their way into the port of Colombo, there was a king at Kotte, not five miles away from where their ships rode at anchor, who claimed the overlordship of all the Sinhalese; there were two military commanders or kings ruling over two areas in the western part of the island; there was a king of Kandy; the kingdom of Jaffna in the north was ruled by its own king.

Of the existence of political disunity in Ceylon at this time there is abundant evidence; its consequences could not differ markedly from those observed elsewhere by moralists and pedagogues who have reflected on kingdoms divided against themselves. The political decadence of those times has, not surprisingly, been attributed to the poor state of Buddhism in the country, for throughout the recorded history of the old kingdom the one had been identified with the other. It is true that the king and the *sangha* (the order of *bhikkhus* or Buddhist religious) were different, their spheres of authority were distinct, but the character of both state and religion depended upon a peculiar relationship between both, hard to define but quickly sensed in all the records of the past. The king was secular head of the state; he was also regarded as secular head of Buddhism which was protected by him, though he claimed no religious authority over the *sangha*. Its activities were ideally concerned with the religious life; *bhikkhus* never attempted to wield political authority themselves directly. Yet the *Sasana* (the religion) constituted a 'fully-fledged state department'.[4] This relationship was probably of much more interest to the chroniclers than the economy which maintained it, so that the decline of one of the two merely argued the lapse of the other.

It was unfortunate that at this particular moment of time in the ebb-tide of state and church (if this term could be used of the *sangha*), new and revolutionary forces should have affected both. They could perhaps have withstood further shocks of invasion by any South Indian kingdom whose star was temporarily in the ascendant. Such experiences belonged to the common stock of hundreds of years of history. Shaken though both may have been, they would have rallied, and though set back could have reconstituted their forces. The arrival of the Portuguese in Ceylon was a new order of events, from the consequences of which neither could recover. The monarchy was doomed. Within fifteen years the newcomers had extended their 'protection' to the king of Kotte.

The religion as an institution was affected too. It could not have been otherwise. More than independence of foreign rule would have been required to restore it to its ancient character. Successive generations of religious who continued to remember the past while it was receding further and further away, would have found this difficult to grant. Had they recalled their own view of the ancient identity of state and religion, it would have been seen how the subtlest change in the one could not have failed to alter the other too.

The *Culavamsa*, a continuation of the Pali ecclesiastical history of Ceylon, which related the happenings of the sixteenth century two centuries later, made no reference to the arrival of the Portuguese in the island. Its silence discloses how deeply lodged in the unconscious memory of the custodians of the past the traumatic experience had been. A Sinhalese chronicle, the *Rajavaliya*, added a legendary embellishment to the coming of the Portuguese. It told of a strange new race of white men who drank blood and ate stones, the noise of whose cannon was louder than thunder. This extravagance was compounded of hatred – the Portuguese were given all the attributes of devils – and of satisfactory rationalization of the inability of the people of the country to deal with the new arrivals. Though the Portuguese did not come as invaders but as emissaries of a foreign power anxious to conclude a treaty of friendship with the Sinhalese monarch, it was clear to the anonymous writer of the *Rajavaliya* that they were, by the time the poem was composed, the paramount power in the coastal regions and the loathed enemies. That is why they were described as devils, although white men had visited Ceylon long before, guns had been known to the Moors (as the Moslem traders in the Indian Ocean were called by the Portuguese), and both bread and wine were familiar to the Sinhalese. The poet was anxious to suggest that visitors like these could not be opposed.

The ships of the Portuguese were blown on to the island in 1505; their last stronghold on it, Jaffna, surrendered to the Dutch in 1658. In those years they lived up to the reputation conferred on them by the *Rajavaliya*. They fought and conquered, they destroyed (and were defeated) throughout the greater part of their sojourn in Ceylon. Had they fought less they could hardly have survived; they could scarcely have fought more than they did. The small noblemen (*fidalgos*) of the little Iberian kingdom, which was able to send an expedition to the East to outflank the might of Islam which cut off Mediterranean Europe from trade with it, could never have achieved what they did achieve had they not been intrepid and desperate fighters. Their 'empire' stretched from South America to the China Seas, and included territories in West and East Africa, the Persian Gulf, the west coast of India, Ceylon, Malaya and the East Indies. It was taken by force and held by force. The clerics who accompanied the forces and had their plans for a spiritual conquest of these regions, were much better organized and more farseeing than the soldiers whose excesses they deplored. But had the soldiers not waged warfare so determinedly, the clerics would never have had the opportunity to initiate the plans which could be developed by their successors who remained when the defeated soldiery withdrew.

It is true that the Portuguese controlled only a small part of the whole island; that it was some time after they first built their factory and church in Colombo that they began to interfere in the politics of the country. But their very presence as a maritime power which had destroyed their rivals in Asian waters; the fortified positions from which they gradually infiltrated deeper into the country; and the proselytizing fervour of their missionaries – the various orders allowed to proceed to Colombo because the king of Kotte could not prevent it – radically affected the already altered balance of relations between the Sinhalese state and church. As it did this, it marks the beginning of a new stage in the history of Ceylon. Even those parts of the island where they failed to set up their power were influenced by change which their presence in Ceylon accelerated.[5]

Though, like the other Europeans who succeeded them, they made no revolutionary change in the way the country was administered, there is evidence to show that the holding of land, taxation, the economy of the maritime regions they controlled, were manipulated by them in their own interests. Don Juan Dharmapala, the first Christian king of Kotte, was only the shadow of a king, and his kingdom was a satellite of the Portuguese. On his death he bequeathed the whole of Ceylon (though he had been recognized as ruler only of Kotte) to the king of Portugal – then Philip II of Spain and Portugal. Of course this bequest was only a meaningless flourish, since what he had power to give had long been in the hands of his legatees. The rest of the country they had already tried to take, and would try again, whether it was granted

to them by its rightful owner or not. But the cession of the kingdom was formally promulgated on the king's death by the Portuguese, and at a Convention allegedly held at Malvana the Sinhalese,
through their headmen and army commanders, were asked how
they wished to be governed. Naturally they replied: 'by the laws
of their king' (the Sinhalese king). This was a pleasant interlude,
and much could be made of it, but as the kingdom came to be
ruled, Portuguese and Sinhalese military commanders did exactly
as they chose, with a disregard for any law but that of their own
convenience.[6]

Yet the Portuguese, hated as they were – legends of their
barbarity still flourish in Ceylon – came closer to the people of
the country than either the Dutch or the British. This was not
because they had no consciousness of colour as their successors
had; far from it.[7] In spite of their assumption of superiority to the
native, their pride in birth and 'caste' could be understood by a
people who appreciated pride. Would it be too fantastic to suggest
that as they often had been in desperate straits in Ceylon they
reached a level of experience common to the masses of the country? Neither the Dutch nor the British were to come so near to the
common humanity of the native. The Portuguese attitude to life,
in its mixture of superstition and resignation, touched a responsive
chord in the Ceylonese. Their language became the *lingua franca* of
the East. It survived in Ceylon long after English had become the
speech of the educated Ceylonese.

Their priests, notably the religious they trained among the
native populations of India, came closest of all to the people of
Ceylon. The stories of the masses whom St Francis Xavier converted in Ceylon do not explain the extraordinary success of
Roman Catholicism in Ceylon. His example may have counted for
much, but it was the zeal and devotion of numerous humbler
priests, notably the Oratorians from India, which kept alive the
faith of thousands who were ready to suffer persecution for it
under the Dutch. Some who were converted to Christianity may
have found the transition easy from a decadent Buddhism overlaid
with the traditional rites of the old folk religion and more recent
Mahayana additions. But what these converts were committed to
when the Portuguese, whose state religion they had adopted, were
driven from Ceylon was not easy. Roman Catholicism remains a

great force in Ceylon today, as well worked into the texture of thought of its adherents as any religious system can be.

The Portuguese were not colonizers as the Dutch and the English intermittently tried to be, yet they succeeded in acclimatizing the most significant part of their culture in Ceylon. There was a fair-sized mixed population left by them in their settlements in Ceylon. Colombo in the early seventeenth century has been described as a Portuguese city with its numerous churches. Portuguese names – the honorific 'Dom' in particular – gratified the vanity both of those who embraced Christianity and those who did not. Queyroz remarked that 'all the Apuamis or gentlefolk, when they are baptized add the name Dom to their baptismal name and though they know that many Portuguese gentlemen do not use Dom, yet they do not give it up, not to lose that mark of prominence.'[8] Tavernier in the eighteenth century wrote of what he had been told of the success of the Jesuits in their Colleges around Colombo: 'they found that the youth of Ceylon were so quick and intelligent that they learnt, in six months, more Latin, philosophy and other sciences, than Europeans acquire in a year'.[9] In this way, too, the Portuguese were the pioneers of change.

Cinnamon which grew best in Ceylon (it was for long believed that it grew only there) kept the Portuguese in the island as long as they could maintain themselves there. It had been an article of export from Ceylon for two or three centuries previously, carried by Arab traders to Red Sea and Persian Gulf ports and thence to Europe. Its importance to the revenues of Portugal is underlined in the letter of Don Joao III: 'As regards Ceylon in particular, try to retain the friendship of the natives in order that the Faith may be spread, as well as on account of the cinnamon from which my custom-house receives great profits.'[10] Portuguese policy with regard to cinnamon, and to every other article of export, was to exploit them as much as possible and to exercise a monopoly over their shipment. But the royal treasury which should have benefited from such policies did not receive the profits due to it. The corruption of officials in the East, which plagued all European nations trading there, was a byword in Goa and Colombo. From the Viceroy down to the humblest tally clerk all were guilty. The growth of Dutch sea-power and the irrepressibility of the Moors as coastal traders added to the difficulties of the Portuguese in making their commercial policy effective.

Cinnamon, according to Baldaeus, was the Helen which drew the ships of the Dutch to the East. Their expeditions, however, were no fatal adventures. They did very well in pursuit of their Helen, and Amsterdam in the seventeenth century was the envy of the European world on account of its wealth, its counting houses, its buildings and its port. The Dutch controlled the Maritime Provinces of Ceylon from 1658, when they finally expelled the Portuguese from the island, till 1796, when they in turn had to give way to the British. Though cinnamon was the major export on which the wealth of the Company in Ceylon was based, the Dutch decided that it was not to be included in the Revenue and Expenditure Account of the island. It was in effect the 'tribute' levied by the authorities at home on their possessions in Ceylon, in much the same way as the Portuguese had levied tribute payable in cinnamon on the king of Kotte.

In order to balance their budget in Ceylon therefore the Dutch were committed to spending as little and making as much as they could outside the cinnamon trade. Self-sufficiency, particularly in the matter of food, and the development of other sources of revenue, were forced upon them. War – with the Kandyan king in particular – was to be eschewed as an expensive luxury. He had to be placated, because a great deal of the cinnamon exported was produced in the jungle of his territory.

Other sources of revenue had to be developed in Ceylon. The Dutch, in this way, began the systematic exploitation of their possessions in the country so as to ensure as much profit and as little expense to themselves. The most significant part of their work in Ceylon, from which the British were to learn a great deal, arose out of the very humdrum nature of this essential preoccupation of theirs with balancing their books. They devoted volumes of paper to it, most of them yet to be sifted. The detail with which their various ventures were discussed with Batavia and with Amsterdam shows the practical interest which drove them to try to make themselves independent of the Kandyan kingdom with regard to cinnamon and to develop other crops: coffee, sugar, coconuts, cotton, tobacco. Thoroughgoing as all these schemes seemed on paper, the Dutch were unable to break even in their management of Ceylon. They were forced to keep going too expensive a military force; it became impossible to deal with the corruption and inefficiency of officials in the Indies; in the eighteenth century their East India Company was getting more and more involved in financial difficulties; finally the growing strength of both England and France in Indian waters was too much for their weakened sea-power.

During their 138 years in Ceylon the Dutch organized their Maritime Provinces with some measure of success. They introduced their own system of law; they expanded the use the Portuguese had made of the native hierarchy, entrusting minor provincial administration to it and later assigning more important duties to these *Mudaliyars* – a class which gradually acquired more political influence and power and could be a minor irritation to the rulers unless they were wholeheartedly in support of the government.

In the comparative peace of those times there were signs of prosperity on a modest scale and of marked social change in the provinces they ruled. A German traveller to the court of the king of Kandy noted with satisfaction that 'among the Sinhalese who live in the territories of the Company, one sees finer and better houses than in his royal capital.'[11] The Moors, whom the Dutch had failed to eliminate as the main trading community in the island, were, like the class of minor officials, prospering economically and in possession of money. They formed an important element in pre-British Ceylon; they knew the country well and were ubiquitous. The Burghers – the small class of Dutch and half-caste officials of the company – knew how taxes were collected; what dues were traditionally owed by the Sinhalese to the company; how justice was organized; in fact how the country was run by the Dutch. They were an urban and Christian population whom attempts to turn into pioneers of land colonization had failed signally.

As the Dutch when they became the paramount power in Indian waters took over from the Portuguese, so the British displaced the Dutch. But what drew them to Ceylon was not the old Helen, but naval strategy. The British, emerging as the most powerful nation in India, had to maintain themselves against their French rivals and Indian princes. Effective control of the three major British possessions in India depended on sea-power and a harbour in the Bay of Bengal where ships could be repaired. Anglo-French rivalry in the Indian Ocean in the middle of the eighteenth century made Trincomalee a great prize. It has been shown that as long as the Dutch were not involved in European wars against the English, they had no objection to British ships using Trincomalee for refitting and repairs.[12] During the War of American Independence the French had, for a time, secured Trincomalee for themselves, but were forced to return it to the Dutch by the Treaty of Paris in 1784. In 1782 the Madras Government sent one of their civilians, Boyd, to the King of Kandy to negotiate the port for themselves. Boyd failed because the British had little to offer in return and the Kandyans wanted a more important official than himself to treat with.

But the lesson of the War of American Independence had been learnt by the British. In 1794, when troops of the French revolutionary government moved into Holland and the Stadtholder fled to England, the Madras Government acted quickly. An expeditionary force took Trincomalee, after a few days fighting necessitated by the Dutch commander's refusal to acquiesce in the Stadholder's instructions to the Dutch overseas to accept British garrisons in their possessions. In Colombo, to which the British addressed a similar demand, the Dutch could not make up their minds how to act. In the meantime the British expeditionary force was advancing along the western coast and another British emissary had been sent to the Kandyan court. The British were ready to sign a treaty with the king, by which in return for Trincomalee and his help in turning the Dutch out of territories which he claimed as his, they would assign him what he had long sought to secure for himself: a port in some favourable situation for his trade with South India. This treaty, largely on account of the excessive cautiousness of the Kandyan king, was never ratified. In the meantime Dutch dilatoriness and the loss of their mercenary regiment inveigled from them by the intrigue of Hugh Cleghorn, made smooth the British expeditionary force's road to Colombo, which capitulated in 1796 after a slight burst of fighting on its western approaches. The British were in possession of the Maritime Provinces of Ceylon without the necessity of having had to make any concessions to the king of Kandy.

16

The Dutch still hoped that diplomacy in any European settlement of the French war would give them back what their forces could not keep. But the British Company in Madras having obtained both Trincomalee and Colombo was determined not to part with them. It administered the Maritime Provinces for two years, until Parliament stepped in and placed their government under the Crown. Early in 1802 the possessions in Ceylon were made a Crown Colony. In the same year the Peace of Amiens finally made them over to the British.

As for the king of Kandy, he found himself in much the same position as his predecessor in 1638, who had signed a treaty with the Dutch by which they would help him to expel the Portuguese from Ceylon in return for which they would be the most favoured nation in Ceylon's trade with Europe. He was completely deluded by his allies who kept what they took with his aid from the Portuguese. His plight was described at the time by the Sinhalese proverb: *inguru dila miris gatta* (we gave ginger and got pepper in exchange). His successor found himself in the position of the man who, in another Sinhalese proverb, fell from a tree and was gored by a bull, for Rajadhirajasinha in 1796 got nothing for himself and now had the British on his hands. What he might have done will not be known, for he died soon after, childless. His successor, put on the throne by the First *Adigar*, Pilima Talauva, was a young man of nineteen who assumed the name of Sri Vikrama Rajasinha. It was his capture which moved Brownrigg to tears in 1815.

CHAPTER 2

THE AGENTS AND THE DEVELOPERS
1796-1805

In 1796 the British took over the Dutch Maritime Provinces in Ceylon almost peaceably. There had been some little fighting in Trincomalee, and as the British forces drew near Colombo there was a skirmish with some Dutch and Malay troops at Mutwal. But Pieris notes that, when the British encamped just outside the Fort of Colombo, 'no further opposition was offered, and the only excitement was caused by a couple of buffaloes straying within the British lines; for the alarm was given and the guards firing wildly had the misfortune to kill two of their own men'.[1] Dutch power in India, exhausted, passed away in sullen silence. The transition to British rule was like the passage of time which none could gainsay.

The Honourable East India Company in Madras had acted promptly as soon as the opportunity for action presented itself. Lord Hobart, the British Governor of Madras, threatened the Dutch with force 'because he was determined not to allow them to prolong negotiations until reinforcements could be sent to the Trincomalee garrison or the French took the initiative and seized the port themselves'.[2] The importance of Ceylon to the British in 1795 was, naturally, very much subservient to their stake in India.

In England, however, visions of empire were then regarded as uncomfortable nightmares. From the highest motives – briefly mentioned in the preamble to the 42nd Clause of the Act of 33 George III cap. 52 (1792): 'to pursue schemes of conquest and extension of dominion are measures repugnant to the wish, the honour and policy of this nation' – as well as on the prosaic ground of expense, adventurous acquisitions of territory were discouraged. Yet there were in Pitt's cabinet men like the dutiful

Henry Dundas, the Secretary for War and President of the Board of Control, who could have been described as alive to the importance of Ceylon to the Indian Empire. Associated with him, but not in the Cabinet, was another Scots lawyer, Sylvester Douglas, afterwards Lord Glenbervie. This official was in a key position. He was extremely able and owed his rapid rise in politics to his marriage with Lord North's eldest daughter. He was to become the most influential figure in all matters concerning Ceylon. As his brother-in-law Frederic North wrote to him from that island, where he was Governor, on 1 October 1801: 'Your exertions have changed the Face of everything here. From being a miserable Wretch in Chains, threatened with Prosecutions and disgusted with my Situation, I am become the most flourishing Governour in the World.'[3]

Once the Peace of Amiens finally made over the Dutch possessions in Ceylon to the British in 1802, Pitt could describe them in Parliament as 'the most valuable colonial possessions on the globe, giving to our Indian Empire a security it had not enjoyed from its first establishment'. These words recall Sylvester Douglas's comments on the dispatches sent to Dundas on 19 September 1800: 'nobody can entertain a rational doubt of the importance and value of Ceylon to this country and our E. India Company, or think that its possession would be too dearly paid for, if the whole expense of guarding and retaining it were to fall either upon the Treasury of the Company, or that of the Empire at large, without its being able to contribute anything from its own resources'.[4]

The demands of naval strategy had temporarily placed the Dutch possessions in Ceylon in the British company's hands. It did not really know what it had succeeded to; what the extent of the Dutch possessions was, or what rights were possessed by the king of Kandy. Sylvester Douglas, the filter through which communications from the Governor of Ceylon permeated to Dundas, observed that the Governor 'represented it as a fortunate misconception by the two parties of their respective interests, that the ratification of the Treaty of 1796, though solicited by us, had been deferred by the Candians, and that he was well assured, that nothing would more contribute to the continuance of amity with that court, than to allow the Treaty to expire in embryo . . .'[5]

As the British succeeded the Dutch in circumstances of temporary expediency, it was not to be expected that great differences were going to mark the way in which the Maritime Provinces were administered by the British Company until their ownership was finally settled by treaty. One difference, however, might have been foreseen – that between the military rule of people unacquainted with the country and the civil administration of those who had established their own system of government in it for more than a century. Military rule has rarely been marked by enlightenment. The military commander in Colombo and his aides and civilian helpers in the country were not oppressors by design; their rule was distinguished by that lack of understanding which is another characteristic of military governors. The British in 1796 were attempting to perform what they were unable to comprehend. Very wisely they decided to carry on the administration of the country as the Dutch had done, but they did not understand the Dutch method of farming taxes. The Dutch in Ceylon who did were enemies and held themselves aloof; the Mudaliyars who might have helped, were looked upon with suspicion by the Company's civilians and the army as a presumptuous set of persons whose powers were dangerous. The cost to the Company of the expedition against the Dutch and the maintenance of the army had to be paid for. Robert Andrews, the Superintendent of Revenue, introduced a new tax to be paid in silver by all owners of coconut trees. Not only was the tax unfair, it could not be met by the mass of people who had no specie at all. Futhermore Andrews, in order to weaken the power of the Mudaliyars, decided to abolish service tenures.

The results of one and a half years of this sort of attempt at 'making no difference to administration' can be guessed. There was chaos, and the masses, at first unconcerned as to who their rulers were, reacted with vehement opposition to the difference in the way they were treated by their new ones. They chased and beat up minor officials, shouted their grievances and advanced threateningly against some of the more important functionaries of the new government. As the military were in power these disturbances were short-lived. But the civilian government of Madras was alarmed. So was Dundas.

Lord Hobart decided to go to Ceylon and to investigate the

situation on the spot. In London Dundas thought the erstwhile Dutch settlements should be controlled by the Crown and not by the Company, since their fate would be a matter to be decided by the negotiations then proceeding on a peace settlement in Europe. With that instinct for compromise which was rooted in a Parliamentarian he felt that the East India Company should be responsible for administration and revenue, while a civilian Governor, commissioned by the Crown, should be responsible for the government of the country, but he should be subject to orders he might receive from the Directors of the Company, or from the Secret Committee, or from the Governor-General in Council.

Hobart when he arrived in Colombo from Madras in 1797 found that it was impossible to administer Ceylon unless it was known how the Dutch had set about it. He therefore appointed Pierre Frederic de Meuron, once commander of the regiment secured for the British from the Dutch by Cleghorn, to preside over a Committee of Investigation into the revenues of Ceylon and how they were collected. Associated with him was Lieutenant-Colonel Philip Agnew, another military man, who had very strong views on a subject agitating the company in India: the inadvisability of uniting executive and judicial powers. Though Robert Andrews was the third member of the Committee, its report reflected the views of Meuron and Agnew who, in fact, were sitting in judgement on Andrews's administration.

It has been for a long time now assumed that the disturbances which led to the setting up of the Committee were due entirely to the misdemeanours and rapacity of the Madras officials, who took advantage of a situation which placed them in control of areas which might well have ceased to be administered by them ere long, to benefit themselves and their myrmidons. Administrators in the East (and elsewhere), at a time when they were officially allowed to engage in private trade and expected to enrich themselves against their retirement to England, were likely to have been very much alive to the chances presented to them. Besides, the inhabitants of Eastern dependencies and colonies were accustomed to being fleeced by their own native overlords. In Ceylon in 1797 it was not the degree of extortion which caused the shoe to pinch, but the new and unexpected mode of levy. What was responsible for this was the ignorance of the Madras officials in attempting to carry on a system with which they were unfamiliar, and not their avarice.[6] The 'union of the powers of renter and magistrate', adduced in Meuron's report as one of the causes of the disturbances, was not as iniquitous a proceeding as it seemed, for it was known in Dutch times and native chieftains exercised similar powers. It was given such prominence because the echoes of the discussion of Cornwallis's principle of separating judicial from revenue functions were still reverberating in Indian administrative circles. Cornwallis was certain that 'where the power to redress oppressions, and functions that must always have a tendency to promote or screen the commission of them, are united in the same person, a strict adherence to principles of justice cannot be expected, and still less can it be hoped that the people will feel a confidence of obtaining justice'.

When the old system was restored and the new tax on coconut trees was withdrawn, everything was quiet. It was in this climate of calm after the storm that the first civilian Governor appointed by the Crown arrived in Ceylon in October 1798.

This did not mean that henceforward British administration, better informed as a result of Meuron's report, would revert to the old Dutch mode. It would have been surprising if this would have been so. There was all the difference in the world between the British and the Dutch. Dutch Company rule had already been replaced by a joint administration of British Crown and British Company. Most important of all, the agent through whom these dual powers were going to be used was a man with ambitions and a will of his own. Qualities like this had surely been exhibited by Dutch Colonial Governors, but they were representatives of a commercial company. The Honourable Frederic North, the first civilian British Governor of Ceylon, was never that. He had far too many notions of his own to be anything but a highly individual and eccentric English milord at a time when the species could throw off extraordinary examples.

Frederic North, the younger son of the second Earl of Guildford – the Lord North of the long Tory administration of George III's reign – was the first of a succession of Colonial Governors of Ceylon, who were, particularly in the early years of the British connection, personally extremely important agents of change and developers of the country over which they had been placed as rulers. There were in the one hundred and fifty years of British rule of the island changes in the source of supply of Colonial Governors, but it could be said of practically all of them that they took their responsibilities seriously and had minds of their own. The names of most of them have faded from the memory of the people of the island. Streets and squares once named after them have had their designations altered, but as persons they left their mark on the structure of British rule in Ceylon.

Frederic North is worth remembering not so much for what he did as for the man he was. An aristocrat with the best possible social and political connections, he had a large field in which to exercise his abilities. He had served for two years in Corsica under Sir Gilbert Elliot, later Earl of Minto; he was the personal friend of Wellesley, Governor of Madras and later Governor-General of India; Sylvester Douglas, Dundas's right-hand man was his brother-in-law. He was therefore in the particularly strong position of a person with influence, known to those who might have curtailed his freedom. Besides, like all Colonial Governors until the steamship reduced the times taken for dispatches to reach Ceylon from England, he enjoyed considerable discretionary powers. Sylvester Douglas noted that 'it is impossible, at the immense distance between this country and Ceylon to foresee, and, by anticipated regulations, to direct, every measure which necessity or sound policy may render it a duty in the person entrusted with the delegated authority of government to pursue'.[7]

Accordingly North, in spite of his own feeling that he was inordinately hampered by the responsibility he owed as representative of the British Crown to the Company, had a comparatively free hand. No one at that time – in London, in Calcutta, or in Madras – had clearly worked-out policies relating to the future administration or development of Ceylon. There was no grand imperial design which dictated what had to be done, apart from the understandable consideration that any threat to the security of a British possession had to be countered. Decision on most matters was going to be left to the man on the spot. North's importance lay in the fact that he was that man.

Like all the other early Colonial Governors of Ceylon – the men on the spot – before the Colonial Office had come into being and established its own routines, principles and traditions, North was something of an autocrat. This should not be surprising, for here were men invested with power, not because they sought for it or were ambitious to exercise it in this particular field, but who in the course of their careers came to fill a position of power, calling for abilities they were confident they possessed and which they were not reluctant to put to the test. To them Ceylon was, as it was to Frederic North, their 'domain'. They were so personally involved in the country they ruled as representative of His Britannic Majesty that they were in fact the country. There was no one to gainsay this unspoken claim of theirs. Below them were their British subordinates – civilian and army officers, from whose personal jealousies and spite they had nothing to fear but needless irritations. They could, and did, regard the great mass of the natives of the country with contempt tinged with forbearance. As Barnes described them in his first letter to Bathurst of 31 July 1819, they were little better than primitive tribesmen: 'The Cocoa nut in this part of the Country supplies all their wants, which appear to be extremely small for, generally speaking, they are, with a *very small* exception of covering round their waist, in a perfect state of Nudity – indeed some of them are compelled to be so by the Cast regulations.'[8] A troublesome Chief Justice or an awkward Officer Commanding the troops might have been carried away by notions that they were as important as the Governor, but these were inconveniences which could soon be dispelled.

This identification of themselves with everything planned and worked out in the colony accounts for the extreme touchiness of all of them – North, Maitland, Brownrigg, Barnes and Horton – to anything savouring of criticism or reproof. They knew the country and what was best for it; to question this axiom was a personal affront to them. North and Brownrigg at the end of their careers in Ceylon were physically ill when their conduct of affairs had been criticized in England. They awaited the tardy arrival of their successors with vexed impatience. Maitland's continual proclamation of his imperviousness to criticism makes the reader feel that he did protest too much. Barnes and Horton saw in the inclusion of Ceylon in the inquiries of the Colebrooke Commission a studied personal attack on all they had stood for in the country.

Barnes reacted with icy anger to its presumptuousness, which he felt must be regarded 'as an inquiry into my conduct, for such it will be considered'; while traces of the 'bitterest mortification' run through Horton's letter to Viscount Goderich on the Colebrooke-Cameron Report. Later Governors could not so easily feel themselves to be the personification of the country, for by the 1840s the Colonial Office, European interests and a small group of natives profiting from the education they were receiving, could dislodge from the Governor's mind any notion that the sum of things in the colony amounted to His Majesty's representative. But by the time the Colonial Governor had altered his stance and was addressing himself to the role of abstract Justice holding the balance and mediating between conflicting interests.

The first man on the spot was North and it is important to consider what kind of man he was. If it is possible at this distance of time to say anything about North's character which does not depend on the prejudices of his friends and his detractors, it is that his vanity would not let him rest content with the advantages he derived from his birth and family connections. He burned to prove himself well able on his own to leave a name to posterity. He was not without ability; some liberal ideas knocked about in his mind, notions about freedom which were mixed up with his admiration for Greek institutions; more than everything else he was enthusiastic about his undertakings at a time when the word 'enthusiasm' implied an impulsiveness in need of the restraints of reason and judgement. He had for a short while been a member of Parliament; later he had been Secretary of State to the Viceroy of Corsica during the British military occupation of the island in 1795–6. Corsica was already familiar to the English in North's childhood since Pascal Paoli had become an intimate of the Johnson circle and inflamed English imaginations with his fight for freedom. North must have seen himself in the role of liberator and lawgiver if only he had been given the opportunity. In another island in 1798 this seemed to have come his way.

He set out before his Commission was ready and at Bombay was fretted with impatience that it had not as yet arrived. (Incidentally the phrase 'I fretted my guts to fiddlestrings' occurs so often in his

letters that it throws light on the extreme volatility of his character.) He had brought with him a little court of his own in the
island he was going to rule – his 'domain' as he called it. These
were the eight persons he had personally selected for office.
Among them were the nephew of Sylvester Gordon and another
close relative of his. The ninth was Cleghorn, handsomely rewarded by the Directors of the Company for his share in helping
them to acquire the Dutch possessions, and now returning as
Colonial Secretary to the scene of his successful exploit. Though
North and himself got on well together during the voyage to
Ceylon, it would have been surprising if two people each with a
well-developed sense of his own importance could endure each
other for long.

North soon found various details in the Commission issued to
him – notably its provisos – irksome. He was right to complain,
but it was not before 1801 that changes were made through a new
bill. Dundas, in the same year, suggested in his dispatches the
creation of a council in Colombo over which the Governor would
preside. The others on this advisory Council were to be the
Officer Commanding the troops, the Chief Justice, the Principal
Secretary to the government and two other officials nominated by
the governor.

Even if he had not been determined to exercise authority and
power, North would have found impossible the unworkable controls placed upon him when he first arrived in the island. He soon
came to think of the Honourable Company and its servants in
the island as the greatest obstacles to his fulfilling his functions as
governor. His quarrels with various high officials show how
touchy he was on all matters connected with his dignity and
importance as the King's Governor of Ceylon. The King's Commission of 19 April 1798 for which he anxiously waited in Bombay
is no longer to be found in the Ceylon Archives. Jennings suggests that North probably carried it off with him when he retired.
If he did this, it must have been out of pride in the powers
entrusted to him, but so far it has not been discovered among his
papers.

Whether North's passion for freedom was the cause or the
effect of his readiness to see oppression and hostility everywhere,
it is impossible to escape noticing his obsession that practically all

those with whom he came in contact were either, as members of a group, oppressing others, or, as individuals, hostile to him and anxious to affront his dignity as King's Governor. All the systems of government he had encountered in Ceylon – that of the company, the Dutch, the Kandyan king – were to him 'oppressive', 'tyrannous', 'vicious' etc. The inference, clear in his opinions and actions, was that he felt himself called upon to free the oppressed.

When he decided to intrigue with Pilima Talauva, the Chief *Adigar* of the Kandyan king, North was fulfilling one part of his plans to free Ceylon from oppression. (Of course he himself would have the credit of attaching a new possession to the British Crown.) He must have seen, as any one else could have seen it, that the position of the Kandyan king in 1799 was going to be extremely difficult and even untenable. Douglas, who knew the situation through him, noted:

Our sovereign possession of that uninterrupted belt which follows the whole circumference of the Coast, and encircles and hems in the entire kingdom of Candy, places that kingdom virtually under our control and dominion, as to every supply from abroad, and particularly of that essential article of necessary consumption salt, and every export of their own commodities. By the possession of the cinnamon gardens which may easily be rendered sufficient to answer the consumption of the world, we do not in any manner depend upon the Candians for that article, formerly the great source of their power and revenue, but now of no value whatever to them but at our pleasure; and our command of the sea and harbours makes us masters of the other chief source of riches in Ceylon, the Pearl Fishery. Such being the case, is not the independent sovereignty of the King of the interior of the Island, a name more than anything else?[9]

Judicious comments of this kind could never compete in North's mind with his vanity and his emotional hatred of oppression. He therefore carried on intrigues with the king's chief *Adigar*, but had nothing to offer either king or *Adigar*, because he was not empowered by either Company or HM's Government to embark on such negotiations. Of course he kept Dundas informed of his schemes for getting a treaty with the king, by which his kingdom would be placed under British protection and the British would have a road from Trincomalee to Kandy and supplies of beef, without which the army could not exist.

The complete story of these intrigues has yet to be pieced together. The documents on the English side were carefully gone into by Pieris. It is to be regretted that such scanty evidence exists on the Kandyan side to show what Pilima Talauva's demands and promises really were. Obviously he was plotting against his king, but it is impossible to tell whether he deliberately and conveniently broke his promises to the British. The perfidiousness with which the Kandyan was so often accused was due in great measure to the difference between European and Oriental modes of speech. Although earlier the European conquerors in the East held that fidelity and truth need not be maintained by Christians in their dealings with pagans, by the nineteenth century they had begun to place a moral value on frankness and straightforwardness in speech, however unpleasant these may have been. By contrast the Oriental mode valued pleasant social communion. Its object was (and still is) to give pleasure by what is said, even to the extent of withholding the jarring reality. The speaker wishes to produce the agreeable feeling in the hearer of falling in with his wishes. Forster renders this remarkably well in *A Passage to India*. Mrs Bhattacharya was not guilty of falsehood in promising to send her carriage for the two English ladies and then forgetting all about it. Conventionally, according to the best usage known to her, she was showing them the greatest goodwill. It is possible that the English misunderstood Pilima Talauva.

Having failed to extract what he wanted by intrigue, North tried force. The First Kandyan War (1803–5) was in the nature of a punitive expedition sent by him to demand satisfaction for the alleged maltreatment of some Moorish traders, the British King's subjects, by the Kandyans. History repeated itself. The Kandyans were no match for well-equipped and armed European and native troops in the open, but they were adepts at guerrilla tactics and had no difficulty in harassing an enemy unable to maintain his lines of supply on account of the absence of roads, torrential rains and the ill-health of his forces. Whether the unfortunate Major Davie, left in charge of the small British force which had got to Kandy and taken possession of it, had secured safe conduct for his troops when he tried to get back with them to Trincomalee, is not known. Most of the three hundred and seventy members of that force were cut down by the Kandyans or took their own lives rather than fall into the hands of their enemies.

North extricated himself as well as he could from the consequences of this disaster. He could, and did, place all the blame on the perfidy of Pilima Talauva. Yet the real cause of the ill-success of the expedition was his enthusiasm and his confidence in his own powers. In 1800 North's brother-in-law foresaw what was likely to happen in such an eventuality as led to the disaster of 1803. He wrote to Dundas: 'If any difference of opinion should arise in regard to the urgency or expediency of the steps he has taken, which I trust will not happen, his justification will be, besides such sanction as they may have received from the Governor-General, that he has been obliged to exercise his best discretions and that he has lost no opportunity of transmitting account of what he has done, and the reasons and motives of his conduct'.[10] North certainly used his discretion, and he lost no time in flooding Governor-General, Governor of Madras and Whitehall with accounts of a catastrophe for which he was not to blame.

The 'war' continued desultorily. The king's troops could do no more than advance towards the border of the Maritime Provinces and threaten some forts there, but they were unable to meet the British forces in the open. For the next two years North pursued plans for avenging himself on the 'perfidious' Kandyans, but the new Commander-in-Chief, Wemyss, was not to be pushed into any schemes which were not militarily foolproof. The Kandyan 'war' dragged on for two years, with all the pillage and horrors associated with such activities. The chief sufferers were the Kandyans. Their chieftains continually intrigued with the British, and the resources of the country were being drained away. North wrote to Douglas on 6 March 1804, and for once was quite correct in his judgement of the situation on the Kandyan side: 'I believe that the Candians long for Peace; but I will certainly not make Peace with the present King or the Adigar; and indeed my Object is the Annihilation of Candy as a separate State altogether.'[11]

The same enthusiastic reaction against oppression, accompanied by personal vanity that he was to be the liberator, marks North's fiscal, educational and social policy. The sanguineness of his hopes with regard to the finances of Ceylon is a case in point. His Commission and the instructions given to him made over the control of the revenue of Ceylon to the company in India. The least he could have done in the situation was to ensure that the wishes of the Secret Committee were carried out and that revenue was increased in order to meet the company's commitments on the military establishment. Hobart had advised the promotion of trade with Kandy by bartering rice, salt and cloth, for cinnamon, pepper and betel-nut. Wickremeratne notes that the authorities at home had pressed North on this matter too: 'That these instructions were reiterated almost at the end of this period is again evidence of North's unwillingness to promote the Kandyan trade.' What might have been the reason for this unwillingness? In the first place trade with Kandy implied maintaining the *status quo*. This North could not tolerate. Furthermore, he had his own grandiloquent notions about the money to be made through the Pearl Fishery. He was convinced that the fisheries of 1798 and 1799 had been ruined through the rapacity of the officials of the Madras Government. This time the oysters were the wretched victims of exploitation. He was so confident of the vast sums to be made out of pearl fishing that he had a large house built for himself at Arippu with a colonnade of Doric columns, from which he saw himself looking out at the boats bringing back their rich freights from the sea.

Once again his enthusiasm was too strong for him. He knew too little about the natural history of the pearl oyster; he had insufficient experience of the business acumen of the renters of boats. But in the end he was convinced that his schemes had been defeated only by the doubtful honesty of some of the British officials and by the cunning of the renters.

North disliked service tenures intensely. To him they were the reactionary vestiges of a feudal order which tied the unfortunate holder of land to the soil and prevented him from exercising his rights as a free man to make money where he could. This would account for his preference for the Moors to the Sinhalese. The former, as he saw them, were an enterprising and industrious set of persons, unfortunately oppressed by having to pay a traditional capitation tax (*Uliyam*); the latter were so devoted to their service tenures and the communal ownership of land as to be lacking in enterprise of any kind. Dundas had noted in red pencil on one of Douglas's papers: 'The great Desideratum in the Island is a proper management of the territory and agriculture of the country. Till this is brought into a better state the subsistence of the inhabitants of the country rests on a precarious footing – a better system in this respect would likewise introduce a territorial revenue . . .'[12] As North saw it, communal ownership of land, an unfortunate peculiarity of the Sinhalese, had first to be eradicated before agriculture could be developed.

The disturbances of 1797 which led to the appointment of the Committee of Investigation resulted in the recommendation that service tenures should be restored. North was uneasy about this, but had to acquiesce. In 1800, however, he produced a variant to service tenures, allowing them to be commuted by payments in money whenever this was possible. But he was disappointed in the reaction to what was to him a liberalizing measure. Very few persons took advantage of the alternative, and it was withdrawn in 1802.

His attempts to work enlightened changes in the fiscal system came to nothing. The one new tax which he proposed – 'Joy' tax, so called because it was levied on jewellery, for which the Portuguese word was *joya* – might have been sensible, had it been part of a well-integrated system of taxation on all sources of wealth. But North's 'Joy' tax was no real tax but the levy of a flat rate on all persons who wore jewellery. It was strenuously resisted and was ultimately withdrawn.

North was most successful in his educational policy, if such a phrase could be used of some differences he made in the restricted field of schooling in English in Ceylon. Here the very limitation of the area in which he introduced change, as well as favourable circumstances, enabled him to be modestly successful. What he wanted to do was what the small circle of those likely to benefit from his plans heartily wished for. He was no innovator, but the inheritor of schemes already tried out and found successful in Portuguese and Dutch times. Colonial administration and missionary endeavour had proved the usefulness of an *élite* trained in the language of the rulers. Their numbers came from the circle of the families of chieftains and headmen and the class of European descendants. North, like every other Englishman in his time, believed in the humanizing and civilizing value of English and Christianity. He saw, as the Dutch had seen it very clearly, that

31

there was some immediate gain in propagating the language of the rulers and their religion: a small group of loyal minor officials. He resuscitated the Dutch schools and established the Colombo Academy in 1799, from which, as the first Chaplain and Principal of Schools reported: 'The British interests in the island have already experienced essential benefits . . . . (it) has not only, for a long time, supplied the place of a translator's office, but likewise furnished confidential interpreters to the various departments of government.'[13]

North's decision in 1802 to accept no petitions except those written in English was not, as Pieris suggests, due to his contempt for the Sinhalese language. He was only seeking to make English financially attractive to the students of the Academy who would draft these petitions. Like the Portuguese religious and Dutch Governors, North had schemes for sending a number of youths yearly to the mother country for higher education. But for such extravagances there was no money.

Had he been able to break down the influence of the Mudaliyars as he wished to do, North would have done the state some service. Like all Britishers in the early years of British rule in Ceylon he was cautiously suspicious of them, and personally felt that their position was the obverse of the 'poverty and slothful submission to vexatious and undefined authority' of the mass of the people. But in order to do without them North would have had to revolutionize the holding of land and so to attack caste. It is too much to have expected this of him or of any other Britisher in the nineteenth century. They were there as rulers who would change the existing social and political structure only so far as it suited them to do so. North saw, as others did, that the 'black Agent', as he termed the minor Ceylon official, was most often corrupt. For instance, he wanted to have superintendents in the cinnamon gardens who 'should be entirely without suspicion of corruption or any temptation to it'. His conclusion was: 'I do not think that these concerns can safely be entrusted to the daily uncontrolled management of a black Agent.'[14] Even without this decision of his, Britishers would have been placed in the highest supervisory positions. It is ironical, however, that North with his own experience of his venal countrymen should have believed so strongly in their honesty. Whether his opinions were ill-judged or wise, the sense of North's minutes was in keeping with official British policy throughout the period of their rule in Ceylon. While it is possible to say that one kind of corruption was kept down to a minimum in high places, it seems to have been taken for granted that the corruption of the minor hierarchy was a necessary evil.

From North's time onwards British rule seems to have been characterized by the combination of two contradictory impulses: an acceptance of an objectionable social structure and the determination to improve the island's resources. The interdependence of the social and economic structures was not always seen, but there are hints that some colonial governors did observe that economic changes were powerful political solvents. North writing to Douglas remarks, after the disaster of 1803; 'I heartily hope that solid Amity may then be brought about by the gradual operation of the Causes on which I had formerly endeavoured to establish it; viz. in the increasing interest of the Candian Nation collectively and individually in our Commerce, both of Export and Import, and in the very circulation of our Paper-currency, so admirably calculated for the Purpose of avoiding the Rapacity of irregular and arbitrary Injustice.'[15]

When North left Ceylon in 1805 the Civil, Judicial and Military Servants of His Majesty (most of them his cronies like Robert Arbuthnot and William Boyd) presented him with an address and a piece of plate worth one thousand guineas. Anderson, an officer in the 19th Regiment and later Paymaster in the Company of Pioneers organized by North, offered the tribute of verse:

> Upon this darling of Ceylon
> May Seva, mighty name!
> Protector of this mundane egg
> Bestow eternal fame![16]

The Native Headmen, who proffered a 'Humble Address' to him, did better than Anderson, for though they were as infelicitous as he was, at least they had something to say: 'Your Excellency's Care for their [the people's] well-being extended itself so far as not only to favour them with lands for Cultivation but also perceiving that the Small Pox made every Year a sad slaughter Amongst the Natives (who from Nature are fearful of the same in the Highest degree) did not spare any expense to accustom them to inoculate, by which Means at present, that fatal Complaint being extirpated, the Old men and Women in the Interior of the Country declare that they are become happy parents through the preservation of their Children through inoculation.'[17] This should be sufficient atonement for all North should not have done and all he did not do.

CHAPTER 3

CLEARING THE GROUND

1805-32

North, when he left Ceylon in 1805, had not done very much to clear the ground for the subsequent development of British rule in the island. He had merely swished with his cane at a few shrubs that stood in the way and he had indicated what he would have liked to do had he the power to do it. The task of clearing the ground in preparation for the structure of British rule in the island was really left to his successors. The three who followed him came from the class of army officer who had seen some active service. The least they could do for the new British acquisition – to ensure that it would be militarily defended – they were never called upon to do, for Napoleon's Eastern ambitions were unrealized and the French threat to India receded into the background. They were free therefore to clear the ground in the new colony, each in his own way. This they did as much by deliberate policy as by their personal attitudes and ambitions. Brownrigg (1812–20) was impelled by ambition to hail himself as Conqueror of the Kandyan kingdom. What he effectively achieved was, as will be seen, the removal of the obstruction of the old feudal order from the site which had to be developed.

The man on the spot was free, as Brownrigg was, even to disobey his instructions, provided that he was successful.[1] He was not unduly restricted in the plans and schemes he initiated. The colonies were administered as part of the office of the Secretary for War since 1801. There was an Agent for Ceylon appointed in the same year – an office which Huskisson held, receiving a salary of £800 a year for his duties. Though this was later increased 'in token of the value of the services he rendered to the Colony', he had little to do in formulating any policy for

Ceylon, nor did his financial expertise make any difference at all to conditions in the colony.[2]

Not until 1812, when Earl Bathurst became Secretary of State and Henry Goulbourn his Under-Secretary, did a Colonial Office begin to take shape. But Whitehall was responsible for what happened in Ceylon, and on occasion Parliament did intervene, as for instance in 1804, when there was talk in the House of Commons on an inquiry into the conduct of North's 'Candian War'. Such interventions were often part of the strategy of party warfare in England. They were none the less a possible check to the activities of colonial Governors. Glenbervie, writing to North on 21 April 1804, remarked of Creevey, who had raised the matter of the 'Candian War' in the House, that 'his object in the first place was no doubt to make a speech and a motion quelconque, and in the next place to shoot a Bolt at the Ministers – and not at you'.[3] But he did think it prudent to appeal to Minto on behalf of his brother-in-law: 'I wish to suggest to you that the turn the debate that day on the Ceylon business took, seems to me to make it very necessary for Fred North's personal friends to attend to its progress. The words 'inquiry' and if necessary *censure, and punishment* were used.'[4]

Despite these possibilities the Governor of Ceylon was comparatively free at the time even to ride his hobby horse as hard as he wished, provided that the Commission and the Instructions issued to him did not emphatically place a veto on certain types of action. Sir Thomas Maitland, who succeeded North, was an aristocrat, a man of private means and a genuine eccentric. He had seen some military service in India and on his return to England entered Parliament and proceeded to identify himself with the Whig opposition in the vehemence with which he espoused causes. The appellation 'honest Tom', gained as a result of his early career in the Commons, shows the quality on which he set store. Like North he was self-regarding and narcissistic, but he had common sense and canniness – probably the result of his Scots upbringing – casting a very cold eye on everything which suggested theoretical vaporizing. In it he diagnosed a fundamental dishonesty, which, as far as he was concerned, his vanity led him to oppose.

When he arrived in Ceylon in 1805 as Governor and Commander-in-Chief, Maitland had already made a name for himself as a man of affairs. He had an excellent yardstick in his pocket with which he measured all schemes and enterprises: did they pay? If they did they were necessarily good and were to be recommended. If they did not, they were clearly inefficient and had therefore to be discarded. This simple pragmatism led him to look askance at practically everything he found in Ceylon on his arrival. Once he had given himself time to get a good general view of the British administration and the 'war' against the king of Kandy, still dragging on since there had been no peace settlement, he acted. Charles James Napier, who got to know Maitland well after his term of office in Ceylon, described with approval his mode of operations in the Ionian Islands, of which he became Lord High Commissioner: 'He gave to his "resident" in each island considerable power, with a corresponding degree of responsibility . . . he created himself "dictator", and was well designated by the appellation of "King Tom": he did more; he made his residents dictators in their respective islands.'[5] In fact Napier's own test of successful colonial administration sounds like an echo of Maitland's principles: 'Perhaps no better rule could be established for appointing governors, than removing all those who do not make the colonies they govern pay, each, its own expenses.'[6]

By this test Maitland's administration of the Maritime Provinces of Ceylon was extraordinarily successful. When he took office the colony was in debt and a nuisance to the Treasury; when he left all the debts had been cleared and he had made Ceylon pay its way. But his tenure of office should be remembered not for this financial success, but for two decisions which he made and acted upon. One of his successors might perhaps have been compelled by the force of circumstances to do as he did, but it should not be forgotten that Maitland's convictions on these two subjects led to important changes in the way the country was governed and developed.

If the country was going to be well administered, its civilians had to give all their attention to their administrative duties and to nothing else. He therefore forbade civil servants from engaging in trade. To tighten up financial control he insisted on previous sanction from the Governor for any item of expenditure incurred by them as collectors. While they should have complete control of the collection of revenue and the management of their districts, expenditure should be authorized only by the newly constituted Commissioner of Revenue. Civilians were expected to learn the native languages (Portuguese being reckoned one), and in the revised scale of salaries promotion was dependent on proficiency in them. Annual reports were called for, and collectors were instructed to look into the conduct of Mudaliyars and minor government officials in order to prevent any oppression of the people or corruption.

The result of these changes was a better organized civil service and efficiency in the collection of taxes. Sir James Mackintosh, the Recorder of Bombay, who visited Ceylon for a few months in 1810 but did not actually meet Maitland there, left a warm appreciation of his administration in his diaries:

> It is impossible for me to do justice to General Maitland's most excellent administration, which I am convinced never had an equal in India. By the cheerful decision of his character, by his perfect knowledge of men, he has become universally popular amidst severe retrenchment. In an island where there was in one year a deficit of £700,000, he has reduced the expenses to the level of the revenue, and with his small army of five thousand men he has *twice in the same year* given effectual aid to the great government of Madras, which has an army of seventy thousand.[7]

Frewen Lord, Maitland's earliest biographer, thought that the eulogy was projected by Mackintosh's awareness of his own ineffectualness and his consequent over-valuation of the slightest signs of decisiveness in other people. Be that as it may, Maitland was always efficient, whatever private weaknesses he may have had.

His other important decision was the consequence of his desire to develop the resources of the colony. In 1810, after several earlier efforts to interest Castlereagh in his scheme for making land available to European 'speculators', he persuaded Lord Liverpool, the Secretary of State, to allow Europeans to own land in any part of the British possessions, provided that no single holding exceeded 4,000 acres. Dundas in 1801, following similar policy on the part of the East India Company in the two Presidencies, had ruled that except in Colombo no European could own land. Maitland saw that the solvency of the colony depended on raising its revenue from agriculture, which could not be developed without the use of capital. As only Europeans could be expected to possess this, land had to be made available to them. It ought to be stated that what Maitland had in mind was not turning vast tracts of the Maritime Provinces into plantations, but stimulating the native to embark on cultivation by 'the example of two or three Individuals cultivating here, either Corn Coffee or Cotton to their individual Benefit'. Whether he was sincere in this belief or not, he stated that this would 'go further to remove the Prejudices of the People than all we could ever say or all we can ever do as a Government to effect this important Object'.[8] What was in Castlereagh's mind was not primarily plantations on the scale or in the pattern of those in the old colonies, but 'the productions of Provisions, especially Rice'.[9] Liverpool, who was 'happy to be able most completely to concur' with Maitland in these proposals to make land available to Europeans, went on to say in his dispatch of 5 June 1810:

The large supplies of Rice which Government have been obliged to import annually from the Continent, previous to your assuming the Government, would alone suggest the vast advantage which must arise to the Colony from its raising its own Supplies, and I cannot help thinking that was it invariably to do so, the Exchange must be greatly benefitted, at least that it would promote the Circulation of Capital within the Island, and prevent the Transfer of so large a Portion of the Revenues out of the Colony in order to effect the above mentioned purchase.[10]

The Dutch long before had tried sugar, tobacco, cotton and coffee in Ceylon. A small quantity of the last had been exported to Europe, and during North's governorship a Hollander by the name of Conradie, who did have some capital and wanted to launch out into trade, exported some coffee to Great Britain. North gave the project his blessing and wrote to Glenbervie: 'Pray, as Head of Trade, encourage the Importation of our Ceylon Coffee. It is very fine and I am going to take proper measure to correcting the Errors now existing in the Method of pruning it, and am making Extracts out of all the learned Works I can procure on the Subject.'[11]

Maitland could not foresee the results of the removal of the embargo on European ownership of land, since all he was interested in was the immediate increase of revenue. Large-scale development of commercial crops had to wait until the hills of the Kandyan country, more suitable for the cultivation of coffee, were available for settlement. But the principle laid down as a result of Maitland's intervention with the authorities at Whitehall was to affect the whole economy of the island in a short time.

The rest of his administration can be summed up in terms of the simple equation of Efficiency = Profit which dominated his thinking. Increase of revenue and efficiency were synonymous with happiness, both of the rulers and the ruled. He did not therefore move a finger in the Kandyan 'war', except to try to secure the release of Davie, which could not be effected without recognizing the authority of the king of Kandy which he was reluctant to acknowledge. Despite the protests of Wilberforce and the growing pressure of the Evangelical lobby in the House of Commons, he saved money on education and was critical of Christian missionary activity. With the admirable scepticism which characterized him he concluded, correctly on the whole, that the religious convictions of converts depended on where their profit lay. Missionaries had to wait his departure before they could spread their wings under the patronage of a governor of Ceylon.

He reorganized the judicial system as soon as he could have Alexander Johnston, a man in whom he believed, as Chief Justice. The effect of these changes was that the customary law of the Sinhalese was replaced by Roman-Dutch law which had already been in use since Dutch times. Maitland was far too practical a person to have thrust English common law, as he really wished he could, on a people unaccustomed to it.

He has been described as a man who knew what the word 'trusteeship' meant long before it came into use.[12] This is an exaggeration, if by the word 'trusteeship', in the context in which it has become familiar in writing on colonial administration, is meant the wielding of power on behalf of the ruled on whom it must in a short or a long time devolve. With such notions Maitland, if we judge him on his dispatches to Whitehall, would have had no patience. If he was a 'trustee', it was for the benefit of the British people, since he had been given a commission by His Majesty's Government. As an administrator to whom the honour of His Majesty's service was paramount, he would carry out his duties to the best of his ability. He was too much of an autocrat and too narrow-minded, in spite of his early Whig days in Parliament, to think of the ruled as being anything but a mass for whom he was able to decide on all subjects. Phrases like 'black intelligence' (in the sense of worthless information provided by natives), 'black intrigue' appear too often in his writing to make one feel that here was a man in advance of his time. In spite of his oft-quoted statement that 'the sole object of government is and always ought to be considered to be to ensure the prosperity of the island solely through the medium of generally increasing the prosperity and happiness of the natives', he was at the end of his administration as 'convinced as ever that the best surety for good government was the plenary power of the Governor'. For him happiness and prosperity followed on good administration and whate'er was best administered was best.

Brownrigg who succeeded Maitland in 1811 had neither the advantages of aristocratic birth nor the wealth of his two predecessors. He was a professional soldier with a long record of service. He was besides the protégé of the Duke of York. With the Maritime Provinces quiet, a fairly well organized government and no deficit in revenue, he could dally with a prospect which would have appealed to any military man – the subjugation of the kingdom of Kandy.

There were two factions at the Kandyan court: the Sinhalese and the Malabar, or rather the anti-Malabar and the rest. The king, Sri Vikrama Rajasinha, had developed into a much stronger monarch than his First *Adigar* Pilima Talauva, had anticipated and in 1811 turned tables on the latter by having him executed. Pilima Talauva was succeeded as First *Adigar* by Ehelepola who, like practically all Kandyan noblemen, was intriguing against the king and sooner or later would be sounding the British.

Open hostility between the king and Ehelepola led the latter to refuse to present himself at court at the king's command. Instead he crossed into British territory, leaving his wife and family in the king's power. They unfortunately suffered the penalty meted out by Kandyan law to the relatives of traitors, the precise mode of their punishment being transformed by myth into a story of such sadism that it still features in accounts of the fall of the Kandyan kingdom. According to this story, which was given the widest publicity by the British, the wretched wife of the traitor Ehelepola was forced to use a pestle and mortar to pound the heads of her children who had been executed before her eyes. Sinhalese vilification of the Malabar king turned him into a devil in just the same way as the *Rajavaliya* metamorphosed the Portuguese.[13]

Brownrigg, when the odds were in his favour, moved against the Kandyan militia with two British and five Ceylon regiments which he commanded in person. But no military engagements marked the 'Second Kandyan War'. It showed the British once again that if the Kandyan kingdom was to be held, military roads linking Kandy with Trincomalee and Colombo were absolutely essential. Though the campaign was undistinguished militarily, the engineers on the British side performed notable feats by supporting the infantry with cannon which had to be parbuckled from tree to tree up the wooded heights of the pass of Balane.[14] The king fled from the capital with his queens and Brownrigg found the way clear to Kandy.

With the capture of the king on 18 February 1815 formal arrangements for the domains over which he had ruled had to be proclaimed. These were the substance of the Kandyan Convention of 2 March 1815. They followed the lines of the proclamation issued by Brownrigg on 10 January of the same year when he launched his 'war'. A 'tyrannous' king would be removed and his descendants for ever excluded from the Kandyan throne; the dominion of the Kandyan Provinces was vested in the sovereign of the British Empire and was to be exercised through the Governors of Ceylon 'for the time being' and their accredited agents; the laws, customs and religion of the Kandyan chieftains and people would be respected and maintained. The terms of this Convention, drafted largely by John D'Oyly, the British adviser on Kandyan affairs, was in the form of an agreement between two high contracting parties: the king of England and all those Kandyan chieftains who were there to append their signatures to it. D'Oyly had long been conversant with the Sinhalese language, he knew a number of the chieftains personally, was trusted by some of them, and he was interested in their institutions. Years earlier when Mackintosh saw him during his brief visit to Ceylon, he remarked how little different from a 'Cingalese hermit this Master of Arts of Cambridge seemed to be.[15]

Article 5 of the Convention read as follows: 'The religion of Boodhoo professed by the Chiefs and Inhabitants of these Provinces is declared inviolable; and its rites, Ministers and Places of worship are to be maintained and protected.' This emphatic wording was to lead later to much controversy and great heart-burning, both in Christian England and in Buddhist Ceylon. Zealous Christian opinion was outraged that the Crown had been committed to support and protect paganism; Buddhist nationalism was equally bitter that guarantees so solemnly given had been so lightly disavowed. Bathurst was at pains to point out to Brownrigg in his dispatch of 30 August 1815 that 'if, however, the Term "inviolable", in the first Clause of the Article, is (as I do not conceive that it can have been) understood as precluding the efforts which we are making to disseminate Christianity in Ceylon by the propagation of the Scriptures, or by the fair and discreet preaching of its Ministers, it would be very much at variance with the Principles on which His Majesty's Government uniformly acted for guarding against so great an Evil'.[16] Brownrigg hastened to assure Bathurst that he had had no intention of acting at variance with the principles of HM's Government.

Brownrigg was not being deliberately untruthful; he was temporizing. He was anxious to have no trouble on his hands with regard to any part of the Kandyan adventure. D'Oyly should have known better. He knew enough of the Kandyan people to realize that their devotion to their religion had to be recognized and that he was committing the British sovereign to the role of defender of the faith of the people whose territory had been annexed in his name. A formal contract which set out rights and duties had to legalize the conclusion of the war and the beginning of the British annexation. Neither the governor, nor his adviser, nor the chiefs to whom the document was read, realized what these high-sounding abstractions would in the course of time come to mean in the harsh light of everyday life. The chiefs were probably unanimous in consenting to the exclusion of Sri Vikrama Rajasinha and his heirs from the throne. After all in times gone by their ancestors had rebelled against former kings. Ehelepola was confident that the British would appoint him king. The words 'for the time being' in Article 4 suggested (even if they did not mean it) a temporary settlement. The ordinary man in Kandy was neither thrilled nor interested in any of these things. Marshall, who was there when the Convention was signed, noted: 'That portion of the population which had returned to Kandy evinced no concern in the business which was going on at the Palace. They did not leave their ordinary avocations even to look at the troops which were assembled, in review order, in the great square before the audience hall. Apparently, they regarded the transfer of the government from an Oriental to a European dynasty with perfect indifference.'[17]

The document having been signed, the Kandyan Provinces were formally annexed to the British Crown and were adminis-tered separately. D'Oyly was appointed agent for them with various collectors in the provinces. A Board of Commissioners and not the Supreme Court, of which Johnston was Chief Justice, administered law. Forts to secure military occupation were built, and trade began to flow freely across boundaries which once cut off the British colony from the Kandyan country.

D'Oyly worked hard to maintain good relations between the government and the old hierarchy of chiefs and influential pre-lates. But neither the British Government nor the Kandyan hierarchy had quite foreseen or understood the consequences of the substitution of British rule for that of the king. Everything was changed, in spite of the attempts of the British to minimize or disguise this. Moors and low-country traders poured into the Kandyan country. The dignity of the chiefs was diminished, their revenues were reduced with the removal of the old boundaries and their tolls, and British law rejected their authority and certain privileges and institutions which were repugnant to it. Similarly affected were the *bhikkhus*. The loss of position, influence and income by both feudal chieftains and *bhikkhus* did produce a re-sentment against the new order. *Pax Britannica* in the first two years after the Kandyan Convention brought many alien forms to a people conservatively attached to old usuages. Their resentment, too, was natural.

The Rebellion which broke out in 1817 was the last convulsive shudder of the Kandyan kingdom before its end. It was also the violent protest of feudal suzerainty in Ceylon against British rule. Like the Indian Mutiny of 1857, described by Nehru as 'a feudal outburst, headed by feudal chiefs and their followers and aided by widespread anti-foreign sentiment',[18] it represented the last strenuous effort of Sinhalese feudalism against the new order. Both were national struggles – such national struggles as could be led by a displaced and crippled feudal class. Both struggles looked not forwards but back. Their objective was the restoration of the *status quo ante*. In both instances the event was the necessary prelude to the imposition of new forms of economic, social and political organization on the conquered people.

For a few months the position of some of the British forts was precarious. But time and circumstances were against the rebels, however hard they could press British forces in isolated positions. They had neither the discipline nor the resources to defeat an enemy who had practically all India to draw upon. When the Tooth Relic of the Buddha, which had been spirited away from Kandy by the rebels, fell into British hands, the courage which had sustained irregular forces against well-trained regiments failed. One year after the men of the remote district of Vellassa had first turned against the British resident of the area, the Rebellion was over. With it, feudal leadership of the nation, such as it was, was over too.

The rising of 1817–18 was the first and last rebellion of the Sinhalese against their British overlords. That it should have taken place in the Kandyan country is easy to understand. There the old, so sure to pass away but yet so slowly tarrying in the hills, roused itself against what it was unable to understand but of which it disapproved. In 1796 there were the strongest and clearest differences in character and level of development between the Maritime Provinces and the Kandyan country. Twenty-two years later at the end of a rebellion which had been put down with great severity, these contrasts were sharpened. The Maritime Provinces had moved further along the road of change, the future to which their inhabitants were being schooled was incomprehensible to the Kandyan villager. He belonged, by contrast with the new, to the undeveloped and backward parts of Ceylon, for which the future was as definitely dark as it seems now to world opinion for the underdeveloped whole of the island. When, not long after, the Kandyan country was opened up by European planters, the Kandyan villager was not one of the involuntary beneficiaries of the new order. By the time he awoke to its reality more than a century had elapsed.

The Rebellion marked a further stage in the decline of the influence of the Kandyan chiefs. Brownrigg claimed that the Kandyan Convention, signed by them, had been abrogated by their rebellion. They therefore lost practically all their rights as independent feudal overlords recognized by the British, though in the village and in remoter districts they continued to enjoy a much restricted field of influence. According to Brownrigg the chiefs were to be reduced from 'an aristocratic faction to the rank and office of stipendiary organs for effecting the regulations and orders of the supreme executive authority'. This was to be the British Governor, who became in show and reality the 'king' of the Kandyan country and of all Ceylon. All dues payable in kind to the chiefs were abolished; so was *Rajakariya*, or the traditional labour owed to overlord or king, except for work needed for roads. Only temple lands were exempted from taxes, nor would they have to pay for services rendered by their tenants. The old system of land tenure was further broken up and Roman-Dutch law was soon to run through the Kandyan kingdom. Kandyan custom which enabled the seller of land to buy it back within his lifetime was altered by law, and the Proclamation of 28 October 1820 required signed and witnessed documents for transactions in land.

Two characteristics of British rule in Ceylon could be illustrated by the Rebellion of 1817–18: the suddenness with which the British rulers were surprised into recognizing that there could be any trouble at all, and the unco-ordinated nature of the expression of discontent by the people who made trouble or showed their disapproval of their rulers in various ways. British officialdom rarely could sense what the people over whom they ruled really felt and thought. Too great a gulf was fixed between white rulers and the ruled in their numerous gradations, divided by racial groupings, caste and locality. What characterized the ruled in their moments of mass consciousness was an intensity which had nothing to express but the inarticulateness of its rage. No rebellion marked the remaining one hundred and thirty years of British rule in Ceylon, for the same reasons which made the best the rebels of 1817 could achieve sporadic and ill-sustained successes in a minor key. There were various disturbances and some trifling commotions in 1823, 1824, 1834, and, most famous of all, in 1848 and 1915. Ceylon, long broken up into small kingdoms which European powers vanquished, in the last struggles of one of them showed strains of division and disunion which had marked most of its history. Even this 'Great Rebellion' of 1817–18, as it was called, mustered only a part of the Kandyan people. A number of chieftains, including some of the highest, stood outside. Brownrigg in his Proclamation mentioned some fifteen whose 'loyalty and adherence to the Lawful Government merits favour'. A mass uprising would, in the end, have been crushed by superior British power, but it might have left a residue of some sense of unity among those who had waged their hopeless fight. One consequence of the rebellion was clear for decades after in the minds of the colonial British. To them the Kandyan was synonymous with artfulness, perfidy, treachery and sullen unregeneracy. This myth was as durable as that of the sadism of the last Kandyan king.

Brownrigg did more than he ever knew when he 'conquered' the Kandyan kingdom. After four centuries a small island composed of various racial groups in various stages of economic development was again united, in the picturesque phrase of the Pali chronicles, 'under the one umbrella'. This time it was under the British who could do more than any other rulers of Ceylon could ever have done. They had the whole island under their control at a time when they had become the strongest power in the world and industrially the most advanced. Had Brownrigg obeyed the Prince Regent's instructions and left the Kandyan kingdom alone, the omission would probably have been repaired by some later governor, for the only logical future for Ceylon was what had been maintained throughout its history as its political destiny: an island ruled by the one sovereign power.

Sir Edward Barnes who succeeded Brownrigg secured effective military control of the whole island in his two terms of governorship between 1820 and 1831. He was a great autocrat. A wealthy military man, he had been wounded at Waterloo and had earned the personal commendation of the Duke of Wellington. He saw at once that roads were needed, both to prevent the recurrence of any such difficulty as the British forces had to contend with during the Kandyan rebellion, and to give the colony as good a chance as it could have of paying its way and becoming – as he hoped it might – a colony of settlement. He was certain that militarily the defence of a possibly refractory Kandyan country could not be based on fortified posts, if there was no effective communication between them and Colombo. He assumed responsibility for putting an end to the earlier policy of building more fortified posts and concentrated on developing roads. In a personal communication to Bathurst on 19 May 1820, he wrote:

The several Corps of Pioneers . . . are chiefly employed in the construction of carriage Roads through the principal parts of the country . . . an undertaking which will tend more than any other I could adopt to consolidate the new with the old provinces, improve the commercial intercourse of the two, remove the principal difficulties that we experienced in the late military operations, if unfortunately the necessity for such operations should recur, and diminish the vast expense in the conveyance of commissariat supplied.[19]

Barnes pushed on with his programme of road building, using army engineers and not scrupling to make unwarranted use of *rajakariya*. He thought Kandyans, both chieftains and ordinary people, 'artful' and not to be trusted. To use *rajakariya* as it had never been used before was presumably an excellent mode of getting even with them. Lieutenant-Colonel Forbes, writing in 1850, considered that the Kandyan peasant had been exploited in being forced to build roads from which he was not to derive any great benefit: 'The great lines of road in the interior of Ceylon were made prior to 1833, and principally at the expense of the lives and the unpaid labour, of the native proprietors of rice land. But the greatest benefit of these roads is derived by those British capitalists, who in no way contributed to their formation.'[20]

When he decided to encourage a plantation industry in Ceylon by using Maitland's order in council that land was to be made available for development by Europeans, Barnes was improving upon Dutch example. Colonies – British, French and Dutch – had already for a hundred and fifty years been producing such crops as sugar, tobacco, cotton and coffee for the benefit of colonist planters. Cinnamon in the 1820s was no longer the profitable article of trade it had been; inferior grades from the East Indies and cassia had depressed its price in the world market.

Barnes' policy was significant in its mode of operation. He saw that coffee could profitably be developed, particularly in the new territories now controlled in the Kandyan country, only by government encouragement. He saw, too, that little use had been made of the powers given to the government to grant land to Europeans. Since Maitland secured the concession there had been only one speculator who was interested and even he had not been encouraged by the terms on which the offer had been made.[21] Barnes took up coffee planting himself, and moving the Royal Botanical Gardens from Slave Island in Colombo to Peradeniya enlisted its services in the development of coffee culture. Moon, the Superintendent of the Gardens, was instructed by Lusignan, the Secretary for the Kandyan Provinces, to give his attention to 'the growth of coffee which His Excellency has particularly at heart to see increased throughout the Island.'[22]

These early attempts on the part of Barnes and another Englishman by the name of Bird to develop coffee in the Kandyan country were not immediately successful. Not until the duty on Ceylon coffee imported into the United Kingdom was lowered in the mid-thirties did the exploitation of the hill country by the new plantation industry begin. But Barnes had envisaged large-scale enterprise under the aegis of a government interested in helping planters. The roads his administration provided were the springboard from which they plunged into hills and woods, soon to be the scene of the transformation of old Ceylon into a nineteenth-century colony of the British Empire producing for the world market a commercial crop on which its whole economy depended. In principle this can hardly be described as change at all: instead of cinnamon it was now coffee, and before the century was out it was going to be tea. But economically and socially it was going to

49

have far-reaching consequences, because of the political control exercised by the British over the whole island. The Dutch, with their suzerainty of only one part of it, had done no more than obtain for export all the cinnamon their company could collect – from the king's territories and from their own plantations – over which they jealously maintained monopoly rights. Now with the annexation of the Kandyan country a political entity had ceased to exist; the land was going to be developed by the private speculator; its surviving social structure was to be thrown into the discard and Colonial Governors would have to reconcile the welfare of the people they governed with the profits of commercial interests.

Barnes left Ceylon in 1831 to take up the important assignment of Commander-in-Chief in India. But it was impossible that a soldier from the last century like himself should have got on well with the new Governor-General, Lord William Bentinck, who professed that while he governed in name, it would be Jeremy Bentham who would govern in fact. Such notions must have seemed frenetic to Barnes, who was as sceptical of Bentinck as his hero Wellington had been. There had been Englishmen in Ceylon with extremely liberal views. Eighteenth-century enlightenment had no better representative in Ceylon than Sir Alexander Johnston, who spent a great deal of energy in emancipating slaves, introducing the jury system and liberalizing the existing code of laws. When he retired to England he was responsible for the foundation of the Royal Asiatic Society and was consulted by Whitehall on Ceylon. Barnes had unfeigned contempt for his fussiness, regarding him as being no better than 'a grand Mountebank'.[23] Whether this was fair comment on Johnston's undoubted self-importance or only prejudice, the future, so far as Whitehall's pronouncements on the empire went, belonged not to the old-time professional soldier but to the professional administrator, whose element was the new climate compounded of Benthamism, Evangelicalism and high ideals too hard to preserve intact. Self-interest of an enlightened kind was going to be identified with the public good. A government providing for the moral good of the people over whom it ruled would benefit commercially from their increased wealth and prosperity.

Barnes was on the way out of Ceylon when William Colebrooke, one of the members of a Commission of Inquiry appointed to investigate 'the manner in which its resources were managed', arrived in the island. This Commission had originally been the suggestion of Robert Wilmot when he sat in Parliament. Since then he had been Under-Secretary of State and was now Sir Robert Wilmot Horton, the new Governor of Ceylon (albeit reluctantly, as he would have much preferred the governorship of Canada). A man of much colonial experience and a superior person, he resented the Commission as another gadfly to irritate a Colonial Governor. He was able; he professed high ideals; he was convinced that moral good and economic improvement were one and the same. Byron, whose cousin he was by marriage, disliked him intensely, referring to him in one of his satiric epistles as

> Wilmot the small wit
> Ward's creeping Companion and Louse,
> Who's as damnably bit
> With fashion and Wit
> That he crawls on the surface like Vermin.
> But an insect in both,
> By his intellect's growth
> Of what size you may quickly determine.

This was prejudiced comment. As a public figure Horton would have spoken the same language on most matters of general principle as Colebrooke and his fellow Commissioner, Cameron. But on specific matters of detail he was aware of two advantages he possessed which they lacked: he had experience and he was the man on the spot. Barnes, for the same reasons, was of the same mind as himself.

Between the end of 1831 and the middle of 1832 Colebrooke and Cameron presented their reports on their investigations into the 'Laws, Regulations and Usages .... into every other matter or thing in any way connected with the administration of the Civil Government, the State of the Judicial Civil Military and Ecclesiastical Establishments Revenues Trade and Internal Resources' of the island of Ceylon. Of inquiries into such extensive subjects carried out by two persons over a period of less than two years no revolutionary or surprising findings should have been expected. But what they did select for recommendation to

Goderich, the Secretary of State, represented a trend towards doctrinaire liberalism observable in the House of Commons, outside it, and even in the much cooler official pronouncements of His Majesty's colonial administrators.

If the assent given by the Secretary of State and Parliament to most of the recommendations of these two Commissioners is thought of as a landmark in the conduct of colonial affairs in Ceylon, surely then it was just one milestone more on a route already mapped out and worked upon by some officials on the spot. Nothing recommended by the Commissioners which was acceptable to the Secretary of State could really be thought of as either daring innovation or previously unthought of break with the past. Practically everything they wished to set up in Ceylon was already in the process of coming into being. Dr Mendis in his admirable and authoritative study of the reports of the Commissioners remarked that 'though the proposals of Colebrooke and Cameron were radical they were not altogether novel'.[24] *Rajakariya* 'had been disapproved already and modified by North and Brownrigg'; vexatious interference with the development of agriculture and industry by farmers of taxes and headmen had been the concern of practically every collector in the island; Sir Alexander Johnston had as early as 1809 forestalled many of the proposals made by Colebrooke. Throwing open various branches of the public service and minor posts in the judiciary to Ceylonese was no new thing. It was the logical result of economies every Lieutenant-Governor faced with the duty of making the island pay for its civil and military establishment had tried to secure. Cameron was quite frank that his scheme of judicature 'could be made subservient to the very important and beneficial purpose of giving to a class of Native functionaries the skill and integrity necessary to render them fit for becoming Judges of original jurisdiction.' 'If this object can be accomplished,' he went on to write, 'a very great saving of expense will ensue. For the salary with which a Native Judge would be amply remunerated is quite trifling in comparison with the amount necessary to tempt a competent European to undertake so laborious an office in so warm a climate, and in so distant a region.'[25]

It would have been surprising had the Commissioners' recommendations really been radical, for they were in line with attitudes associated with Bentham who was by no means a radical. The report was a utilitarian document which owed just as much to Adam Smith as to Philosophical Radicalism. It was in the name of Utility and Economy that Colebrooke and Cameron objected to institutions like *Rajakariya*. With such outmoded nuisances out of the way it seemed to a man like Cameron that Ceylon was destined to be 'the fittest spot in our Eastern dominions in which to plant the germ of European civilization, whence we not unreasonably hope that it will hereafter spread over the whole of those vast territories'.[26] Of course these sentiments were the product of his genuine liberalism. He could not know at the time he expressed them that such notions were not likely to guarantee the growth of anything but that of private profit – scarcely the fine flower of European civilization. Cameron's was, in reality, one of a chorus of English voices in the early nineteenth century in Ceylon proclaiming that the island afforded unlimited opportunities for the English to increase civilization, encourage knowledge, diffuse Christian benevolence and consequently augment the general happiness.

Outwardly the most marked of the changes effected by the Colebrooke-Cameron Commission was the logical outcome of Brownrigg's annexation of the Kandyan kingdom. After 1815 it continued to be administered separately from the Maritime Provinces. Even after the rebellion of 1817–18, though the powers and privileges of the chiefs had been further curtailed, administratively the Kandyan Provinces continued to be an entity on their own. Colebrooke's reasons for terminating their separation from the rest of the island included the familiar reference to the dangers of maintaining the influence of the chiefs. For a long time to come the latter were going to be viewed with suspicion by a large section of British administrators (and others) as the sole cause of all the government's woes in the Kandyan country. But if the truth were known, by 1832 the chiefs, dispirited and unable to cope with change, were only too glad to let things take their course in their old domains. The older politically active *Adigars* paid for their activities with their lives in the last years of the Kandyan kingdom. Newer families came to the fore in British times, quite ready to accept the changed political situation and to occupy less significant positions in the new order. The Kandyan chiefs were not prominent in the agitations which accompanied the assimilation of the Kandyan people into the rest of Ceylon in the 40s and the 50s.

To the minds of the Commissioners in 1832 the traditional life and economy of the Kandyan Provinces had to be brought into line with the new. They were correct in their supposition that the only viable economy for Ceylon was that of a unified country. But when they suggested integrating the Kandyan and the Maritime Provinces into five new provinces, they did not realize that they were subjecting the old to far greater stresses than it could bear.

For the rest the most important change Colebrooke desired was denied him by the Secretary of State, who on this point could not turn down the advice of the man on the spot. Colebrooke's recommendation was that the power of the Governor should be reduced. The extensive authority of this official at that time gave him sole control of all military administration and judicial power in the country. This was not the case in other British possessions, notably in the colonies of settlement where there were legislative assemblies. The Commission proposed that the governor should be a figurehead in an Executive Council and that he be excluded from taking part in the deliberations of a Legislative Council, on which would sit nominated representatives of both the Europeans and the Ceylonese. Change of this kind was strenuously opposed by both Barnes and Horton. Barnes condemned the proposal out of hand: 'I am therefore under all circumstances decidedly of the opinion that so long as the present order of things exists, the present is the best form of government that can be adopted.' Horton, in his mortification at these proposals, expressed himself bitterly: 'If however it is destined that the suggestions of the Commissioners are to prevail, and that I am to be made (to use the expressive words of Mr Gogerly the Wesleyan Missionary whose letter I enclose) "a Political puppet possessed of a name, but destitute of authority", I trust I may be freed from all appearance of responsibility, and that the Council, from one of which I am to be excluded, and the other to be made a cypher, may have the credit or discredit of administering the Executive Government.'[27]

It was impossible for the Secretary of State to disregard this opposition, since it came from the person who had to be credited with the most knowledge and experience on matters vital to the colony and its orderly government. Goderich therefore concurred:

I do not consider the objections which have been urged against involving the Governor with the members of the Legislative Council, are of sufficient weight to counterbalance the disadvantages which would result from his absence ... In regard, however, to the principle of Legislation recommended by the Commissioners and the revision of the existing Laws, I deem it more advisable that the course suggested should be the result of local arrangement than that it should be adopted without limitation by Instructions from home.[28]

Two significant differences made by the Commission were, first, the introduction of representatives 'in equal proportions from the respectable European Merchants and Inhabitants and the higher classes of Natives' in order to convince 'the population that the laws made for their government, proceed from persons participating in their own interests and general opinion'. One phase in the political development of the colony begins here.

But was the satisfaction given to the few nominated representatives of one class, here designated as 'the higher class', that they had a voice in the control of affairs 'a notable advance on the constitutional side'? Only to the historian of constitutions perhaps. Notable advance came later when these nominated representatives made their voices heard. For some time to come they could not be more than a resonant sounding board to the Governor's pronouncements.

The second significant difference was a recommendation with which Horton was glad to comply. Like most colonial administrators of his time he was convinced that the only way towards the future development of the colony politically, socially, economically and morally lay through education. In the same dispatch as that quoted above, Goderich requested Horton to give early attention to 'the establishment of a college at Colombo, with the object of giving encouragement to the elementary schools, and affording to native youths a means of qualifying themselves for different branches of the public service'. Horton had been ready to do as much and more. He was enthusiastic about the desire for education in English, and in an earlier undated dispatch had written: 'The attainment of the Young Men at Jaffna may justly be characterized as extraordinary – I propose to attach immediately two of those Young Men who have finished their education, to the Medical Establishment of this Colony as Sub Assistants, and I look with confidence to extreme advantage resulting from Natives so competent to learn, receiving an English Medical Education.'[29]

CHAPTER 4

RAISING THE STRUCTURE
1833-47

The political and economic structure of British rule in Ceylon was raised not through the legislative enactments which followed the acceptance of the majority of the recommendations of the Colebrooke–Cameron report, nor even as the immediate result of Barnes's attempts earlier to develop large-scale coffee growing in the country. The consequences of both were important. As a result of the work of the Commission, Ceylon after 1832 was administered as a single unit of five provinces with a single judicial system under control of the Supreme Court: *rajakariya* was abolished; Executive and Legislative Councils, over which the governor presided, were set up; a fillip was given to education in English. Barnes had long before tried to stimulate the investment of capital in coffee planting by abolishing export duties on coffee in 1820. A year later new land laws made village land alienable and the right of the Kandyan villager and his descendants to repurchase land they had sold was thereby removed. By a regulation of 1825 no tax was claimed on coffee plantations; and in 1829 all those who worked on coffee plantations were exempted from *rajakariya*.

In spite of these efforts the actual pioneers of the coffee industry in Ceylon made no conspicuous success of their enterprise. George Bird, who first began his plantation at Sinnapitiya in Gampola on four hundred acres 'granted to him free of taxes for 10 years, after which he was required to pay an annual tax of six fanams'[1] (a peppercorn rent), died in Kandy on 1 March 1857, 'having been the means of conferring signal advantages on others by the energy of his character, while to himself, the pioneer of coffee cultivation, his best efforts served only to prolong his disappointment'.[2]

The actual raising of the structure was due to the running down of the economy of another part of the British Empire, when the West Indian interest in the House of Commons could no longer prevent the removal of tariffs specially favouring the producers of coffee in Jamaica and other Caribbean islands.

The impetus given by these events outside Ceylon accelerated change, altering the face of the country and setting up the foundations of that structure which, with a few modifications, still dominates the island economically and politically. If coffee, first planted on a large scale in Ceylon because of the opportunity afforded by the collapse of the industry in the West Indies, became 'king' thirty years later, it must be remarked that even in its early stages it maintained itself with some of the characteristics of an oriental despot. Everything in the island came to be subordinated to its will. Once established it was a more powerful solvent of everything which belonged to the old Ceylon than legislative enactments or official pronouncements.

Until 1835 coffee still remained 'a peasant crop and Ceylon's increasing exports were mainly grown by the natives of the island, either by the roadside, or in the lands surrounding their homes'.[3] In 1827, 1,792,448 lbs of coffee were exported from Ceylon to the UK, most of it, like the quantity going to India, the results of garden cultivation by the villager, who benefitted from the peace and security of the time to turn to advantage what cost him little in energy and outlay of money. In this way the peasant was able to pay for his purchase of a large new class of imports into Ceylon, for Forbes noted in 1836 that 'every article of British manufacture which natives might require or could afford to purchase, was hawked through the most remote native hamlets, was offered for sale at every cabin door and might be procured at prices which would barely remunerate the importing merchant and native pedlar.'[4]

In 1835 the import duties on West Indian and East Indian coffee were equalized, and the Ceylon planter obtained what Governors like Barnes had been pressing upon Whitehall since large-scale coffee plantations had first been tried in Ceylon. The demand for land to be opened up followed. In 1836 3,920 acres had been sold – nearly ten times as much as in the previous year.

In the eight years which followed nearly 255,000 acres of land were sold by government, most of it described as Crown property and practically all of it for the production of coffee. The land was knocked down to the buyer at the upset price of five shillings an acre, the government paying for the costs of surveying it and accepting one-tenth of the purchase price at the time of sale, the purchaser contracting to pay the remainder within a year if the sale was to be considered valid. These terms were certainly 'not in any way unfavourable to investors'.[5] As the price of coffee in the British market rose nearly 300 per cent in these eight years, coffee fever, like gold fever in Australia and California later, seized all those with some money to invest.

The first period of coffee planting in Ceylon – until the depression of the 40s extinguished many bright hopes – was characterized by all the symptoms of an epidemic: the mass infection of all potential victims (in this case the moneyed section of the community), feverish speculation, the delirium of visions of immense profits, and fits of rage that the Ceylon Government or Parliament was withholding the legislation which could have ensured these. Estimates of the fortunes to be made by buying land, planting it, recouping oneself for one's capital investment and work and then selling it at a handsome profit were extraordinary. Lieutenant de Butts, an army man who knew little about coffee planting and its prospects at first hand but who heard from planters about the money to be made, reckoned in his *Rambles in Ceylon* (1841) that in the third year of enterprise the speculator recovered 50 per cent of his outlay and working expenses. At the end of the fifth year he would be making a profit of over £4,000 per annum; retiring nine years later with close upon £30,000 for his fourteen years spent on his three hundred acres in Ceylon.

Of course such items as the wages of coolies who worked 365 days in the year entered in his book-keeping make his calculations seem fantastic. But more sober records – such as this from the *Ceylon Observer* of May 1842 of an estate in Hantane near Kandy – prove that Butts, in spite of his silliness, was not completely deluded:

The O-Estate was commenced in July 1837 – Extent of Forest 1,892 acres.

Dr.

Total expenditure up to December 1841, including purchase of forest, planting 305 acres, stores, machinery, etc.

£6,938 7 3

Cr.

1839 Sale of seed and 42 bags of coffee	£445	18 6¾
Sale of 176 acres of forest	176	0 0
1840 Sale of seed and 796 cwt of coffee	3,017	10 5
1841 Estimated value of 2,000 cwt shipped	8,000	0 0

11,639 8 11¾

The crop of last year, 2,000 cwt, which is now going home, was gathered off 200 acres and only about 50 acres of that in full bearing. The crop of the coming season is estimated at 3,000 cwt and it will be gathered off about 250 acres. Judging from the experience of these two years, when the whole planted part (about 350 acres) is in full bearing it will give fully 5,000 cwt.[6]

The crash came when the depression of the 40s caused a steep drop in the price of coffee. The Ceylon Government was blamed for all its sins of commission and omission and the home government for its failure to protect the Ceylon planter. In 1845 plantation coffee (as distinct from 'native coffee' produced in the peasant's garden) was fetching forty-five shillings a pound on the London market; in 1849 the price had dropped to seventeen shillings. Sir Samuel Baker who was in Ceylon in the years of the depression, on very different business from that of speculating in coffee planting, wrote rather sombrely 'a rapid fortune can never be made by working a coffee estate'.[7] He was right. The day of the amateur intent on quick profit taking was over. But the problems which had harassed him in the course of his fortune-hunting remained to engage the attention of later planters.

The first was that of the land itself. Coffee, as proved by Kandyan peasant and Governor of Ceylon, would do best on the Kandyan highlands, at that time most of it in virgin forest. Except on altitudes over 5,000 feet where low jungle covered the heights, tall trees of the tropical rain forest came down the slopes where the villager halted them with terraced rice-fields – still a beautiful feature of the terrain – and gardens where the mixed cultivation of vegetables, fruit, the areca palm and the pepper vine made his living easier. Forest land in Kandyan times was the king's. It afforded him the twin sources of protection on which the country greatly depended; the formidable buttress of mountain and forest. But the right to use this latter for pasture and for crops of grain and vegetables, slashing down trees and undergrowth while the crop was raised for a few seasons and then the jungle allowed to resume the area again, had been the peasant's who tilled his fields in the valleys below.

It is difficult now to envisage the hill country of Ceylon as it must have looked before commercial crops were grown on it. So much has changed since then that the descriptions of the country by the earliest Englishmen who knew it read like accounts of an unimaginable landscape in forgotten times. Skinner who trudged through it in the 20s and the 30s, pitching his tent, or 'wigwam' as he called it, in the wilderness while working on his one-inch map of the Kandyan country described it as follows: 'So inaccessible were the interior districts at this time [about 1820] that Kandy was only approachable by narrow jungle paths, so steep and rugged as to be quite impassable for any description of vehicle, and often dangerous as a bridle-path. Commissariat supplies, and ammunition & & etc., were from necessity carried, to the capital and numerous outposts of the interior, on men's backs.'[8] Tennent who remembered the same country remarked:

To judge of the difficulties which beset such an undertaking (as Skinner's mapping and triangulation), it must be borne in mind that till very recently travelling in the interior of Ceylon was all but impracticable, in a country unopened even by bridle roads, across unbridged rivers, over mountains never trod by the foot of an Englishman and amidst precipices inaccessible to all but the most courageous and prudent. Add to this that the country is densely covered by forests and jungle, with trees a hundred feet high, from which here and there the branches had to be cleared to obtain a sight of the signal stations.[9]

It was this land which speculators in the 30s wanted for coffee cultivation. The majority of them were officials – of the Ceylon Government, of the East India Company in India (with more money at their disposal than their Ceylon counterparts), soldiers (of the regular armies and of fortune too) to be joined later by hopefuls from Britain. Few Ceylonese were qualified to join in the rush; they had neither the necessary money nor the influence to secure the best portions of land.

Stewart Mackenzie, the Governor, took up the position that as the Kandyan kingdom had been ceded to the British, the king's land legally belonged to the Crown. Addressing Normanby on need for a survey of Crown lands on 16 July 1839, he wrote: 'But thinking, as I do that the burden of proof [of private ownership] should lie with the private party and that conquest (?) of the Maritime District, and Cession, under treaty of the Kandyan Provinces, give the Crown a Catholic right to all land, not proven to have been granted at a former period, and of which neither title or registry can be proven or traced . . .'[10]

The difficulty was that the rights of an individual proprietor which could be validated in a court of law in the 1830s had never been envisaged by the custom governing the use of land in the Kandyan kingdom. There were individual owners of land in Kandyan times, but most cultivators tilled fields held by service tenure. They grew fine grain in forest clearing, or *chenas*, and pastured their cattle in forest land about whose ownership no one was concerned, as long as the age-old right of the peasant to use it was undisputed.

The speculator in the 30s, however, wanted land with a clear title to it. The Ceylon Government could neither establish this, nor could it provide the surveyors to divide land into insulated blocks fast enough to meet the demand. The Governor in Council attempted to frame legislation to deal with the pressure put upon officials by the private capitalist. This naturally had to have the sanction of the Colonial Office. Stewart Mackenzie, the Governor, spent a great deal of energy trying to persuade his reluctant superiors in England to allow him to declare as encroachers on Crown land all those who could not validate their claim to individual ownership. The Colonial Office disallowed this, as the Governor himself stated in his opening address to the Legislative Council on 19 October 1849, because a period of prescription in favour of the occupant had not been fixed. But Lt-General Colin Campbell, who succeeded him in 1841, was able to secure Colonial Office sanction to Ordinance No. 9 of 1841, which removed the protection afforded by an earlier Ordinance (No. 12 of 1840) to claimants to land occupied by them in the Kandyan Provinces.

His success in establishing the right of the Crown to make inroads upon the forest domains of the Kandyan kings regardless of the prescriptive rights granted by the earlier Ordinance, coming as it did upon the previously unavailing efforts of his predecessor to move the Colonial Office, led one scholar to suspect 'collusion between the Colonial Office and the Governor.'[11]

In an able and convincing piece of research on the evolution of the two Ordinances, K. M. de Silva disposes of the suggestion that the Colonial Office had been party to a fraud. On the contrary he shows that if there was a conspiracy, all the conspirators were to be found in the Colonial Government: 'Stewart Mackenzie and the Ceylon civil servants preferred to provide as little information as possible on this issue. In fact they deliberately and consistently misled the Colonial Office on these ordinances.' If anyone in the latter was to be blamed for not having looked more carefully into the dispatches from Ceylon it is James Stephen, who 'It would appear took this legislation extraordinarily lightly'.[12]

James Stephen was Permanent Under-Secretary of State at the Colonial Office in these years. He was regarded as being virtually its ruler – Mr Oversecretary Stephen was his nickname. A man of outstanding ability and integrity, the nephew of Wilberforce and an earnest Evangelical Christian, he was throughout his public career a lawyer, to whom justice in the abstract and the rule of law were positive values. Dr de Silva agrees that lightheartedness on all controversial issues was not his usual mode of approach.

On the receipt of Campbell's dispatch to Stanley of 24 January 1841, Stephen asked for a summary of what had passed with regard to the proposed legislation up to that date. This was provided in a memorandum on 31 March 1841:

In 1840 an Ordinance was passed by the Legislature of Ceylon 'To prevent encroachment on Crown Lands'. It was referred (30 May 1840) to the Law Officers of the Crown, who reported (8 June) that it ought not to be allowed because it gave an unlimited power of summary ejectment, against any party whose original entry was alleged to have been without probable claim or pretence of title. A copy of this opinion

63

having been forwarded (15 June) to Ceylon, and the Ordinance disallowed – a second Ordinance for the same purpose was introduced into the Council, passed and sent home by Mr S. Mackenzie on the 9 December 1840. This second Ordinance was likewise referred to the Law Officers, who reported (26 February 1841) that its provisions were as objectionable as those of the preceding Ordinance, because in every case of uninterrupted possession not exceeding thirty years it allowed a party to be turned out *brevi manu*, leaving him afterwards to make out his title as he might. In consequence of this Report it was determined to amend the Ordinance in this Country and an Order in Council was passed for that purpose confirming the Ordinance subject to the amendment of substituting the period of five years for that of thirty years. This Order in Council was forwarded to Ceylon in Lord Russell's Despatch of 25 August 1841.[13]

In spite of this Stanley, Stephen's superior, agreed to Campbell's suggestion that it would be judicious to amend the law of prescription, to which exception had been taken by the Law Officers of the Crown in England, because as the Governor stated, it was necessary 'under the peculiar circumstances of the colony'. So far as Stephen was concerned, the right finally to decide on these matters was one which, by character and temperament, he was reluctant to withhold from the man on the spot who ought to have known which was equitable or even justifiable. He had stated in 1830, with regard to any difference of opinion between the Colonial Office and the government of an established colony: 'Had I the understanding of Jeremy Bentham himself, I should distrust my own judgement as to what is really practicable in such remote and anomalous Societies.'[14] If he was responsible for the Colonial Office's consent to Ordinance No. 9 of 1841, he is unlikely to have made his decision lightly, but to have reacted in his dilemma with characteristic seriousness.

Between 1841 and 1844, when the world depression began to affect coffee culture in Ceylon, 185,000 acres of land had been sold. Not all of it was planted with coffee; some of it was bought by Ceylonese. But the general trend in these years was towards establishing the new structure of Ceylon's economy: that of a supplier of a commercial crop on the world market. Its immediate effects were not the depopulation of Kandyan villages or the creation of a large class of landless peasants. The villager benefited from the increased prices paid for coffee, and certainly no protest was made against Ordinance No. 9 of 1841. In 1859, when coffee had established itself as the staple industry of Ceylon, planter, Kandyan chieftain, Burgher lawyer, low-country Sinhalese and Kandyan peasant met in public (in the rooms of the Planters' Association in Kandy to be precise) to protest against the iniquity of Ordinance No. 12 of 1840, because it denied the Kandyan peasant the right to sell *chena* land to the planter (European and Ceylonese) with the clear title which such a sale would have demanded. This Ordinance claimed all such land as Crown land in the absence of valid proof to the contrary. Sir Henry Ward, the Governor in 1859, drew attention to 'the unusual combination between the two Races . . . the native element represents the vendors whose interests are, in this instance, identical with those of the European'.[15] By this time it would appear that there was still land to sell and that nearly everybody was anxious to sell if he could.

The extent of the real situation of the peasant in 1841 was not immediately clear. Only when he was left exposed to the sharpness of the economic climate in a time of depression, could he feel what he had been stripped of. In times of booming prices he could forget everything when profits came his way too.

To the planter and speculator the plight of the Kandyan peasant, or indeed of anyone else but himself in pursuit of the sacred right of profit, would have been immaterial. As the provider of a new source of revenue to the colony the planter saw himself as the sole justifiable object of concern to the Colonial Government and Whitehall. James Steuart, a civil servant in those years, expressed himself as forcibly as he could: 'We fear it is too true that the Merchants and Planters of Ceylon, have been taught by partial favours of government, to consider themselves *the Public*, or at least the most important interest in the community.'[16]

At the same time as the planter was pressing for land with incontestable title, he was facing his second problem: that of labour to work the land. The immediate tasks of clearing the forest and building simple huts for labourers and a bungalow for the superintendent did not at first provide problems, for the Kandyan peasant was ready to do these if he was paid for them. Tennent, within three days of assuming the Acting Governorship of the colony on Campbell's departure in 1847, sent a dispatch to Russell in which he set out the results of an earlier questionnaire to the police and magistrates in the Central Province on the important subject of estate labour. More than one of his informants had the same story to tell. The planter might have succeeded in getting some part of his labour force from the village, had he treated his workers fairly. Colepeper, the Superintendent of Police in Kandy, wrote that the villager was not work-shy and would have welcomed the opportunity of casual employment, but he had had galling experiences: 'I have been informed even this season [in 1847] some Estates have applied to them [native villagers] with success. The villagers demand only to be paid at the end of the day and not once a week. The villagers do this from experience, most of them having been employed at the opening of Estates and having suffered the same treatment and disappointment to which the Malabar labourers have been reduced.' In other words they were paid no wages and were beaten for their impudence in demanding them. C. H. de Saram, the Police Magistrate at Gampola, had a similar tale to tell: 'Several Headmen of this District tell me that the Villagers have so often been duped and cheated out of their due that some have given up work and others daily become more averse to work on the Estates.'[17]

But casual labour alone would not have satisfied the needs of the coffee planter. Besides a small number of workers to weed and keep the plantation in order, an active labour force was required between the months of August and early November when the berry was ready for plucking. Such numbers working throughout this period could not have been secured from the Kandyan village, because the villager at this time had his own *Yala* harvest (that before the North East monsoon) to bring in and his fields to plough for the new sowing. Besides he was not unmindful of the fact (even if he had had better experiences with the planter than those related by Colepeper and de Saram) that the cultivation of his small field gave him a traditional status of honour in the community, while the hired labour of the coolie degraded him. Above all, why should he have obeyed the categorical imperative 'Work', which the capitalist had elevated into a moral principle, since with his field and *chena* he could keep himself and his family content. Too often in the accounts of British planters (and of visitors to the island who were their mouthpieces) the Kandyan villager was portrayed as incorrigibly lazy and utterly unreliable. The strong tones of moral reprobation in these comments make the partiality of the writer obvious. Edward Sullivan, who spent a few months holidaying in Ceylon in the early 50s, repeated estate-bungalow talk he must have often heard: 'The Cingalese are of that miserable race that will not work unless forced to do so. Even gold, that all powerful persuader, fails in producing the desired effect; and I feel convinced, that if English energy and Malabar labour were removed, all that has hitherto been done for this island would, in five years, have utterly and entirely disappeared, and the coffee and cocoa crops have sunk to nothing.'[18]

The unwillingness of the peasant (and most Sinhalese were peasants) to forsake his traditional work in the rice-fields for more gainful occupations had long been remarked on by the British. There was, for instance, a profitable (in money terms) trade in vegetables in the vicinity of any small garrison town. But this was not explored or exploited by the native. In 1810 Maria Graham who visited Ceylon observed that Chinese labour had been imported into both Galle and Trincomalee to provide vegetables for the British.[19] Had the local population been interested, they would have learnt in 1810 what they were certainly able to do later.

The reluctance of the Kandyan peasant to become a wage-slave is understandable. Those who preach the virtues of work have tended to profit from the labours of others. To the planter in the 30s and 40s not only was such hard work as he had no occasion to do a moral duty, it was, so far as the coolie was concerned, inordinately well paid at fifteen to eighteen shillings a month. (It is significant that no planter writing at this time ever considered himself well paid, though his earnings were thirty and forty times those of the coolie.) Austin, who planted on Hunas-giriya in the early coffee days, spoke of the high rate of wages in his time (the 40s). This fact was 'proved by the circumstances that a labourer in Ceylon can live on one third of his pay, and save two thirds'. Clutterbuck, who visited Ceylon nearly fifty years later when the rate of sixpence a day had not gone up since the forties, des-cribed the good fortune of the Tamil coolie whose 'pay of sixpence a day is so enormous that he can afford to dress his children in this astonishing way (i.e. with silver rings on their toes, etc.)'.[20] It is refreshing to remember in this connection James Stephen's minute of 16 October 1841 on the suggestion in Campbell's dispatch of 'the great advantages likely to arise from the reduced wages of labour': 'So the rich invariably argue in all parts of the World. Whatever gives them a greater command of the labour of the Poor on lower terms, they, who hire such labour, will always regard as a public benefit . . . One would think that wages were low enough in Ceylon already where you can hire a day labourer for threepence or fourpence, and men live in Wigwams with clothing and food not much better than those of an Aboriginal New Hollander.'[21]

A supply of cheap labour, engaged throughout one coffee harvesting season on the plantations and then to be dispensed with until the next, was the problem. The first coffee planters had made their own arrangements about a contingent of coolies from South India, at that time a depressed area from which overpopulation and bad harvests sent many Indians overseas. But most of these 150 coolies secured by Bird and Barnes for their plantations (their pay was twelve to fifteen shillings a month plus a measure of rice) deserted and the experiment failed.

In the late 30s the Indian Government concluded arrangements with Jamaica, Trinidad, British Guiana and Mauritius for the immigration of Indians from the south to work on plantations. But, apart from these government sponsored schemes, the Indian Act No. 14 of 1839 forbade any attempts 'to engage or assist labourers in leaving the country'. In spite of this, as conditions in South India worsened and planters' agents from Ceylon were busy trying to recruit workers for the annual coffee plucking, there was a steady flow of coolies attracted by the prospect of seasonal labour, paid for at rates higher than those obtaining in South India. To this the Indian Government turned a blind eye.

The saga of these immigrants who travelled, some of them with their wives and children, along the coast of South India until they reached a port from which, herded into rice boats, they made the short crossing into north-central Ceylon, has to be conjured up out of the records of government officials in Ceylon. Depressed and wretchedly poor they trekked hundreds of miles through the arid plains of South India and the steamy jungle of Ceylon, banding themselves under leaders called *Kanganis*, the victims of both their own countrymen at home and any Sinhalese in Ceylon who chose to relieve them of their hard-won earnings. Death picked them off on jungle tracks; cholera and malaria frequently completed what the privations on the march had begun. No one seemed interested in their fate, provided that a sufficient number survived to reach the coffee districts in the Central Province of Ceylon at the time their labour was needed. The majority worked for four months on the estates, denied themselves everything which might have made their life endurable in order to take back home as much as possible of what they had earned. Most of those who survived the trek and the hard conditions of labour on the plantations returned to India. Some stayed on in Ceylon, finding more congenial work and more humane employers in the Public Works Department. Tennent's minute to Grey of 19 April 1847 gives the figures of those entering and leaving Ceylon. 'It is only within the last eight or nine years however that the influx of Indian labourers in search of employment attained its present height, commencing with the opening of the coffee estates in the interior.' He shows that in 1839 1,971 men, 182 women and ninety children arrived in Ceylon from South India. In 1845 66,557 men, 642 women, and seventy-nine children made the journey. In 1846 the numbers had dropped to 34,683 men, 257 women and thirty-one children and the planters were alarmed.[22]

In order to assure themselves of this source of supply, systems of 'indenting for labourers' were adopted by the planters. The most popular was that of paying the *Kangani* advances on the number of coolies in good health which he could provide – the coolie, of course, paying much more to the *Kangani* than the sum which had been advanced to him. By this system of 'coast advances' as it was known, the coolie acquired another opponent to contend with – his countryman in the shape of the *Kangani*. Of course there were *Kanganis* who defrauded the planter of the advances paid to them, but as parties to a contract they could be proceeded against in a court of law. Further since a number of coffee planters were civil servants and military officers in the service of the Indian Government, it was impolitic for a *Kangani* to risk default.

Faced with the human problem of this trek through the jungles of Ceylon and the accumulating evidence of the bad treatment of the coolie by the planter, the Ceylon Government tardily intervened. As most of the immigrants disembarked at Arippu and various ports on the north-western coast, hospitals were provided, staffed with medical sub-assistants, at Puttalam and Kurunegala, and 'rest houses' (thatched shelters with a supply of drinking water) on the much frequented road from Puttalam to Kurunegala. There was, however, no government hospital at Kandy, the centre of the coffee-planting district. A small institution founded in 1838 by the Friend in Need Society, to which both the government and some few plantations made contributions, had to deal as well as it could with the medical needs of a large new element in the population.

Everything so far had been conducted according to the rules of *laissez-faire*, and in order to hold the ring legal cognizance had to be taken of the situation. Ordinance No. 5 of 1841 upheld the solemn nature of the contract entered upon by employer and employee. As in all legislation of this kind, the scales were weighted against the unfortunate wage-slave in the open market. He now had the full force of the law invoked against him by the planter, who could, in rare cases, even be both accuser and judge. In any case the coolie who dared betake himself from the estate where he was ill-treated would find himself before a friend, or crony, of his employer and suffer accordingly for his temerity in breaking the law. Knighton's *Forest Life in Ceylon* (a novel which deserves reprinting as a social document) gives an excellent picture of what the coolie came up against in the name of justice.

Little could be hoped for from the civil servants, for most of them had taken to coffee planting when the economy proposals of the Colebrooke–Cameron commission withdrew their pensions, cut their salaries and diminished their prospects. 'The character of the [civil] service is materially deteriorated' wrote one of its prominent members, Anstruther,[23] himself a coffee planter. He had been asked while on leave in England to set out his views on the state of things in Ceylon. He wrote strongly about the frustration felt by members of the service, about the poor quality of the new entrants. He had no comments to make on the neglect of their duties by civil servants engaged in coffee planting, because most government officials were coffee planters, and in any case the Colonial Secretary, the Chief Justice, the Archdeacon of Colombo, etc., etc., did not actually plant on their estates.

Although no civil servant was allowed to take part in trade – a prohibition copied from that of the Indian Government – he was allowed to buy land and to sell its produce. 'The Governors encouraged the civil servants in their enterprise, for at that time they were almost the only Europeans in Ceylon who had capital to invest, and the one hope of making revenue balance expenditure was to develop the new industry.'[24]

By 1846 the Colonial Office, in spite of the protests of the service, had dealt with the problem of the civil servant coffee planter. Those who had bought land prior to 1845 and had had it cultivated were allowed to continue, but in future no civil servant was allowed to 'acquire any land in Ceylon save a house and grounds, nor might he sell the produce'. The wisdom of this measure, which ultimately distinguished planters from civil servants, freeing the latter for concentration on their duties as administrators and magistrates is to be seen in the changed relationships between the two groups of Britishers. Knighton, in the novel already referred to, remarks of his fictional character Mouat, the Police Magistrate of Rumincadee: 'It must not be supposed that Mr Mouat is presented to the reader as a sample of Ceylon magistrates generally – quite the reverse, he was an exception.' At the time Knighton wrote the ban on civil servants owning coffee plantations had just come into effect.

In the course of time resentment began to smoulder among planters that the civil servant, who seemed unnaturally devoted to the interest of the Kandyan peasant and the Tamil coolie, was not sufficiently aware of the planter's right to special favour as the mainstay of Ceylon's economy. This is tartly expressed by Duncan in *The Private Life of a Ceylon Coffee Planter*. Writing of civil servants he says 'it never enters into their brainpans, that if coffee planting were done away with, it would be necessary for them to wear their pocket-books shorter than at present, as the number of rupees which would fall to their share would be considerably reduced'.[25]

The drop in numbers of immigrants in 1846 disturbed the coffee planters. There were public meetings and three European members of the Legislative Council used their right to suggest legislation to introduce the draft of a proposed Ordinance 'for the protection and encouragement of Indian Labourers resorting to Ceylon'. On this subject, as on all others, the planters wished the government actively to engage itself in meeting their demands. Whatever the Ceylon Government might have thought – Campbell during his governorship tried to help the planter as much as he could, Anstruther his Colonial Secretary writing all his dispatches – the home government was unwilling to interfere. If the planter wished to procure labour for his estates, he was free to do so. Whitehall and Westminster, wedded to free trade and *laissez-faire*, would not move. Tennent in his dispatch, already referred to, suggested recruiting labour on long-term contracts (as the PWD was doing). Among other proposals of his were a special officer, designated Protector of Coolies, to be appointed to look after their interests; increasing the number of magistrates in coffee-producing districts to deal with infringements of the law; coolies to be allotted plots of land in which they could grow vegetables and rear poultry. The cost of all this 'would be entirely borne by the immigrants themselves, or defrayed out of advances made by their employers'. The planter would benefit; so would the government – from the revenue of the stamp duty on the contracts; the coolie would derive advantages for which he would pay.

Tennent went further. He developed an ingenious suggestion that as 'the great object of the Colonial Government should be to create a permanent and indigenous supply of labour within the Island', immigrants should be induced 'to settle permanently in Ceylon' by giving them grants of land in the Northern Province (at that time it included the whole of the ancient Sinhalese kingdom of Rajarata), a country which resembled their own, and which at one time had been extensively cultivated. The desire to settle the island's labour difficulties became one of Tennent's *idées fixes*. In order to understand what would seem today to be an extraordinary proposition, it should be remembered that Tennent was an ambitious careerist intent on impressing the Colonial Office. He later denied that he had ever made a suggestion in these terms. At the time he sent it in, however, he justified himself by stating: 'It is a fact very important to this inquiry, that the inhabitants of this once productive locality were not Cingalese but Malabars, induced to settle here under the dominion of Cingalese sovereigns; and the language of the few individuals scattered over the province is, to the present day, not Cingalese but Tamil.' He was, of course, either misinformed or ignorant.

The Colonial Office, interested though it might have been, took no further action in the matter. It could not, however, postpone intervening in the immigration of Indians to Ceylon, for the Indian Government could no longer keep up the pretence that a movement of its people to Ceylon did not exist. In 1858 the Coolie Immigration Ordinance set up a fund, contributed to partly by the government and partly by the planter, to create an Agency in India and an Immigration Board in Ceylon to facilitate immigration to Ceylon. The coolie was to pay a capitation tax of three shillings; in return he was to receive transport by chartered steamer and medical attention at depots organized by the government. In 1872 Ordinance No. 14 aimed at providing for the medical wants to coffee districts, where large immigrant populations had settled.

Exiguous as these benefits were, the immigrant worker seemed in the 1860s, and was still in 1965 represented as being, at an advantage over the indigenous villager in the planting districts. In the years when coffee was the major industry of Ceylon – that is, up to the end of the 1870s – no concern was felt for peasant or worker except when economic distress produced the troubles of 1848. But even at that time, in the inquiry held into the 'rebellion' as it was termed, the precise relation of this new element – immigrant worker – in the working population of the island to the rest was not examined. Here beside a land-owning or rice-growing peasantry, Sinhalese, Buddhist, enjoying a comparatively fair standard of living, was planted a large group of badly paid wage-slaves, Tamil, Hindu, completely isolated from the peasant and his life, maintaining within the confines of the estate a hard life reminiscent of conditions in South India in everything but the mode of making a living and its terrain. Between these two elements of the working population there was to develop suspicion and hostility as sharp as that which unhappily divides the agricultural worker from the industrial. When pressure on the land later worsened the plight of the Kandyan peasant, it was not difficult for him to think of the immigrant coolie, now long settled in Ceylon and every whit as depressed economically as himself, as being specially favoured. The raising of the structure of colonial rule was producing in Ceylon, as elsewhere in the world, tensions and causes of conflict bound to break out later.

The third of the planter's problems was that of transport of his crop from the hills to the port of Colombo. Anstruther, in his memorandum of 23 November 1840 already referred to, was explicit that there could be no development of the plantations without roads: 'Already complaint begins to be made that it is difficult to find lands fit for sugar and coffee near the high roads – and how can a planter be expected to purchase lands to which there is no reasonable prospect of a road being opened.'[26]

The fiercest of all the campaigns waged by the planters was that waged first on the provision of roads, and later on the railway from Colombo to Kandy. The planter learned the value of organization early. In 1842 the Ceylon Agricultural Society was founded, with Anstruther, the Colonial Secretary, as its President. It reflected, on the matter of roads, the opinions of Anstruther and of every civil servant who felt that the colony's annual contribution of £24,000 to the expenses of the military stationed in the island was unnecessary and inequitable. No other colony had been saddled with such an impost and the money could quite easily have been used for schemes of development such as communications. For close upon twenty years this was a constitutional issue which united all those whose profits were linked with coffee. In this way the planter, with his allies among the nominated members in the Legislative Council and aided by newspapers and public meetings, first used mass agitation for political purposes in Ceylon.

When coffee began its reign military roads built by the Royal Engineers and a locally recruited company of Pioneers connected Colombo with Kandy, and Kandy with Kurunegala and Trincomalee. There were few bridges and until loads of coffee berries had to be transported on them traffic was light. As more roads were built, for which tolls were charged, the costs of maintaining them grew. When heavily laden bullock carts began to use them their loosely held gravelled surfaces deteriorated quickly and caused long delays in the columns converging on Colombo from the hills. In his budget for a coffee plantation in 1841 Butts included £60 for 'bullock bandies and bullocks'. These in a continuous stream from plantations descended on Colombo, returning from there with rice and provisions for the labourers. Vanden Driesen notes that in 1833 only £11,393 or 2·5 per cent of the country's revenue was spent on roads; by 1860 there were 1,800 miles of major roads in the island, 'a continuous metalled line extending from Galle to Colombo, Kandy and Nuwara Eliya'. By this time nearly 20 per cent of the revenue was spent on road building and maintenance, but before this the collapse of the first scheme to build a railway between Colombo and Kandy to help Ceylon coffee to compete with Brazilian had fired the planting interest in the island with the desire for constitutional reform. With logic that seemed justifiable the planting interest claimed that as coffee provided the greater part of the revenue, the coffee planter and the merchant should be more effectively represented in the legislative assembly. The demand for constitutional reform arose out of the self-interest of the planter. That it was taken up by other sections was an omen for the times.

CHAPTER 5

THE STRUCTURE COMPLETED
1848-99

The structure of British rule in Ceylon was completed only after the depression of the 40s. In the ten years between 1845 (when the depression in the UK was first beginning to be felt in Ceylon) and 1855 (when trade and commercial prospects had revived), the planting of coffee had been transformed from the interest of the private speculator into a major industry, in which the capital involved was no longer the sum total of the personal assets of persons anxious to enrich themselves quickly. The depression finished off most small investors. Those who had invested their savings and their limited resources in plantations were resentful of what they interpreted as two body blows to their enterprise: the home government's reduction of differential duties which had given Ceylon coffee an advantage over the Brazilian, and the Ceylon Government's 400 per cent increase in the upset price of land. One of those who survived wrote of his fellows at the height of the depression:

> Capitalists were induced to enter into coffee cultivation at a time when land was cheap, and when the protective duty amounted to 150 per cent in favour of the British grower: but no sooner were numerous estates formed and a very large sum invested than the price of land was raised 400 per cent, while the protective duty, our great stay, was lowered to 50 per cent, so that the British cultivators were at once placed in a false and a most unfortunate position.[1]

The recovery of the UK from the depression, the boom in industry, the increasing demand for coffee in England and Europe and the export of capital from England into the colonies finally set coffee firmly on its feet again. Its British rulers could see no other future for Ceylon than that of a country producing a commercial crop for which there was a demand, the revenues from which benefited British planters and merchants and contributed to the cost of running the island, paying for its defence, its administration and its development. Were there any other possible choices before them? They were men of their time, and their course of action seemed recommended by both political economy and Christian morality. What they were doing was not only for their own good, but also for the benefit of the people of Ceylon.

D. Wilson, a planter writing in 1847, estimated that two million pounds had been invested in coffee and sugar in Ceylon between 1840 and 1844.[2] As his pamphlet was intended for the consumption of British parliamentarians at a time when affairs in Ceylon were being investigated by a Select Committee of the House of Commons, it is likely that he was slightly exaggerating the amount put in by his compatriots in their efforts to improve themselves and the economy of Ceylon. But certainly much more than this was invested in coffee after the 50s. The old proprietary planter still dominated the scene, but he got his money now from banks and agencies in Ceylon and in the United Kingdom. Vanden Driesen reckoned that 'the total capital invested in the plantations was something like £12–£13m'.[3] This was not, by British standards of that time, a very large investment. But it was, in relation to Ceylon and its possibilities, an immensely important factor of change in the monetary sphere alone. Money was coming into Ceylon, and though the return from it – its accumulated profits – went to the UK, a great deal of it stuck in the island and was responsible for the altered structure of the island's economy.

But before that happened in the 50s, Ceylon too had been caught by the vagaries of the economic climate with consequences similar to those all over the world. It caused the disturbances in 1848, called the 'Rebellion' by many writers on Ceylon then and now. The Ceylon Government, engaged in planning fiscal reform at the instance of the Treasury and the Colonial Office, found itself faced with falling revenue in 1847 on account of the depression instead of anticipated surpluses. To make up its deficit a series of new taxes, of which Whitehall approved, was presented to the Legislative Council in 1848 by Torrington, the Governor, who was incidentally a cousin of the Prime Minister, Lord John

Russell, and owed his appointment to this connection. The Queen, who knew Torrington and had no high opinion of his capabilities, was surprised at his selection for the office of Colonial Governor.[4]

Seven new taxes, including one on firearms and another on dogs, were to be imposed at a fixed rate. In addition there were taxes in lieu of work on the roads, from which only the military and the Governor of the Colony were exempted: all males over the age of eighteen and under sixty-five having to pay three shillings annually, or work six days on the roads. These taxes were as unimaginatively conceived as that on coconut palms in the second year of the rule of the Madras Government in Ceylon. The reaction to both was similar.

Tennent had recently assumed office and was innocent of any practical knowledge of Ceylon, though he had already begun his preparations for writing his compendium of information on the country. There might have been some excuse for his ignorance had no opposition been expressed in the country to the government's tax proposals. But there was immediate and vehement objection to them which he, with confidence in his intellectual parts perhaps, undertook to demolish by argument. A sample of this was provided in Kandy early in July 1848 by his asking his subdued audience of chiefs and the populace (carefully controlled by a strong detachment of police), whether it wasn't better to pay the gun tax rather than to receive several lashes. Whatever he thought of the success of these arguments at Kandy, he could hardly have been in doubt of the outcome of the debate in Galle, where the hostility of the audience to his thesis forced him to take flight in the Government Agent's horse-carriage, from which he was precipitated into a water butt.

Although the Governor, most of the military, some British officials and practically all the coffee planters regarded the disturbances which followed the promulgation of these taxes as a serious 'rebellion', it was the manifestation of deep-seated peasant unrest, the unrest of a people who had lost the feudal leaders to whom they were accustomed and had found no leadership to replace it in their desperation at the exactions imposed on them. They tried to recreate the past which was beyond recall by going through all the rituals which once had belonged to it: a pretender to the Kandyan throne – he was a low-country man from Mora-tuva; the bandying about of the names of some chieftains and *bhikkhus* who had promised their support; a few indifferently armed bands. That was all. In 1848 in the Kandyan country some of the rural poor had tried to influence the course of events by direct action in the only way in which they could envisage it. After that date they disappeared from the political scene until 1936, when they were just beginning to realize the value of universal franchise as a weapon.

The events of this 'rebellion' of 1848 were unimportant in themselves, but like everything connected with it are of the great-est significance in elucidating the stresses of British rule on life in Ceylon. First of all, the unimportance of what happened in the few days of the disturbances at Matale and Kurunegala was an index of the changed character of the country and of British con-trol of it, when it is contrasted with the rebellion of thirty years previously. Then for over a year irregulars were fighting a losing battle against the British. There could be no question now of any threat to the absolute control of the country by its new rulers.

Contemporary accounts of the 'fighting' might be amusing reading,[5] had not the consequences been oppressive for the Sinhalese involved in them. The government, convicted of negligence by its failure to understand and foresee the course of events, seemed determined to create a state of emergency in dealing with which it could salve its wounded self-esteem. Inflamed by tendentious reports from Kandy and Matale, Torrington who had already called out the military to deal with a peaceable crowd in Colombo, allowed himself to be influenced by Sir Herbert Maddock, the Deputy Governor of Bengal, then in Kandy on a visit to his coffee plantations in the Matale District. Martial law was declared and Maddock proceeded to take a leading part in a 'council of war' consisting of Lt-Colonel Drought, Captain Bird of the Ceylon Rifles and himself. He seems to have been in con-trol, both of the military (despite the fact that the Officer Com-manding the Troops and a number of senior officers were in Colombo) and also of the Governor who travelled to Kandy.

In Colombo a crowd of a few thousand had assembled on the northern outskirts of the town, intending to proceed to the Fort, there to present a petition to the Governor, complaining of the injustice of the new taxes. Torrington was alarmed, alerted the police and called out the military. It did not require more than the efforts of a single Irishman, Dr Christopher Elliot, to persuade the assembly not to break the law of the land by entering the Fort in such numbers. He undertook to present the petition to the Governor and the meeting broke up, but not before some of the participants were soundly belaboured by the police. Nothing more was heard of any 'disturbance' in the Colombo area.

The unfortunate inhabitants of the Matale, Kurunegala and Kegalle districts were, however, experiencing the zeal of army officers with martial instincts aroused against a foe unable to retaliate. Houses were burnt, cattle and personal property confiscated, all in the name of law and order. Courts martial primed by informers (British and native) and determined to discourage anything which could remotely be interpreted as connection with, or knowledge of, the 'rebellion', were sentencing people to be shot in batches of four at a time. In spite of the protests of the Chief Justice who was proceeding on Supreme Court assizes to Kandy, martial law was not lifted until six weeks after the so-called Pretender had been captured. There was the extraordinary spectacle of the Chief Justice presiding over sessions in Kandy, while not twelve miles away courts martial were dispensing a justice of their own.

The conduct of the military and of some of the planters has to bear the responsibility for the savagery with which 'the rebellion' was suppressed. Both military and planters seem to have been bitten by Maddock's madness that the lives and property of every European in the island were at stake, and only the utmost severity could save the situation. The Ceylon Government caught the infection and went mad too. Troops were urgently demanded from the East India Company and were landed in Trincomalee – all to deal with a rebellion which never took place.

The second conclusion provided by a study of the 'rebellion' is that though the time was long past when British control of the island could have been disputed militarily by its inhabitants, political control had not reached the stage when it could rely on the support and loyalty of the masses of the Kandyan country. Had there been no troops in the island Ceylon would still have remained British, but this would have been due to the conviction

that opposition to them was hopeless and not from any attach-
ment to their rule. Chiefs and government officials had been in-
corporated into the official hierarchy. Their interests would be
identified with those of the British ruler and the maintenance of
law and order. But even these native officials – the chiefs especially – were not whole-heartedly trusted by the British administrator.

Worst of all, the administrator seemed to be – if he is to be
judged by his actions during the 'rebellion' – unable to understand
the people he ruled. To take one example: Waring, the Police
Magistrate of Matale, informed by Maha Nilame Dullewe that a
band of disaffected persons was approaching his station, immediately left it. This discretionary action does not discredit his processes of reasoning, but it does show that they did not include any
faith or hope in dealing personally, by virtue of his high office,
with people in a moment of stress. Quite often in the evidence
given before the Select Committee witnesses spoke of the poor
showing of the civil servant of that time. There can be no doubt
that a number of Britishers in the island felt that the 'rebellion'
might never have taken place at all and that its worst consequences
might have been avoided, had officials been better aware of the
condition of the people. Skinner, who had spent thirty years in
Ceylon and knew the Kandyan country well, was quite emphatic
that 'had there existed less ignorance of the social condition of the
people, the late troubles might easily have been averted, even at
the eleventh hour; while to that ignorance is to be attributed the
(in my humble judgement) exaggerated view taken of the nature
and extent of the disaffection; the consequent severity of the
punishments inflicted on those implicated in the revolt.'[6]

Finally, the British official's lack of understanding of the
people, his failure to feel the pulse of the country, was matched by
the inability, or unwillingness, of the native hierarchy to transmit
to its superiors the real state of feeling in the country. No investigation has yet been made into one feature of the history of
nineteenth-century Ceylon: the composition and ethos of the
Mudaliyars of the Maritime Provinces and their counterparts, the
chieftains, in the Kandyan country. Such an inquiry will have to
determine to what extent this important class of native official,
supernumerary though they might have seemed in relation to their

British superiors, really did know the people of the country, and to what extent, too, they were ready and able to communicate their knowledge. It will have to study very carefully the social process in Ceylon and the psychological development of the Ceylon character. It seems as though a great deal of the local knowledge of the British with regard to Ceylon – its ultimate conversion to Christianity, to take one example – in the first half of the nineteenth century was based on information conveyed by the Mudaliyars that the populace was shortly going to be weaned from its adherence to Buddhism. Did the Mudaliyars – for on this subject the Kandyan chieftain held different views – really believe that the ordinary man would, as readily and understandably as they had done, change his religion? It is difficult not to believe that as they were Oriental in their unwillingness to disappoint the European inquirer, they were over-anxious to please with their answers rather than to inform. Perhaps some of them had, as a result of the divisive social trends of the time, become quite as isolated as their white masters from the people whose language they spoke and whom they represented. Maria Graham relates an episode during her brief visit to Ceylon in 1809. She was warned by the Maha Mudaliyar not to enter a Buddhist temple in Weligama because the devil was worshipped there. Of course faulty English may have accounted for this statement that the devil was worshipped in such a place. But the inability of most British writers on Ceylon, who depended for their information from Mudaliyars, to distinguish between Buddhism and exorcistic rites suggests that their informants did not trouble to correct their misapprehension. Miss Graham knew better than the Maha Mudaliyar; she put down his obsession with the idea that Buddha and Satan were identical to his Dutch Protestantism.[7]

These speculations have been indulged in only to suggest that it was not easy for the British official to acquaint himself with the state of feeling in the country. If he betook himself to accepted authority – the Mudaliyar who was supposed to be the fountain of all knowledge – he would perhaps have had his prejudices confirmed and his suspicions strengthened. As for the native official at a disadvantage in his dealings with a master with unpredictable reactions and strange language habits – he would feel safer in complying in advance with his superior officer than setting himself up as critic or opponent. Those who faithfully performed their duty in reporting, in their own way, what was astir in the countryside did so in language modes which must often have left their British hearers mystified. Here is the sworn statement of Maha Nilame Dullewe:

> On Wednesday the 26th of July last, I went from Kandy to Matele; on my way, at Kellalpittiye, I met two Koralles, Tibbotowe Koralle and Kahawittegedra Koralle; I told them there was a report of a rebellion, and asked them whereabouts it was; they answered, 'there is such a report, but we do not know much about it'. I proceeded to Matele, and went direct to the house of Mr Waring. I told Mr Waring 'there is a report of a rebellion at Dambool, but it is too late now to talk about it, I will go to my lodging, and call upon you tomorrow morning'. I inquired after his health, and went away. Mr Waring said, 'very well, come in the morning'.[8]

In the Maha Nilame's words is reflected the sulkiness of the old-time chieftain (actually he was eighty at the time and the only surviving signatory of the Kandyan Convention) at the changed way of life in the Kandyan country. Once upon a time he would himself have dealt, or would have had to deal, with such matters as reports of a rebellion. Now this had to be conveyed to his British superior who would deal with all such affairs. What he probably intended to say to Mr Waring was 'You people have come here and upset everything. I have done my duty in telling you about the report of some discontent; now you had better look after things yourself. I have done my duty and am off.'

The Maha Nilame behaved correctly; he reported everything he heard; he obtained Mr Waring's permission for everything he did. He took it for granted that as his lot was cast with the British, he would have to escape if these 'rebels' descended upon Matale. As Mr Waring had a horse, the Maha Nilame assured him that he certainly would outdistance any pursuers, since the 'rebels' were on foot. So the old chieftain went his ways, returning the next morning after a quiet night to inquire what had become of Waring.

The Maha Nilame was an old man, and perhaps rather senile, but his attitude, particularly in its lack of enterprise and initiative which angered Buller, the Government Agent of the Central Province, could represent that of native officialdom: what have we to do with these things; they concern the rulers of the country, not us. These native officials were not passing the buck; they were only acknowledging their lack of power and their inferiority to the rulers of the country. To a great extent this denial of any responsibility to the native headmen (Mudaliyars and chiefs) in all but trivial matters persisted throughout British rule in Ceylon. One result of this over-concentration of power in British hands was the greater isolation of the British administrator from the people through whom they were kept in touch with the country. Many British civil servants knew the landscape of the country well; they were interested in its antiquities, its flora and its fauna. Very few of them indeed knew its people. Their contact was on an official level with minor public servants, towards whom they behaved correctly, condescendingly at times, but whom they rarely knew as persons. It would have had to be an exceptional civil servant – in the days when practically all of them were British – who could say that he moved freely and naturally with the people he ruled.

The unimportance of the native official, like the Mudaliyar, had one unfortunate consequence. Deprived of real responsibility, and quite obviously outside the ranks of the ruling caste, he compensated for his loss of status by adding inches to his stature in his dealings with the ordinary man. 'The evils of the headman system' became a cliché in the next century, because in actual life the brief authority in which the Mudaliyar was dressed made him a tyrant to his countrymen below him in the social scale.

The government's opponents lost no time in mounting their attack. Both Torrington and Tennent were disliked by important sections of Colombo society: the English business man, the Burgher lawyer and the trader resident in the Pettah. Besides there was a real newspaper (and not a government sheet as previously) in the Colony, which had been started by two Colombo businessmen fourteen years before. It was then edited by Dr Christopher Elliott, who had given up an appointment in the colonial medical service to turn journalist. He made up for the lack of a large circulation by the fiery devotion he gave to popular causes. During his tenure of editorship the *Observer* persistently criticized the government. Colonial Governors were very resentful of the influence he had over his small English reading public, and were always nervous of the possible reaction of the Colonial Office to his fire. The language of dispatches from Ceylon in the forties and the early fifties still glows with the scorn of Governors and Colonial Secretaries at the impudence of a mere journalist.

Elliott's campaign against the Governor was based on more than support from his Colombo readers. There had been widespread concern about the courts martial and the recklessness with which the military had behaved. For the first time in the history of the colony the organized public meeting, with resolutions, became a feature of the political scene. Reference has been made earlier to Elliott's success in persuading the concourse of the discontented at Borella to give up their plan of marching to the Fort. That was not a mass meeting, but the well-known Sinhalese custom of taking a grievance to the ruler. It was the accepted and official mode of procedure at the time of the Kandyan kings. It was not a meeting of people to discuss anything, it was an assemblage of people who had already decided to go to the ruler. Knox who knew the custom well and had himself taken part in one of these gatherings, refers to it.[9]

The small meetings at Hultsdorf harangued by Elliott and others with their resolutions and petitions, copies of which were addressed to the British Government in England and were circulated among members of Parliament, produced the effect intended. Ceylon, not for the first time, became a subject for debate on the floor of the House of Commons. The wind raised by these meetings blew a gale there which threatened to topple Lord John Russell's government. To its opponents Ceylon was as good a weapon as any other in their assault on the Prime Minister and Earl Grey, the Colonial Secretary.

Thomas Young McChristie, a barrister who had been in Ceylon in 1846 and had contacts with Elliott, was the agent by whom members of Parliament like Joseph Hume were informed of what had happened in Ceylon. McChristie was obviously shaken by the results of his work, as he stated later that he never expected that the petitions presented by him would have caused such a stir:

When I presented these petitions to Parliament, or when I procured the favour of some honourable members to present some petitions, I acted as a mere agent, and without any personal feeling whatever; and throughout, I considered that the inquiry desired might be obtained without much difficulty, and I might almost take the liberty of saying without any angry feeling whatever. I never contemplated making myself a party in any way whatever, but when I found that there was considerable feeling on both sides, I desired to withdraw from any further proceeding.[10]

It is necessary to draw attention to this mode of appeal to an authority more eminent than either the Colonial Governor or the Colonial Office, because it was going to be used in the future by all those with strong opinions to express about the state of things in Ceylon. As there was an appeal from the highest court of law in the island to the Privy Council, so the canvassing of the interest of members of the House of Commons became an institution.

Though for a time it looked as if Russell's government would be in difficulties in the House, the delinquencies of the administration in Ceylon were not sufficiently grave an issue for such consequences as the fall of a ministry. A Select Committee of the House was appointed in 1849 to 'inquire into the grievances complained of in Ceylon, in connection with the administration and government of that Colony, and to report their opinion whether any measure can be adopted for the redress of any grievances of which they may be shown just reason to complain; and also whether any measures can be adopted for the better administration and government of that Dependency.' Peel, Hume, Disraeli and Gladstone served on the committee. Of course Russell had his own men on it too. Despite its general terms of reference, it concerned itself only with the question whether the Governor had handled the situation as well as he might have done. It recommended a royal commission which would visit the island, repeating this in its Third Report on 24th July 1850. This was resisted by Russell and by Grey who, as a matter of principle, stood by the Colonial Governor. A few officials from Ceylon were ordered to England for examination. In 1850 Torrington was recalled and asked to resign his governorship. A year later the whole political rumpus blew over in England.

The record of the evidence given before the Select Committee is dreary beyond description. The crowd of British civil servants and military men who appeared before it were almost without exception anxious to grind their own axes and to whirl them about the heads of their professed and secret enemies. Few seemed aware of their human responsibilities towards the people they ruled. There were political, administrative and judicial considerations involved. Through the meshes of this official network of duties the people of the country, semi-civilized savages to be controlled by the hand of authority, slipped without much comment. Anstruther, who was looked upon as a civil servant of the good old days, was a coffee planter with 2,500 acres in the Ambegamuva district, accustomed to raise the voice of authority and to be obeyed. Sympathy and understanding were not notes often sounded by it.

Wodehouse and Tennent, both dismissed from the Ceylon civil service, got off more lightly than Torrington, for both of them were subsequently back in official life. Tennent's luck did not desert him. He was offered the Governorship of St Helena, but never took up the appointment. His book on Ceylon appeared in 1860, when he had been Secretary of the Board of Trade for eight years. Since that time his two volumes have been regarded as holy writ on Ceylon, though they are much in need of some higher criticism. Wodehouse went on to serve overseas, ending up as Governor of Bombay.

In Ceylon the agitation died down with Torrington's recall. When in the 50s coffee was doing well again, the troubles of 1848 became a thing of the past, to be referred to only in the obsequious addresses of welcome to Governors presented by local Mudaliyars in the south, anxious to demonstrate their superiority to the perfidious Kandyans.

With the return of better times coffee was firmly established as Ceylon's major export and the foundation of its economy. Cinnamon became a minor article of export; its cultivation was taken up by the small landholder in the Maritime Provinces. During the inquiries of the Select Committee the total extent of Kandyan land in coffee was given as one-thirtieth of its whole territory. It is difficult to say whether these figures were accurate, since the witnesses never stated what they understood to be the whole extent of Kandyan territory. The greater part of the hill country of the old Kandyan Provinces was still in forest. This did not long remain so, for by the 70s the total acreage under coffee in European plantations and native holdings had increased to 272,000. In 1874

Birch, the Government Agent Central Province, complained that 'there have been no land surveys for the last year and applicants have been waiting for their title plans for eighteen months and two years – It is absolutely necessary that the question of forest reserves should be no longer delayed and in the absence of all surveys planters are encroaching on the Crown forests with apparent immunity.'[11] By that time all but the higher elevations where coffee did not do well had been stripped of their forest cover.

It is true to say that, as coffee supported the whole economy, the government despite its routine interest in other sources of revenue did not trouble itself unduly with any alternatives to it. Rice, which the increasing population of the island needed more and more, could always be imported from Bengal. Despite the reports of a few civil servants who worked in the North Central Province and the personal interest of governors like Gregory, little was done to grow more rice or to tackle the enormous task of bringing into cultivation the old rice-growing areas of the northern plain. Coffee dominated the scene; everything in the island took its cue from its price in the world market. R. L. W. Herbert, in his minute on Gregory's dispatch on famine conditions in the North Central Province of 15 February 1874, made the obvious comment: 'Previous Governors do not seem to have been aware of their duties, for they were not justified in expending large sums for the benefit of the planters in the more prosperous districts while large portions of the island were totally neglected.'[12]

Sugar was never really persisted with, nor were its pioneers encouraged. Bertolacci writing to North on 10 January 1811, after Maitland had succeeded in rescinding the order prohibiting Europeans holding land in the island, mentioned a sugar project in Kalutara: 'At last the order for granting lands to Europeans has been received and a very fine plantation is begun at Caltura under the superintendence of Mooyart who you will recollect used to join our musical parties.'[13] Private speculators tried the cultivation of sugar-cane in the Southern Province and in the Northern Province with indifferent success. It was not refined and there was a prejudice against it. Besides it could not compete with cheaper West Indian and Javanese sugar.

Something might have been done for cotton, had there been any plans to diversify the plantation economy. Governor Ward had sent some samples of Ceylon grown cotton to Lytton, the Secretary of State, in 1859. The Cotton Supply Association of Manchester, to whom the samples were directed, were favourably impressed: 'They consider it to be of excellent quality worth nine-pence per pound and that it will find a ready and extensive sale in their districts. They have added an expression of their hope that you would use your best efforts in directing the attention of the inhabitants of Ceylon to the speedy cultivation of cotton on an extensive scale.'[14] But again little was done.

But the health of the economy was not long to be charted by the graph of the rise and fall of the price of coffee. In the 40s coffee came in like a fever; it went out in the late seventies with a plague. The Botanical Gardens, transferred to Peradeniya by Barnes in order to help his attempts to develop a plantation in-dustry, had always been watchful of the interests of the planter. The staff had been experimenting on other crops; on the simple machinery used for pulping the berries; and on such things as rats and leaf diseases which had troubled the coffee planter. Cocoa had been tried out in the Kandy district; the first large-scale planter of the new crop was Tytler on Pallekelly. The prospects of cinchona had also been investigated.

By 1869 a new blight appeared to be afflicting coffee – an orange red splotch on the leaves which, as it spread, gave the hillsides an autumnal splendour but gradually destroyed the crop. For a long time the warnings of the staff at the Gardens were unheeded, for prices continued to improve and, as more land was brought under cultivation, the fall in the money value of the crop was masked. Jenkins, an experienced planter, remembered that in 1869 'the peculiar appearance on the leaves had already caused alarm'. But at the same time 'land for coffee, and coffee estates, rose to their highest values, and prices – till then undreamt of – were freely asked and paid . . . the abnormal state of the Mincing Lane market accounts for this'.[15] Even a very capable administrator like Gregory disregarded the forebodings of the experts at the Botani-cal Gardens and invested some of his money in coffee. (In this case the itch to gamble, strong in an Irishman, must have got the better of his judgement.)

The promised doom overtook coffee by the end of the 70s, when it became impossible to control the disease which by now had spread to every district, even to Uva which had been comparatively free from it. A large number of people were ruined; a great deal of coffee land and forest land bought for the cultivation of coffee were abandoned; and a new start had to be made. Fortunately the debris of the old order was still serviceable and the Peradeniya Gardens had succeeded in recommending the advantages of subsidiary crops like cinchona (from the bark of which quinine was prepared) and cocoa. After a period of hardship for himself (and for the country too), until the planter had learned how to manufacture tea and the city of London discovered a bright future for the new product, the run-down plantation economy was again set going.

Cinchona had been tried out with success at the Botanical Gardens at Peradeniya. Its cultivation for a time eased the difficulties of the transition from coffee to tea. But it never had a future in the island and over-production depressed world prices.

It was different with tea, which had attracted a few experimenters in Ceylon even before coffee had become the major crop. The tea bush had been discovered growing wild in the jungles of Assam in 1830. The Governor-General, Lord William Bentinck, set up a Tea Committee in 1834 to investigate the possibilities of its cultivation in the Presidency of Bengal. In 1836 the first Assam-grown tea was sent to London, and tea seed from Assam was received at the Gardens in Peradeniya in 1839. But before this tea was mentioned in documents at Peradeniya, according to the official history of the Royal Botanical Gardens. 'Tea was introduced before 1828 and was found growing on the site of the old Botanical Garden at Caltura in 1841. A reintroduction took place in 1839.'[16] In 1841 Maurice Wörms, of the Rothschild family, tried to raise the China tea plant in a specially prepared clearing at Labookellie on the slopes of a Ramboda Pass. A Chinese 'tea maker' was imported to prepare the leaf, but his methods were so expensive that it was impossible to produce a pound at under £5. Other coffee planters who tried tea as a subsidiary to coffee had similar experiences, the finished product being expensive and undrinkable.

But when coffee collapsed and there was urgent necessity that tea should no longer fail, it succeeded. Planters from Assam helped with their experience and knowledge of making the leaf into a dark tea of good quality. Tea seed, not *bohea* but of the *viridis* variety from Assam, was imported as soon as supplies were available. The first tea sold in Ceylon was made at Loolecondera Estate in 1872. In 1883 Ceylon tea was recognized on the London market as possessing qualities of aroma and flavour distinct from the Indian and the Chinese. Soon various grades of Ceylon tea, from the best grown at heights at which coffee would not thrive to low-country teas planted a few feet above sea level, established the reputation of the Ceylon product. Gradually the dark teas of India and Ceylon began to oust the Chinese from the market in the UK.

The city of London welcomed an empire controlled source of supply in preference to the uncertain Chinese product. So tea, which to most upper-class Englishmen and women for close upon three centuries had been 'the infusion of a China plant', by the end of the nineteenth century was the characteristic product of Ceylon to all the common crowd in the UK delighted with a cheap, strongly sweetened and stimulating beverage. When Thomas Lipton, the successful owner of a chain of grocery stores, invested money in 1890 in plantations in Ceylon and sold his product direct to the customer, bringing his proprietary brand 'straight from the tea gardens to the teapot', the island naturally became 'Lipton's tea garden'.[17] The average consumption of tea per head of population in the UK rose from 1·22 lbs in 1840 to 6·07 in 1900.

Tea is an evergreen which could be grown in all parts of the island where rain and sunlight in sufficient quantities ensure a good flush of fresh leaves. The plucked leaves – the two leaves and a bud – are put through five processes of withering, rolling, fermenting, firing and sorting in the factory. The product is then ready for export.

The cultivation and processing of tea requires a fair-sized labour force engaged all the year round in the multifarious tasks of a large plantation which secures economies of scale and is the most effective unit. Rainfall restricted the development of tea to the central massif, the wet zone of the low country and the highlands of Uva. The north-central plain, the north and the east lay outside regions where tea could be grown. These areas therefore were untouched, as they were in the coffee days, by the development of the new plantation industry except indirectly. They lay in jungle, ill populated except for the northern peninsula of Jaffna.

In 1867 no tea at all was exported from Ceylon and only ten acres were cultivated with it. In 1874 4,700 acres had been opened up. By 1894 as much land as had ever been planted with coffee was producing tea – over 330,000 acres.[18] Within eighteen years of the failure of the coffee industry tea had taken its place as the mainstay of Ceylon's economy. To the old coffee planters who survived the crash and remembered the rigours of their pioneering days, the tea planter had everything made easier for him as a result of their years of toil and agitation. To a great extent this was true. But resourcefulness and energy were needed on the part of those who now had to turn to tea, destroying high forest in their desperation to recoup their losses. Besides this the enterprise of the new race of capitalists who provided the bigger outlay needed for the new industry should not be forgotten. But neither would have succeeded on its own, had not the soil and the climate been ideally suited for tea and the government been more than ready to help. As early as 1873, when the first consignment of Ceylon tea was exported, Gregory began to feel that the future really lay with it. It had long been accepted that the economy of the island was soundly based on large-scale plantation agriculture; if coffee could no longer be produced then a substitute would have to be found. This was the view of the government, the planters, and all those, British and Ceylonese, who had any opinions to express.

Before the end of the century a new possibility opened out before the planter and smallholder in Ceylon. Rubber had been introduced with some success and a new tribe of planters, made rich by plantation agriculture, appeared on the scene, with, for a change, quite a few Ceylonese among them.

Markham 'kidnapped' the cinchona tree in the 70s; not long after Charles Wickham, with considerable self-assurance and bravado, 'kidnapped' some 70,000 *Hevea* rubber seeds – at that time a prohibited export from Brazil – shipped them to Le Havre and then rushed them off to Kew where they germinated under glass. The extraordinary story of this exploit, first told by Wickham himself, has been so often repeated that it need not be recounted here.[19] Some of the plants raised in Kew were sent to

Ceylon in charge of a gardener. They were planted at the Henerat-goda Botanical Gardens (an offshoot of those at Peradeniya), for which Gregory was responsible. They throve there and from Heneratgoda seedlings went to Malaya. The parent trees still stand in Heneratgoda, in their girth and height most unlike their slimmer, neater looking progeny in Ceylon. Wickham had the satisfaction of being photographed beside them when he visited the island years afterwards.

After a period of trial and error, and experimentation on the best seed, the best terrain, and the most suitable instruments for 'tapping' the tree, rubber of the *Para* variety came to be planted on a large scale in the low-and mid-country of Ceylon. The steamy river valleys of the Western and Southern Provinces, and the slopes of the foothills of the mountain ranges were found to be good rubber country. There is a line above which rubber fails to do well, so that mixed plantations of tea and rubber – common at a time when tea prices were not satisfactory and rubber was planted as a good stand-by – belong to the low-country and the mid-country.

As most rubber land lay in the populated Western, Southern and the new Sabaragamuva Provinces, about half the acreage opened out in it belonged to Ceylonese whose title to the land could not be disputed. In the hinterland of the western coast where there was already a nucleus of people who had some money and some experience in business dealings with the Britisher, a great deal of land was planted with rubber. As in the case of tea, large estates were generally capitalized in the UK and European-owned. Fortunes were made (and lost) in rubber which seemed to be more sensitive to trade cycles than tea. Industrial expansion in the USA and in Europe increased the demand for rubber; in 1912 Ceylon, with its 217,000 acres, exported fifteen million pounds. The latex (or milk from the incision regularly made in the trunk of the tree) was collected, smoked, cured and then exported in the form of crêpe and sheet rubber for industrial use. As there was no industrial enterprise in the island, it could not be used on the spot and had to be exported.

Coconuts, which had been cultivated all over the island, but chiefly in the old Maritime Provinces, trailed far behind tea and rubber. But with changes such as those referred to above which made it possible for the demands of a world market to be supplied by exports from the island, it is not strange that the cultivation of the coconut palm developed on a scale similar to that of tea and rubber. Practically all coconut land belonged to Ceylonese, the commonest unit being the few trees in a village garden, some of them as a result of the wasteful partition law of the island held by as many as two hundred owners.[20] Large plantations of coconut by the end of the century were within the means of the small class of wealthy Ceylonese, for they needed no extensive outlay of capital, no costly machinery, nor a permanent labour force. Most of the produce was raised for domestic consumption, the nuts and the oil being sold on the local market. But with the development of the port of Colombo at the behest of the planting industry, the possibilities of supplying a foreign market could be exploited. A trade developed in copra (the desiccated kernel of the fruit) and in coir rope, obtained by retting the husks. In the Eastern Province a few old-established British families opened out fair-sized coconut plantations. For the most part wherever a village existed there a coconut grove would be found, providing its owners with the hundred and one commodities for which the palm was famed. There is no nineteenth-century book on Ceylon which does not list all its various uses, leaving on its reader the conviction that life under the shade of this palm must truly be idyllic, and that the wants of those it blessed with food, drink, shelter and fuel must indeed have been few.[21]

The economic structure set up by Britain in Ceylon in the nineteenth century assured all Britishers, whose capital and enterprise went into its construction, of a major share in the profits of the island's economy. The plantation industry – it was at the end of the century a sizable industry undertaking the cultivation and manufacture of tea, rubber and coconut products – could not but bring into being minor trades and crafts associated with it, so that some small share of the increased productivity of the country went to those who waited on it in humbler capacities: as carters in the days before the railway, bringing coffee to the port; as carpenters and blacksmiths responsible for maintenance and repair; as clerks in storerooms and warehouses or in the minor administrative posts of the numerous government departments created to deal with the demands of the new order; and, lastly, as traders supplying food and all the necessities of life to the new populations in and around the plantations and in the rapidly growing town of Colombo. As the country was opened up, small towns with courts of law and government offices provided employment for a new class of lawyers and others with an English education, whose earnings went into forming the beginnings of the small middle class wedged in between the very small group of wealthy British planters and merchants and the mass of the people of the country, whose condition is sometimes glimpsed in the administrative reports of Government Agents who found it hard to reconcile statements about the island's wealth and prosperity with the wretchedness of the people they saw around them.

Not only did the planting industry benefit British capital, the demands of a new market for clothing, food and consumer goods (small though it may have been by comparison with India) enriched the British industrialist and the commercial houses who handled imports from overseas. All this trade was in British or Indian hands. The only Ceylonese with sufficient expertise and tradition to engage profitably in it were the Moors. But they were soon outdistanced by the trader from India with some money, better credit facilities and much more skill at the game.

Strangely enough it was the liquor trade in this Buddhist country, where by precept abstinence from strong drink is an important part of the way of life, that provided the Ceylonese entrepreneur with profits resembling those of a capitalist. The low-countryman with his familiarity with the business of farming rents, and of organizing the sale of drink prospered most from the government policy of making as much money as it could in order to maintain solvency.

Enlightened self-interest, a typical eighteenth-century article of belief, has often been credited with the development of Britain's colonial empire. All such structures have shown very sharp differences in the quality of accommodation they have offered the people of a country. These inequalities have been justified by the claim that without the self-interest of the few whose rewards may have been inordinate, the many would never have been housed or fed. This is a useful rationalization which removes some of the odium from the actions of those accused of being involved in a capitalist conspiracy. In actual fact the enlightenment and the self-interest were rarely united in the same persons. Self-interest was certainly shown by the planter who wanted everything his own way, and was satisfied when it seemed that everything was for the best in the beautiful plantation world. But this is a normal instinct and quite a few eighteenth-century thinkers claimed that without it few societies would survive. On the purely instinctual level therefore it is hard to object to the drive of the coffee planters (and the tea planters who succeeded them) in securing what was required for their survival and profit. In all these cases their gains resulted, as we have noted, in some benefits for those whose labours were less handsomely rewarded. The wealth of the planting community diffused itself gradually and in ever smaller trickles from the commanding heights of the economy right down to all but its lowest levels. Indeed the planter, noting the hostility with which his superior position and his successful demands were entertained, provided just the same justification and recommendation as the economists for the new economic structure he had built. All good things like education, improved communications, the beginnings of medical care, the harbour at Colombo, came from him above.

His self-interest had successfully built up the new economy. But did enlightenment form part of his impulse? For this valuable ingredient in the mixture one would perhaps have to turn to the pronouncements of Colonial Governors, to the nagging minutes of the Colonial Office and the conscience of Members of Parliament. Enlightenment could hardly stand up to the force of instinctual drives when it seemed that self-interest was taking the bit between its teeth. The struggle between the two is a continuation of the age-old debate between judgement and will, and only in the artificial constructs of literature has will been properly abashed.

It is possible at this time to see that this division of self-interest and enlightenment produced a lopsided economy. Some areas of the country – much its smaller part – were highly-developed productive units, the rest was benighted. There were two worlds, completely different in character from each other, not confined geographically to plantation areas and the rest, because even in the pockets of the former lived and worked a depressed and landless peasantry. But little was done to correct this mis-development. One side of the imbalance was noticed by British administrators. All they could do was to try to alleviate the distress it occasioned. Those among the people of the country who could, and did, express an opinion on what had taken place were just as strongly motivated by self-interest as those whom they criticized. All they asked for was a larger share of the cake. A few, and among them the most enlightened, imagined with Utopian fervour a return to the golden age of feudal Ceylon, when the outrage perpetrated on the hillsides of the island would be reclaimed by forest free and jungle scrub, and a new age, the resumption of the old, would be ushered in.

It has been suggested with a great deal of perspicacity that if the 'exploiter' had really exploited the resources of the colonies more, what are now called 'the under-developed countries' would not be in the plight they are.[22] The weakness of the plantation economy was its development of only one section of the country's resources. There were mineral resources in Ceylon, not considerable it is true, which might have been taken in hand. Graphite, for which in the last few decades of the nineteenth century there was world demand, was only imperfectly developed by a few low-country families in whose land it was found. The provision of rice, the staple food of the country, often gave concern to the administrator, but little was done. It was concluded that imported rice would be paid for out of the revenue afforded by the plantation industry. The possibilities of providing consumer goods in the country were never examined. The old crafts fell away, Birmingham and Manchester providing everything wanted by the growing population. Germany and Japan came in later to dispute the British share of this trade. The only machinery or tools actually produced in the island were the uncomplicated driers and rollers needed for the processing of tea.

One of the early Governors of Ceylon had his own ideas about the development of the country, but this was before the plantation industry had been established. Wilmot Horton's schemes had both common sense and intelligence, but they did not immediately appeal to the self-interest of those who actually developed the economy. In his five *Letters on Colonial Policy*, written in 1833 to the Editor of the *Colombo Journal* over the pseudonym

Philalethes, Wilmot Horton applied 'the admitted Principles of Political Economy to the special case of this island' and had some farsighted comments to make.[23] He objected to a *laissez-faire* economy and saw that in the absence of a capitalist class in Ceylon the state would have to take a hand in the development of the island's agricultural resources, using the old tanks and water-courses as its capital in the first instance. He saw, too, that wealth accumulated from colonial trade merely increased the mother country's resources and little of it was used to advance the colonies themselves. He wanted a colony to benefit from 'the inestimable principle' when it was 'in a situation, from population and improvement, to take upon itself the duties of self-government'. And, most important of all, he saw that tariffs should be used 'for the purpose of encouraging the early efforts of Colonial industry'.[24] It is quite clear that he did not think of Ceylon as a colony of settlement, for he stated quite categorically that 'Ceylon is a colony which can never receive with advantage a labouring European population'. But possibly all this was much too enlightened for its time.

CHAPTER 6

TENANTS OF THE HOUSE

By 1900 the structure of paternal Colonial Government raised by the British in Ceylon seemed a classic example of its kind, destined to endure indefinitely. Yet in less than fifty years the rulers had departed and the structure seemed cracked from top to bottom. It survived, however, and still straddles the landscape. The year 1900, which marked the completion of nearly a century of Crown Colony rule of Ceylon, provides a *stans punctum* to which return can be made to glance again at the past and to examine the future issuing therefrom. Indeed most of the contradictions of the present are snarled up in the seemingly well-defined and clear lines of that nineteenth-century past, in which the British connection decided the fate of Ceylon, gave it its particular political and economic setting, and, for a time, its special character. In what its people assimilated of what the rulers gave, just as much as in what they rejected; in their stomach qualms as well as in their spells of euphoria, they have been reacting since 1900 to the first hundred years of British power in the island. Most events which have followed owe some feature of their character to them, a hundred years seemingly so remote in time and feeling from the world of the 1960s. That this should be so can be understood, when it is recollected that the foundations of the economy have scarcely been altered. Everything raised upon them bears the shape they gave. Inessentials may have changed; what used to be is no longer so; yet the lines of the old structure are much the same as they were in the nineteenth century.

Its hundred years were, by and large, years of peace. Such a long period of internal security with the whole country under the indisputable control of the ruling power had been unknown in the history of Ceylon since the ancient monarchy began to break up in the thirteenth century. Most European powers could have given their colonies in the nineteenth century the boon of freedom from internal strife, but the kind of development the British provided – *Pax Britannica* for want of a better description – allowed something of the high motivation accompanying public pronouncements of policy to seep into the dreary realities of their rule. There was no plan to which they worked. Planning, most often, was the tardy recognition that some form of order would have to be imposed on aimlessness too long tolerated. The willingness of the rulers to try to do something even though it might have been too late; the acceptance of some rules of the game (the rule of law particularly), subtly changed on occasion when they were awkward; tolerance towards criticism when it was part of the processes of debate, were the marks of that lack of rigidity which distinguishes their rule from that of other European powers in Asia. 'Imperialism' and 'colonialism' are words which now give a twinge of conscience to those who feel the accusing finger directed towards them, but in the nineteenth century the latter was hardly known in the language,[1] and the former criticized a particular brand of Tory jingoism. It is difficult to calculate on what basis the accounts between rulers and ruled should be presented. However they are prepared they are only a prosaic rendering of figures. Only their translation into human terms can elucidate what has been included and what left out.

When the British established themselves in the Maritime Provinces at the end of the eighteenth century the last of the small kingdoms into which old Ceylon had disintegrated still survived. But not long after it disappeared too and, in spite of British nervousness about pretenders to the Kandyan throne, little trace remained among the people of the Kandyan country of any nostalgia for their kings who had been, for several decades, of South Indian origin. The descendants of the last king, who died in exile in the Madras Presidency in India, soon gave up any pretensions they may have cherished to the Kandyan throne and were content to remain pensioners of the Ceylon Government, making demands upon it for all kinds of supplementary expenditure. The good-humoured tone of James Stephen's minute on one such request suggests that the old royal family was really no one's concern:

A Young Kandian Prince ... wishes to marry two of his first cousins at the same time (or rather his mother wishes it) and the proposal is that 5,000 rupees should be assigned to defray the expense, though the family cannot afford to buy for the Boy a horse which his health requires. Strange as all this sounds in European ears, I presume from the Government acquiescence, that it is right and becoming, although one should be disposed to think the money much better laid out in sending the boy to school and buying him a horse.[2]

Between the new rulers and the ruled there was an almost impassable gulf. In reality two races were to be found in the island: the British, called Europeans in all official documents (a term which signified 'white'), and the indigenous population, the 'natives'. (The word 'Ceylonese' to describe the natives of the country, whatever their origins, was apparently first used by Charles Lorenz in the 1860s.[3]) Officially there was a threefold division – between Europeans, Burghers, and natives. These categories dated from the earliest days of British rule when a distinction was drawn between the new rulers, the old and their descendants, and the rest. But whatever the Burghers were called, they were to the British as definitely natives as any other indigenous group.

The existence of the division between rulers and the ruled was often remarked upon by the rulers themselves. Some may have regretted it, but to most it was as natural as the onset of the monsoon in May. According to Capper, a newspaper proprietor with numerous opportunities to observe what was passing in the world around, there were hardly any contacts, even on the official level, between rulers and ruled. Anstruther, on one of his many appearances before the Select Committee of the House of Commons, referred the troubles of 1848 to the lack of contact between the two peoples: 'There is a complete curtain drawn in Ceylon between the government and the governed; no person connected with the government understands the language; very few of them have the remotest idea of the customs of the natives; they are perfectly ignorant of the people, as ignorant as any gentleman in London could be of the people over whom they rule.'[4]

William Knighton, in *Forest Life in Ceylon* (1854), touches on one reason for the isolation of the two peoples from each other:

'So completely was my conception of humanity mixed up with clothes and white or black skins, that it was, for a time, impossible for me to realize to myself the idea that these gibbering, long-armed, brown, naked animals were fellow-creatures.'[5] The sudden confrontation of a white man with people of a different culture, economically wretched and absolutely dependent on his goodwill, must have been as much of a shock to him as an encounter of an upper-class Englishman with any of the types described by Henry Mayhew in his study of the London poor. It was close to the reaction of a biologist face to face with a new and somewhat repellent species. Attitudes similar to this were general among caste natives towards outcaste *Rodiyas*. They were just as much members of a different species to the native as the wharf coolie was to the character in Knighton's novel.

Both races had their own caste and sub-caste groups. Those in the European community were as easily observable as the more rigid demarcations among the natives.[6] 'Caste' distinctions among Europeans were not the result of their contact with cultures based on caste, but of traditional class differentiation by birth, upbringing, education and occupation. Abuse of one's opponents on these grounds was as frequent among Europeans when tempers were frayed as among natives. From the earliest days of British rule, to judge from North's letters to his sister Catherine, European society in Colombo was full of malicious gossip. North is often catty and amusing when he refers delightedly to infringements of 'caste' taboos:

The ships are just going to sail, which I am very glad of, as they will carry off such a Set of Whores and Rogues as I suppose never was collected in so small a Space . . . General Fullerton, an old Twaddler from Bengal, . . . walks about with a round Straw Hat, and a Green Gauze Veil, on account of his Eyes. He has a Hindoo Wife, whom he carried once to Scotland, where She shocked the Neighbours by plaistering the Walls of her Drawing-Room with Cow-Dung.[7]

Tennent, later on, had his humble origins and his wealthy marriage brought up against him by an officer and a gentleman. Notwithstanding these 'caste' differences the small group of Europeans in times of crisis did show a cohesiveness which was the envy of the English-educated natives.

The official head of the Europeans was the Colonial Governor, who necessarily belonged to the British ruling class. The awe in which the king of Kandy had been held was transferred by the native population to the representative in person of the British monarch. He was, in the Sinhalese term, the *Rajjuruvo* or king. (Even provincial Government Agents and Assistant Government Agents were given this designation and had something of the glory of a king.)

The Colonial Governor enjoyed enormous prestige and power. An Englishman describing him in 1868 wrote:

> It would be infinitely less hazardous to the interests of two millions of Her Majesty's liege subjects if the head of the Government were surrounded by such constitutional restraints as would place him above the imputation of favour, and the people beyond the temptation to servility. The Governor, however, concentrates in his own person all the power of the State, without either restraint or responsibility. He is the dispenser of place, patronage and promotion; and has the virtual disposal of the Revenue. Every individual and every public body in the country, must depend for the benefits they may desire, or for the redress they may seek, on the will and pleasure of the Governor.[8]

He was the chief administrative and executive officer in the colony. He had the right to nominate candidates to the civil service, the highest administrative office in the colony, until 1863 when entry depended on examination. His word was law in the ordinary processes of departmental business in the country; everything proceeding from Ceylon to Whitehall had to go through him, and though he was sometimes restive at control from the Colonial Office, he could always present it with impressive reasons why his stand on any particular matter should be allowed. In the island his visits to provincial capitals and their journeys about the country were in the nature of royal progresses. Roads would be decorated with *pandals*, or triumphal arches, spanning them at regular intervals; there would be addresses of welcome at various stages; levees would be on the model of those at Buckingham Palace. Some Governors enjoyed this pomp and circumstances. There is the story of Sir Arthur Gordon, afterwards Lord Stanmore, who in imperial fashion had his horse represent him at the ceremony inaugurating the new province of Sabaragamuva, because his wife was ill and he could not be present. 'At the function itself, which consisted of a large procession of elephants, tom-tom beaters, chiefs, dancers and the rag-tag and bob-tail of the populace, the pony was led in solemn state, closely followed by the officials. On its back was a saddle, upon which rested a cushion, that in turn carried a silver tray, on which rested Sir Arthur Gordon's message to "the Chiefs and people of Sabaragamuva".'[9]

The figure of the Colonial Governor inspired so much awe in the beholder, even of English educated natives, that the story told by one of them reveals some of the satisfaction derived at seeing the mighty in England, no longer in their high seats but part of the common crowd:

Like great generals, Colonial Governors lose much of their glamour when they lay aside their cloak of office, and become merged with the common crowd. Soon after my arrival in London, as I was walking down Oxford Street, I stopped to gaze into a shop-window that was attracting the passers-by. The man who stood in front of me suddenly stepped back, and in doing so trod on my foot. 'I beg your pardon, Sir,' said he, 'Granted', said I. As he moved away, I recognized an Ex-Governor of Ceylon who, like me, was only a gazer at a shop-window.[10]

Of course most Colonial Governors enjoyed the splendour of office and like all humanity were touched by expressions of esteem, particularly those which accompanied the great on the occasion of their leave-taking of the country. In comparatively recent times a Governor as keen-witted and sceptical of humanity as Sir Hugh Clifford could refer with evident satisfaction to 'all sections of the population, making it more and more difficult' for him to leave Ceylon – sentiments by which he would scarcely have been taken in on other occasions.[11]

Colonial Governors felt the power they enjoyed a prerogative of their position as Her Majesty's representative. On all matters concerned with the distribution of power in the colony they asserted a twofold claim: that they knew what was best for it, and that they were best able to prevent the abuse of power. They confidently contested the right of anyone else – the planters, the Burghers, the politically conscious Ceylonese at the end of the century and Parliamentarians in Westminster – to speak for the colony. Any attempt to curtail their powers was resented and resisted. As a result of their opposition to any change, they became, without quite intending it, reactionaries. Power did not corrupt, it merely fossilized them.

Till the end of the century practically all officers of the Ceylon civil service, appointed by the Secretary of State or recruited by examination, were Europeans. (The non-competitive examination of 1863 to test the 'general attainments' of local candidates was kinder to natives who received the Governor's nomination than that which all candidates, whether in England or Ceylon, had to take in 1870. A few natives did succeed in getting in, and were consequently looked up to by their compatriots as the possessors of extraordinary intellects.) The exclusiveness of the service, the autocratic nature of the power it could wield, and the multiplicity of the functions of the 'civil servant' (the word was used only of a small minority of administrative officers at the top of the official hierarchy) turned it into an institution of immense prestige. Leonard Woolf remembering the Ceylon of 1904 reckoned that 'the civil servant was socially in many ways top dog; he was highly paid, exercised considerable and widely distributed power, and with the Sinhalese and Tamils enjoyed much greater prestige than the other classes.'[12] This has to be remembered if the relations between officials and politicians in the next century is to be understood. The latter were quick to sense arrogance on the part of persons beyond the range of criticism of the ordinary man, while the civil servant reacted to his critics with as much touchiness as the Governor in the late 1920s and 30s, when constitutional changes gave the unofficial member in Council his opportunity. Baiting the brass-hats of the civil service became a sport which gave the politician a deal of unconscious satisfaction.

By the middle of the nineteenth century, when conditions of pay and allowance had been improved and the growing demands of an empire for British officials of all kinds were being catered for in England by the public schools, the Ceylon civil service could offer upper-class young men of ability a promising career. Of course more money would have been made by the young men who went out to a mercantile house or to a plantation, but they would not be as eminent socially. In India the civil servant was better paid and had wider fields for his talents, but service in

Ceylon had its own rewards: it was an easier and more manageable country, and the Colonial Secretaryship in the colony or promotions elsewhere were attractive.

It is not possible to state that a great difference was made by competitive examinations between the old and the new civil servants. The new took up quite naturally and easily the mantle of power donned by their predecessors who initiated them into the mystery of their function. No special course of training (such as was later provided by Oxford and Cambridge for recruits to the Indian civil service) was deemed necessary for entrants from England into the Ceylon service. On arrival in the colony they would be drafted into a Kachcheri, where, as cadets under the supervision of the Government Agent, they would learn by experience the various duties – fiscal, administrative and judicial – they were called upon to perform. Leonard Woolf gives a list of these at the beginning of the twentieth century: doing 'the office work, checking the accounts, issuing licences, going through all the letters, preparing the files and submitting all important questions for decision for the G.A. with perhaps a précis and, if they had any, their own suggestions or proposals'.[13] This practice continued right through the life of the Ceylon civil service. It smacked of the amateur, but a conscientious G.A. could produce efficient officials and it satisfied the energies of those who enjoyed wielding power and ordering the lives of others.

Of the various types to be found in colonial officialdom the best remembered need not have been either the most efficient or the most admirable. The eccentric or the highly idiosyncratic were much more likely to catch the imagination, particularly of those who had no opportunity of knowing them privately. As public figures therefore the civil servants who most impressed their native contemporaries were martinets like Percival Ackland Dyke, who preferred to spend the greater part of his term of service in Ceylon in Jaffna, because he liked it there. He did not mind suffering financially and gave up the post of Acting Auditor General to 'return to this Province [the Northern] to which I was and continue to be so much attached'. He was universally feared, the local population edging itself off the road and into the drain when he appeared in his carriage, flicking with his whip at those not nimble enough to get out of the way. Joseph Grenier, who later became a Justice of the Supreme Court, wrote: 'I have seen respectable natives, out of deference to him, skipping into wide drains, in a painfully obsequious manner, as the "Rajah" drove through the streets of Jaffna.'[14] Dyke was a conscientious G.A. going on circuit twice a year through all parts of the province. He prided himself on the tent in which he lived on such tours: 'I have an establishment of tents and I believe I am the only Agent that has. On the adjoining continent of India such provision is obligatory and liberal allowances are made for it.' Dyke, who died in the tents which gave him so much satisfaction, enjoyed Jaffna as its remoteness at that time from Colombo gave his powers additional scope. Jaffna then was accessible much more easily by ship than by road – journey by the latter being in the nature of a safari.

Woolf's account of the life of a Ceylon civil servant in the first decade of the twentieth century is extremely interesting, but as he differed in outlook from the majority of them, it is unlikely that what appealed to him in the life necessarily attracted them. In his reminiscences there is, however, one clue to the satisfaction such a life must have offered all Britishers who worked in the service – the reassurance it could give the ego. He writes:

I was the only white man in the 400 square miles of the District, and here for the first time I learnt the profound happiness of complete solitude. For a month I never spoke to anyone except clerks, headmen, Tamil villagers, and my own Tamil servants. My life and my work were entirely my own responsibility and there was no one whom I could consult about anything connected with either. I think this kind of complete solitude, with the necessity of relying absolutely upon oneself and one's own mind, is, when one is young, extremely good for one.[15]

It was as the autocrat in a diversity of fields that the civil servant impinged on the rest of the community in Ceylon. In the next century, from the 30s when the proportion of Ceylonese in the service increased, the aura of omnipotence round the European attached itself to the native too. As a result the politician felt that the direction of affairs had to be wrested from those who had wielded it too long. It is possible that the nineteenth-century reservation of power in the hands of a small class, most of the members of which were not people of the country, had two unfortunate consequences: far too high a price was paid for the orderliness with which such bureaucratic rule secured the *status quo*; secondly, so much energy was expended later in eradicating this tradition that the old orderliness went and nothing took its place. If it is claimed that the member of the House of Representatives took over some of the functions and all the prestige of the old civil servant, then there was certainly no change for the better and a definite loss in administrative efficiency. The old order had its weaknesses; the new did not touch the root cause of any of them.

Woolf knew the service during 'the apogee of imperialism', as he termed it. Looking back, more than fifty years later, on his career in Ceylon which he gave up, he wrote that he 'did not want to return to Ceylon and become a successful civil servant in Colombo and end eventually with a governorship and K.C.M.G.' Ceylon did not appeal even as offering a 'final withdrawal', because 'the days of imperialism were over'. But his readers must feel that he was a successful civil servant in the old tradition, and that he immersed himself in official life and its duties as wholeheartedly as any other career man would have done. Certainly his *Journals*, published in 1963, show hardly a sign of self-reproach at committal to uncongenial tasks.

The army officer faded away by the close of the century when only a very small force was left in Ceylon. As he had little to do after the Kandyan 'rebellion', he tended to be more an ornament to society than a military man with tasks which gave him a special insight into the country or its people.[16] In earlier times army officers had performed civilian duties and had worked in the medical services and in the Public Works Department. But by the 60s they had nothing but garrison routine to occupy their working hours.

There are no records of the experience of Britishers in the big business houses in Colombo or on plantations as interesting and frank as Leonard Woolf's of his life in the civil service. Of course an assistant in a large tea-broking firm in Colombo would have had many more opportunities of meeting Ceylonese than a planter on a tea plantation in the hills. But such contacts were more often commercial rather than social. The social life of the Britisher in the East revolved round clubs restricted to Europeans, each gradation of the white community having its own club within its own circle. Life in the East reproduced, as carefully and deliberately as was possible in a tropical setting, upper-class life in the home country. There was a time when jackals, in lieu of the fox, were hunted on the Erabedda plains in Uva. The cult of cricket, rugger, the turf owe their origins in Ceylon to those Britishers determined to provide themselves with what they felt belonged to the ruling race. Within a few years of the annexation of Kandy there was a race meeting in the old capital of the Kandyan kings, and when coffee was established as the main industry there was hardly a planting district without its own race track, its playing-fields and club. The models provided by these institutions were assiduously copied by Ceylonese as soon as they could afford them. Ludicrous as the fetish of the club may seem in retrospect, it gave satisfaction to those to whom it seemed to be natural and it enabled English-educated Ceylonese to solace themselves with a proof of their own attainment: what the rulers could do they could do as well.

In activities of this kind the planting community set its own standards. Only those who have experienced the life and noted its social nuances could write satisfactorily about it. Those planters who did describe their days in Ceylon either fail to communicate anything to those outside the charmed circle, or seem overanxious to justify themselves in the eyes of the reader. This may have been because their life seemed nothing but an attractive holiday to those outside it. The older men certainly seemed to think that the younger and newer men had things much easier than they had.

To the tea plantation were drafted the young fresh from public school in the United Kingdom. As 'creepers' they would, like the civil service cadet, be initiated into their craft by the older man under whom they worked. The life seemed so attractive to outsiders that comments like the following reflected general opinion:

In fact taken all around, the modern Ceylon planter has one of the easiest jobs in the world; some of them do not even find it necessary to work more than three days a week. Yet, at least, these undistinguished by-products of the English public schools are a decent enough set of fellows: their hospitality is renowned and it is not altogether their fault that their intellectual horizons are bounded by the sports columns of the newspapers and that they are in the habit of drinking far more than is good for them.[17]

It was obviously to dispel the prevalence of such opinions that the writer of a *Manual for all Ranks and Ratings of the Fighting Services in Ceylon* in 1945 stressed other features of life on up-country estates:

> Though the conditions under which Planters work have changed greatly since the first pioneers founded the coffee industry (an enter-prise which collapsed owing to a leaf disease and which was largely replaced by tea at the end of the nineteenth century), the European Superintendent still has to face a long and arduous period of training, absence from his home and country, separation from his family while they are being educated and a life spent in a tropical country. It is well to bear these points in mind when comparing his lot with conditions elsewhere.[18]

Geographical position to a great extent determined the possible range of the European planter's contacts with the people of the country. Superintendents of rubber estates in the Kelani Valley and the Southern Province sometimes spoke colloquial Sinhalese or Tamil fluently and knew both Ceylonese planters and the law-yers of the locality. In predominantly European company owned tea estates high up in the hills such contacts would have been rarer.

Before travel to and from England became easier and more convenient, there were not many European women in Ceylon. In 1871 Richard Morgan found his pleasure in the service held in the Thomas's drawing-room at Lindula dashed by the absence of ladies:

> It was a fine sight to see the stalwart men assembled from miles around to join in divine worship. There was a harmonium to aid the singing, which was very fine. There was one want – there were no ladies. The climate is fine and will suit Europeans. It would be a happy thing if each bungalow had a lady to adorn it, and planters would adopt the place as their home, and have each his family smiling round him.[19]

Unions between European planters and Tamil and Sinhalese women, not so frequent now, were well known in the nineteenth century and a small new element, described in official documents as 'Eurasian', was added to the island's various communities. Planters like the villainous Siggins in Knighton's novel must have been rare even in the 1840s, but the practice Knighton refers to of young girls being offered the planter by the wretched (or the scheming) villager is mentioned by other writers too. The off-spring of such unions had no knowledge of their father's world from which they were excluded, nor did they really belong to that of their mothers. Only in those cases where they were well pro-vided for by their fathers could they expect to have an upbringing which could be described as nearly normal. It is unfortunate that the enclave of the plantation, over which the planter held sway, should have produced two groups of people in different ways underprivileged and denied their rights: the coolie, the worst sufferer of all in the system, and the planter's illegitimate children. The tea plantation furnished the two extreme limits of life in Ceylon in the last century (and perhaps even today). The highest and the lowest, the richest and the poorest, the most powerful and the weakest, were to be found together in it.

Though not the most important nor the most numerous group of Europeans in Ceylon, the missionaries exerted the most influ-ence on the people of the country and left the strongest impression on the island. They were, like their compatriots, birds of passage. Few made Ceylon their home, but the nature of their work brought them closer to the people of the country than any other group of Europeans could get. It is open to question whether the characteristic mark of missionary endeavour in Ceylon is to be found in the Christian communities left by them or in the numbers who received through their agency an education in English.

The Roman Catholics were the first Christian missionaries in Ceylon. The existence of a fair-sized Roman Catholic community in the old Maritime Provinces has already been noted. The Dutch Reformed Church had its small congregations from the late seventeenth century onwards. So had the Church of England in the nineteenth century, though the quality of its priests in its early days suffered from the narrowness of political principles which decided appointments in an established church. The less said of early Colonial Chaplains and Archdeacons (and even of latter-day Bishops) the better. In the 1840s James Stephen noted that two Anglican priests, according to the Bishop, 'seem to labour under an unhappy infirmity of temper, deeply to be lamented in a Minister of the Gospel of peace and love'.[20] Such deficiencies were to be found in the priests of all religious groups. Even less need be said about the meanness of the feuds between the various Protestant sects in Ceylon; the Wesleyans and Baptists resenting the unfairness of the advantage taken by the Church of England of its secular and political privileges.[21]

The urge to make Christians of the heathen and the hope that the goal would soon be reached have been referred to already. Undoubtedly some conversions in the nineteenth century were as frankly matters of convenience as later repudiations of Christianity. In Ceylon where the predominant religion was Buddhism, politically unimportant and stagnant for several centuries, Christian missionaries with their organization and their activity were an unusual phenomenon to the adherents of a folk religion no longer endowed with the prestige of being that of the rulers of the country. But what first disturbed the Buddhist – in the Kandyan country particularly – was the loss suffered in the interruption of the age-old connection between Buddhism and the state. By the Kandyan Convention the new rulers of the country had undertaken that the religion of the Sinhalese would be inviolable. This article led to contention; Christian missionaries in Ceylon and missionary societies in England objected to the protection afforded under its terms by the Colonial Government to the sacred Tooth Relic of the Buddha, and certain formalities which required the assent of the head of the state – the Christian governor who had replaced the Kandyan king. The missionaries urged that the representative of a Christian monarch could not, and should not, have any connection with 'paganism and idolatry'. Buddhist chieftains and priests claimed that pledges publicly given them had not been honoured.

When political advantage recommended it – during the troubles of 1848 – the British were anxious to 'protect' the relic in the Dalada Maligava in Kandy in spite of the objections of missionary opinion. But in 1853, as a result of considerable pressure on the government, the relic was formally handed over to the care of the Kandyan temple authorities. For a long time the average Buddhist priest and Buddhist public generally, as they had few opportunities of expressing themselves, apparently took no special notice of the evangelical work of the missionaries. The latter were Europeans; they could not therefore be withstood.

The stress laid by the early Christian missionaries on converting the heathen, with or without the demonstration of the superiority of Christianity to Buddhism, was for some time not resented actively by the Buddhists. Nor was, in the early days at least, the use of schools as media of proselytism. European rulers of the country had been doing this for upwards of three hundred years, so it must have seemed an unfortunate obsession of theirs. As hopes of a Christianized Ceylon receded, the missionary took up the much easier task of providing, under government patronage and with government aid, education in English for those who could afford it. Evangelical work was never given up, but its results were disappointing.

The majority of people in the island – the very small minority classed as Burghers and the very large group classed as natives – were more divided by geographical circumstances than the various groups of the rulers were. The Tamils of the North and the East in the nineteenth century were, by and large, as much isolated from the Sinhalese of the rest of the island as the Lindula planter was from both. In addition, differences of racial origin, upbringing, culture, religion and language divided the people of the country far more effectively than class separated the rulers. Besides, just as clear as distinctions of racial origin were caste and sub-caste categories in some racial groups. Caste distinctions could be noticed even in groups where they were least to be expected: for instance among Burghers, those of Dutch origin reckoning themselves superior to the rest; and in the Buddhist *sangha* where admission to certain chapters was restricted to certain castes.

Caste was not officially recognized by the British who held that according to the rule of law all men were equal. In the actual business of administration, however, the rulers did have to take cognizance of caste unless they wished to have trouble on their hands. (Christian schools in Jaffna and elsewhere came up against the stubbornness of caste taboos, but, as there was an economic gain in schooling, caste prejudices were swallowed while secondary education in English was partaken of.) In the late nineteenth century, and much more definitely later, caste like a bad smell was unmentionable in polite conversation, but, of course, when tempers were high and no holds were barred much vituperative inventiveness could be indulged in. A man's caste may not be re-membered quite so frequently now, but it never has been, nor is it ever likely to be, forgotten.[22] The old occupational groupings of people and service tenures have been superseded by a new econ-omy. New ways of living, much more mobility in the country and the legal right to assume whatever name you choose have done a great deal to obliterate the more obvious marks of caste. A recent article on colonization schemes in the Eastern Province, to which peasants were drafted from other parts of the country, refers to a very popular mode of by-passing caste: 'The low caste people have changed their economic status considerably and they have changed their attire accordingly. They attempt to change their caste by giving new names to their children.'[23] The patrilineal name which gives away its bearer's caste is exchanged for another.

Caste still exists, and on all important occasions – marriages, elections, the bestowal of favours (from portfolios in a cabinet to a poor relief grant) – it can often turn the scale. It is a factor in the relations of people with each other which no one can afford to neglect. If it is true, as it has been claimed, that caste in Ceylon is dying, then it is certainly going through a prolonged death agony. It was never as complex or as rigid as in India, yet this must be poor consolation to those who, in the contemporary phrase, stand at its receiving end. To them caste must have been hardship which they were relieved to escape. Those above the lowest in the caste hierarchy could always fortify their self-esteem by believing and asserting their superiority to what was reckoned the highest caste of all: that of the cultivators or the *Goigama*. The latter have been referred to earlier as the Mudaliyar class, and as they were the focal point of all the social ambitions and hostilities of the rest, it is necessary to refer briefly to them.

They had long been in the position of favoured subordinates of the white rulers and were prompt to make use of this to consoli-date their gains. In common with the Burghers – first in the field because of the special protection given them on account of their European origins – they took up education in English as the most natural mode of maintaining their position. Again, with the Burghers whom Alexander Johnston selected for service as being particularly apt, they secured for their kinsmen posts in the judicial service. They had land (and claimed much more) but these low-country holdings unlike coffee and tea plantations brought no spectacular profits. They had some money, but no great capital. But early in the nineteenth century they were the only group among the natives who could have been described as 'wealthy', except for those of lower caste groupings who had done well out of speculation in farming rents. The Rev. B. Clough in 1830 made a shrewd comment on them: 'The wealth of the country is chiefly among the headmen – and they possess not only the positive riches of the country, but they exercise an influence over the labours, time and little gettings of the lower classes such as no person can at all understand but from *living among them*' (Clough's emphasis).[24]

They resisted with passion any encroachment on rights and privileges they considered exclusively theirs. Other castes, like the *Karavas* or Fishermen and the *Chaliya* or Cinnamon Peelers, had their Mudaliyars too, who were regarded as heads of the clan. In 1853, when the Governor decided to invest a member of the Fisher caste with the rank of Mudaliyar of the Governor's Gate – an honour up till then bestowed only on the *Goigama* caste – there was savage opposition from the latter at this affront to their dignity. The Governor might have given in, but some senior officials were undeterred and the appointment was made. A member of a wealthy and philanthropic Moratuva family became the first *Karava* to be raised to this rank.[25]

The Goigama Mudaliyar class had to cultivate English in order to continue in their favoured position. The first Sinhalese undergraduates at an English university were the sons of the Maha Mudaliyar who accompanied Maitland when he left Ceylon in 1811. They were the first of a small number of the privileged who in the nineteenth century finished their schooling in England.

The process of providing an education in English modelled on the school curriculum and the extra-curricular activities of schools in England was taken up by the Christian missionary societies after the Colebrooke report. Missionaries had already been providing education in Sinhalese and Tamil more efficiently and more economically than the government. State-sponsored education, quite unknown in the United Kingdom at the time, became a feature of schooling in Ceylon as a result of missionary enterprise. The success of mission schools, despite criticism of their standards of teaching and equipment by officials of the Department of Public Instruction, was due to the devotion and interest of many of the missionaries. In this way the missionary scored his greatest success in Ceylon: by providing an English rather than a Christian education. The distinction between the two may be hard to formulate exactly, but it is valid. Most valuable in what came through the missionary to his pupils was in effect neither indoctrination nor familiarity with the Christian story; it was schooling coloured by certain values derived from the teacher's own education in his homeland. What these men and women believed of course influenced their personality as teachers, but it was their character as men and women rather than their beliefs (in so far as they could be separated) which left its mark on those they taught. For all its inadequacies and misdemeanours this kind of education had most effect through the contact of the pupil with persons whose qualities of mind and character had much to give them. One can only regret that contacts such as these were available only to so few.

When in the 1870s Buddhism in Ceylon took up the challenge of the Christian missions, it had perforce to express itself in forms decided for it by Christian activity. The celebrated Panadura controversy between the eloquent *bhikkhu*, Mohottiwatte Gunananda, and Christian missionaries had the effect of bringing the Theosophist Colonel H. S. Olcott to Ceylon. He founded the Buddhist Theosophical Society and the entry of schools under Buddhist (and Hindu) management into the arena of secondary school education affected in time many more than those who actually sought their education in these schools. As the main front of Christian missionary activity was confined to the secondary school, it was in this particular field that the campaign of the Buddhist Theosophical Society was waged. There was considerable mass interest in its activities. Olcott was well aware that the chief significance of his presence in Ceylon and of the visits of Madame Blavatsky and Mrs Annie Besant lay in their espousal as white people of a religion and a way of life regarded as being inferior by the rulers of the country. The battle joined had to be fought with weapons similar to those used by the Christian missionary: hence such things as Buddhist Sunday schools and even Buddhist carols. It was an unedifying struggle, the Christians in particular showing the infirmity of temper which James Stephen lamented in another context.

As the offensive was European-directed what was being injected into Buddhism was Western-European nationalism which it could readily absorb. Buddhist nationalism was as potent an emotional force in the 1880s and 90s as Irish nationalism. Buddhist and Hindu schools may have lacked the éclat of the Christian, but they could more easily than the Christian, involved as these were with the rulers, give their products something of the nationalism which was a highly significant part of nineteenth-century liberalism.

Connected with them were the numerous societies interested in 'cultural uplift', which enabled the English-educated native to work off his dissatisfactions in unexceptionable activities in temperance societies, literary circles and organizations to redeem the national character from the sordid influence of British materialism. The white ruler and Christian missions had temperance societies too, but it must be remarked of the Buddhist 'temperance movement' that its aims were not restricted to the literal sense of the word 'temperance'. Buddhism was in theory absolutely and totally opposed to any intoxicating drink. The campaign against drink was therefore given additional fervour by Buddhist feeling against the fiscal and social policy of a Christian government which not only allowed drink but also made money out of it.

The revival of interest in Sinhalese and Tamil culture under the aegis of Ananda Kentish Coomaraswamy (the son of Sir Muttu Coomaraswamy and his English wife) was again an expression of criticism of the rulers in political terms, which did stimulate numbers among the English-educated *élite* in Ceylon. A. E. Buultjens, a Burgher, turned Buddhist during his undergraduate days in Cambridge, outraging Christian opinion in Ceylon as it was voiced by the Anglican Bishop of Colombo. He returned to Ceylon as a rebel against the established order. Best remembered of all the youthful rebels in Ceylon today is the son of a wealthy Sinhalese family (outside the charmed circle of the Mudaliyars), who changed his name to that of the Anagarika Dharmapala and adopted the style of a Buddhist lay devotee. Almost at the end of his life he was admitted into the Buddhist order. He flitted between the fringes of political circles in India and groups interested in Eastern religions all over the Western world, becoming one of the best known Asian publicists of Buddhism. Good-looking and well-spoken, he touched the impressionable hearts of those anxious to discover a new answer for old disquiet. His main work was the foundation of the Maha Bodhi Society, with its headquarters in Calcutta.[26]

But despite the interest in their personalities and careers, the Ceylon in which they worked was out of tune with their aspirations. Buultjens was the only one of the three to settle down to a career in Ceylon. After being the first principal of the newly-founded Buddhist secondary school (Ananda College) in Colombo, he became a successful provincial lawyer. Coomaraswamy made an international reputation for himself in the USA as an interpreter of Hindu arts and philosophy. Dharmapala, kept out of Ceylon for a while by security regulations, apparently lived more congenially out of his homeland than in it. The wave of nationalism which influenced the younger generation in the next century was the result of their brooding over the waters.

Outside the very narrow circle of the new *élite* were those of the old Sinhalese-educated *élite* unabsorbed, as chieftains and Mudaliyars were, into the minor official hierarchy. The most important among these were the *bhikkhus* and those who practised the traditional medical system of *Ayurveda*. Temple schools and *pirivena* (centres of higher learning in Buddhist studies) still continued, but they had only an insignificant place in the new structure of British rule in Ceylon.

Everything in the country seemed geared to the drive of the British engaged in developing it and, later on, to the less powerful movement of the English-educated *élite* to obtain a greater measure of power in a system which was acceptable, except for its unfortunate limitation of opportunity.

Pressure on the Colonial Government could be exerted in the Legislative Council through the few members nominated by the Governor to represent various interests. The proposal that there should have been any such council at all was resisted by the governors to whom it was first made by the Secretary of State. Barnes and Horton saw in it a curtailment of their rights and powers. The Legislative Council which Horton inaugurated on Goderich's instructions gave the Governor power to nominate six members – three European and three native – in an assembly of sixteen, over which he presided and had power to select subjects and measures for debate. The Europeans, unwilling to agree over their candidates for nomination, threatened to boycott the new Council, but came into it in a last-minute rush before it met for the first time so as to avoid losing seniority to the three Ceylonese already nominated.

Of the sixteen members of the Legislative Council, including the Governor who presided, ten were officials, including the Chief Justice and the Officer Commanding British troops in the island. They tended to have personal opinions and prejudices of their own and sometimes troubled the Governor, until in 1848 the Secretary of State ruled that officials should accept the Governor's directive when he insisted on their voting with him. With his official majority the Governor could expect no difficulty from the nominated members who had a right to take part in debates, but not to initiate any legislation. Only when the coffee planters wanted direct government intervention in their interests, did the voices of the unofficial members disturb the comparative peace and quiet of Council sessions. In the 40s and the 50s European nominated members, with the backing of the planters and the business men of Colombo, began to agitate in newspapers like the *Observer* for a greater share in the business of the Legislative Council. In this they found ready allies in the Burghers, who were on their own account interested in improving the prospects of English-educated Burghers in the administrative services.

Inevitably it was the fixed item of contribution to the Treasury for the British troops stationed in Ceylon which became the target of most criticism. It was a large sum and it seemed an unnecessary burden, when the planters wanted more money spent on roads and the projected railway from Colombo to Kandy. Agitation for reform of the constitution which originated in the demands of one section of the people for satisfaction set the pattern of political activity throughout the nineteenth century. The only varying factor was the pressure group behind the agitation.

For a time the interests of both Europeans and Burghers coincided. Tempers rose in the Council chamber and outside in the 1860s, when both groups could claim to be acting in the national interest: the planters to increase revenue and the Burghers and educated Ceylonese to improve the prospects of the youth of the country. This raised the first wave of political agitation in the island in British times. It was no more than a storm in Colombo and Kandy circles, but while it lasted it produced the Ceylon Political League, whose object was to secure for the unofficial nominated members the right to initiate and modify finance bills. What the nominees of the Planters' Association and the lawyers were after was very clear. Robinson, the Governor, could justifiably dismiss their claims to speak for the 'nation' with the comment that, 'if the wishes of the petitioners are acceded to absolute power in matters of finance would be entrusted to persons who are self-interested and at the same time wholly irresponsible both to the government and the public.'

Once permanent legislation guaranteeing the fixed military and civil expenditure was passed in 1868, unofficial members of the Legislative Council could feel that they controlled the budget. But before that time better coffee prices damped down the agitation. The European nominated members were not long interested in fighting on the constitutional plane for power which they were gradually securing by their control of the economy. The others settled down to consolidate their gains in a period of increasing revenue and more employment. The political scurries, with their speeches, public meetings, petitions to the Secretary of State – the most favoured mode of bringing pressure to bear on the Governor – brought into prominence such figures as Charles Ambrose Lorenz, a Burgher lawyer with a great reputation for his skill as a writer and debater. It is unnecessary to give him an importance he would never have claimed for himself. He dared to stand up against the full force of the displeasure of the Colonial Government as a representative of a small new group whose support he had, in order to press its interests. His views were never radical, nor were those of the Burghers, Sinhalese and Tamils who rallied round him (with a few Moors and one or two Parsees). He was certain that there were educated Ceylonese capable of bearing as great a share in legislating for the country and administering it as any British civil servants. But these were not novel opinions, they had been expressed to the Select Committee of the House of Commons more than a decade before. British officials like Skinner, F. Saunders and H. L. Layard, were quite certain that there were a sufficient number of intelligent natives who should be given 'a larger voice in the government of the country', and that 'members . . . of sufficient intelligence and capacity could be found to take part in the deliberations of the Legislative Council'.[27]

Neither were Sir Muttu Coomaraswamy (of whom Disraeli thought highly) nor James D'Alwis, contemporaries of Lorenz and as keen as himself on increasing Ceylonese representation in the Council, radicals. If that term could fittingly be used of any politician at this time, perhaps only Dr Elliott could have been so described. He did think that the masses, if they were taxed, should be given the right to choose their representatives. It was on this account that this Irishman was suspected of having revolutionary leanings. Lorenz and the others thought of themselves as members of a group justly entitled by their education to the right of representing the Ceylonese; they were far indeed from Elliott's recommendation of putting into the council 'men of the people's choice'. The agitation of the 1860s died down, but the sense of grievance among the English-educated lay beneath the surface, quiescent for the time.

Those with no English education, and therefore not to be found in the two-layered stratum of the *élite*, if they had any grievance, scarcely expressed it directly. But the enthusiasm with which they hailed, as spectators on the fringe, the activities of the nationalists of the 90s showed how closely they identified themselves with their superiors in the social scale. Those of them who were making money did send their sons to English schools in the hope that one day they would arrive in the circle of the *élite*. Those who were not had perforce to spend their time trying to adjust themselves to an order in which small towns were increasing in size and importance and there were some possibilities of improving their prospects. They still had their village connections, a small portion of land, and a place in village life.

But they were, by contrast with the majority of people in the country, tolerably well off. Most Sinhalese and Tamils were predominantly villagers, working on their fields, paying with the grain tax a much larger proportion of their earnings than any other class of persons and struggling with the difficulties of making a living. The main causes of their distress did not as yet include landlessness. The opening out of large tracts of upland forest had not deprived them of ancestral holdings and recent research has shown that the problems of the peasant were not as yet accentuated by the pressure of population on the existing irrigable land. In the wet zone the peasant kept himself going on a subsistence level. There was a slow movement of population to the provincial town and to the capital.

Worst placed of all was the peasant in the dry zone and in those tracts once rice-producing but, as a result of the neglect of centuries, vexed with the problem of an insufficient supply of water for the rice-fields. Famine was known in these areas, though the Colonial Government tried to minimize its incidence. The distress of the peasant could not escape the notice of the Government Agent. In the North Central Province, in particular, administration reports told an annual tale of woe and also paid tribute to the endurance and self-help of the population who tried by its own efforts to make up for the deficiencies of the government.

In his administration report for 1878 Dickson, the Government Agent of this newly constituted province, while noting that revenue had increased in the five years 1874-8, stated that the most important item of increase was 'land revenue' or the tax on paddy. But the greater part of his report is taken up with an appeal to the government to take in hand the work of ensuring a supply of water for the fields. Without it the condition of the cultivator would be precarious:

Just as the drought of 1876 brought distress in 1877, so does the deficient rainfall throughout the east of the province in the end of 1878 promise serious distress in the eastern districts in 1879. Deficient rainfall means deficient crops, and it is to be hoped that the Government will no longer delay the restoration of the magnificent canals and river-fed tanks of supply which will render cultivation no longer precarious, but will bring to it the security of an unceasing supply of water such as it possessed under the rule of the Sinhalese kings. It is on the restoration of these artificial lakes and their connected network of canals that the future prosperity of this province mainly depends and, until they are restored, the Government cannot expect to receive any large return for the large outlay already incurred on roads and other public works.[28]

The restoration of the ancient system of irrigation had caught the attention of Colonial Governors like Ward and Gregory. But money was needed elsewhere: to maintain and expand the new economy on which the prosperity of the western and central hills of the island depended. Very little could therefore be done. In the meantime the peasant tried to help himself and Dickson warmly commended his enterprise and industry: 'It is a common thing to lament the indolence and apathy of the Sinhalese, and if the Kandyans of this district when left alone were not an exception to the general rule, they have at any rate in the last five years shown that they have in them the power and the will to combine together for common objects, and, in spite of poverty and trials and privations, to work steadily on roads and tanks and bring their village works into a state of which any district might be proud, and which no other district has yet attempted to achieve.'

But industry and enterprise alone were insufficient in the dry zone balanced uneasily between inadequate government aid and the unavailing fight of its people against malaria and drought. The area slumped further into neglect.

By the end of the nineteenth century Ceylon, if not the brightest gem in the imperial crown, was certainly a colonial possession of immense strategic value in the days when the British navy ruled the seas and trade followed the flag. Its importance in relation to the security of the British possessions in India had long been clear. With more and more territories in the map of Asia and Africa coming to be shaded pink, the island of Ceylon afforded a valuable base for the navy patrolling the Indian Ocean and keeping sea-lanes clear for British trade to the Far East and Australia.

This was the real value of Ceylon to the British. Their capital was invested in the plantation industry and the island's import and export trade was largely in their hands. But this did not add up to very much in comparison with the British stake in India, Malaya or Australia. Ceylon was comparatively speaking a poor country; it had no natural resources which could at the time have been exploited to produce wealth.

The benevolent autocracy established by the rulers had, in spite of all its numerous differences from the system of rule (foreign or native) to which the people of the country had been accustomed, two features in common with it: the firmness which goes with power which could be used coercively or tyrannically, and the laxity which has continued to defeat the sternest efforts of the firmest rulers. The Governor was no tyrant, but in the last resort he had at his command a foreign army and a native police force, European trained and officered, and, if necessary, reinforcement from the Indian army, with which to impose his will or that of Her Majesty's Government. There was no occasion, except during the 'Rebellion' of 1848, for the massive demonstration of all these powers. Indeed there was no need after 1848 for any display of the force at the government's command. Whatever is thought of the system of British colonial administration, it was during this period of the nineteenth century clear and unequivocal rule. Who benefited and who languished under it were irrelevancies. There was 'a prosperous Ceylon', as a writer in 1890 commented, 'under tea, as there was formerly under coffee; but alongside and outside of this are the people, among whom a large number, if not a majority, are not prosperous, indeed they are more often on the verge of starvation and are dying of want.'[29] The system confined some to the limits of poverty and gave others large areas of freedom in which to pursue prosperity. All known systems of government at the time produced similar effects. But as this was administered in Ceylon it was definite rule, firm and authoritative.

The laxity was the defect or the accompaniment of all systems based on the interests of a minority ready to tolerate irregularities as long as they did not threaten the whole structure. Much rather some malpractice somewhere than the strain of constantly deploying the apparatus of power in order to arrest the inevitable, might have been the watchword. Patronage had long been known in British political life. It still exists and there are valuable advantages to be derived from family connections, the right school and friends in high places. Corruption, too, is not unknown. In Colonial Ceylon patronage was not surgically removed by competitive examinations. The Governor and senior members of the civil service could still in the nineteenth century secure favours for their nominees. Whole new government departments had to be staffed, and if some of those recruited into them had no outstanding qualifications they were probably no worse than those who might ultimately have been selected by another mode of appointment. There was no trade in these favours; those who dispensed them were above receiving payment for them. There were, of course, stories of money made over contracts, purchases by the government and invoices for stores, but such tales are retailed of all officials. No government in the world today can swear that its administrators are innocent of such practices.

The people of the country would not have been greatly troubled either by the firmness or the laxity. They were accustomed to both in stiffer measure in Dutch times and earlier. The rule of native princelings and kings could be tyrannical and also extortionate. To take one example, neither of exaction nor tyranny, but of the custom of the country: in the Kandyan kingdom chiefs and officials were honoured by presenting them with a *bulathsurulla* (a carefully arranged packet of *betel* leaves in which pieces of silver were disposed) on every well-judged occasion. The same tradition in other countries is called 'graft', 'squeeze', 'baksheesh', 'perks' etc. This is not to affect cynicism about public standards of morality, but merely to state that it is unwise to overlook the dead weight of tradition. With British rule this did not cease to exist. Administrative laxity which knew the institution at home allowed old custom to continue. If a minor government employee took bribes, his superior, whose name and career might have been found in the Civil List, received a present as a token of appreciation. So long as it was not scandalous, laxity contrived to 'get by', in the modern phrase. If it did not know its time and place, then it would have been rudely reminded of them with a firmness which was as familiar a feature of British rule as the laxity it reproved.

CHAPTER 7

REPAIRS AND RENEWALS

1900-21

The history of the first two decades of the twentieth century in Ceylon can be treated as little more than a record of the decorous movement for constitutional reform sponsored by the representatives of a group described in official documents as 'educated Ceylonese'. In other words, the events of these years would seem to be no more than a variation in local terms of the universal theme that politics resolves itself into a struggle for power. This may seem too facile a rendering of years in which the structure of empire was shaken during a world war and a mass movement first raised its voice in India. But only muffled echoes of both could be heard in Ceylon. What catches the ear there is the dignified insistence upon changes which seemed overdue. Although, as a result, there seemed to be little significant change in the structure of colonial rule, the repairs taken in hand by the owners of the house showed that even the normal process of conservation did leave a trace of the demands made by the tenants. By the 1920s nothing could be the same as it had been, and other voices were soon bound to make themselves heard. But until then the most obvious trend in the history of Ceylon was the revival of the old claim for the reform of the constitution by a new set of contestants.

A survey of everything else outstanding in these years would include little more than a reference to the expansion of the plantation economy, and the consequent development of areas, chiefly in the south-west of the island, involved in the export and import trade. These in turn increased the numbers of those pressing for constitutional reform.

These years were led up to by what has been briefly touched upon earlier: the realization of a small group of the English-educated *élite* that their chances of advancement economically and socially had come up against the system of colonial rule. They were an *élite*; they hardly belonged to what could fairly be described as a 'middle class'. Their economic status would scarcely have qualified them for inclusion in the middle classes of either England or Europe, where the chances of economic advancement into the class above were much greater. Very few were able – as C. H. de Soysa was – to entertain the Duke of Edinburgh to supper 'off a plate with a knife and fork, all of pure gold, the champagne and wine goblets being of the same precious metal. Upon the spoon were delicately carved wine leaves, and around the stem was worked a row of pearls. Rows of rubies similarly encrusted the knife and fork.'[1] Most of them were professional men who had made money in the 50s and 60s and had invested it in land – the only investment available to them – or those whose income came from the land they owned and whose sons were now in the professions. Hard work and the profit from farming rents or from government contracts laid the foundation of the family fortunes of this group.

Their money was invested not only in land and house property but also in the education of their sons. It has been noted that education in English paved the way to such employment in government offices, the professions and the lower levels of the civil service as were open to Ceylonese. A Governor of Ceylon could write in 1853 (in his survey of the year's accounts): 'It is remarkable too that in the Courts of Law we have men as Proctors and Pleaders who bear some comparison with the bar of England – this is the result of the teaching in the Island alone.'[2] This was not an ironical comment. But overcrowding in the ranks of those qualified for these opportunities provided by education had already been noted in the middle of the nineteenth century. Glenie, the Archdeacon of Colombo, writing in the *Ceylon Magazine* hinted darkly about 'educating individuals above their probable sphere of life'. Glenie was a mean person, so the tone of his remarks is not surprising:

It is very much the fashion in the present day to talk about EDUCATION, which has consequently become, like all other popular matters, a thing more talked of than understood . . . The evil of educating individuals *above*, if we may use the word, their probable sphere in life has been largely experienced already in European countries where education (as in Germany) has been universally bestowed.[3]

Not long after a writer in *Young Ceylon* fretted about the limitations of the prospects before the English educated:

> They give us a poor English education merely to suit their own selfish views, that is to say, they must have Natives to fill the minor offices, and they train them up to do the drudgery: and those who have by dint of their own exertion exceeded the standard benevolently prescribed by the Gentlemen of the School Commission, all that they get for their trouble is irritation at their present condition and ambition without the means of gratifying it.[4]

It was to be expected therefore that those who had both some money and the education required of them could not long remain content with the ineffective role they played in the country. Mudaliyars and other government officials could not, because of their official position, play any role in politics. But their close relatives and friends were in the forefront of the movement for reform of the constitution. The door leading to positions of power in the civil service and the judiciary could only be opened by the Governor. The unofficial member of the Legislative Council in the last few decades of the nineteenth century was trying to get his foot in the door.

The position of the unofficial member, nominated by the Governor, had hardly altered since 1833. In 1860 the Colonial Office took away the right previously enjoyed by Governors to restrict debate to subjects chosen by them. Unofficial members could put down subjects on the agenda except motions dealing with the disposal of revenue. In 1867, as has been noted, the Colonial Office allowed the Council to discuss budget proposals, except fixed items of expenditure such as those concerned with the country's military contribution, which were provided for by Ordinance. Unofficial members could now have the satisfaction that no money could be spent in the Colony before they had the opportunity to discuss the proposed expenditure. This was a slight advance on their previous limited rights of discussion. But did all this amount to the power which Merivale (in 1853) thought unofficial members possessed? He was of the opinion that the radical defect of colonial assemblies lay 'in the anomalous character of the "unofficial" member in a Crown Colony. No one else (in British institutions) has so much power with no responsibility at all.'[5] Certainly something more was required to satisfy the demands of the 'educated Ceylonese', led by P. Ramanathan at the end of the century. He was responsible for the formation of the National Association, which grew out of the Ceylon Agricultural Association founded by C. H. de Soysa to help Ceylonese agriculturists. By that time two new 'unofficial' members – representing the Kandyans and the Moslems – were nominated to the Council.

In effect the unofficial's rights of debate in the Council did not give him real power, as control of expenditure was as far from him as it had been. Sir Arthur Gordon (later Lord Stanmore), a shrewd administrator in the old style, started in 1885 the practice of meeting the unofficial members at tea, during which he talked about government proposals and gave them the feeling (which, from their own account, they appreciated) of being in the confidence of the Governor.

In the Legislative Council itself there was little a nominated member could do to convince its all-powerful president, the Colonial Governor, that change had to come. Those nominated to the Council were chosen because they were men of standing in their particular communities unlikely to be troublesome in debate. Of course there sometimes were acrimonious exchanges between officials and unofficials, but the august atmosphere of a full dress state occasion which hung heavily over its meetings and the substantial force of the Governor's displeasure turned them into parade ground manoeuvres as far as could be from real warfare as trooping the colour. There had been skirmishes in the Legislative Council in the 1860s, but in the 90s proceedings were full of decorum: 'Every meeting was something of a State occasion. The Governor and most Official and Unofficial members wore black or grey morning coats. The Kandyan members wore their ceremonial dress (*tuppotti*), the Tamil members their buttoned-up long coats and turbans, and the Muslim members formal European dress with the addition of the red fez cap.'[6]

The prestige of belonging to this assembly was enormous. It conferred unique social distinction; the initials M.L.C. after one's name (a resplendent combination in a country where such distinctions were hankered after) bestowed on their possessor a sense of power likely to be exaggerated by him the more his own experience showed how little he counted in the assembly. The attitude of Colonial Governors to this much-coveted honour was paradoxical: it was important, as it was the greatest distinction they could confer, but with it often went no little amused contempt for the eagerness with which it was desired, as well as some resentment that creatures of their own making should have the right to discuss their actions. This is to be seen in West Ridgeway's determination to make an example of a Moslem lawyer from Batticoloa who, delighted that he had been raised to the giddy eminence of a M.L.C., made a present of fifty guineas (in a parcel) to the Lieutenant-Governor who had gazetted his appointment. Of course the unfortunate lawyer had not intended to bribe the Lieutenant-Governor who was shortly leaving Ceylon. West Ridgeway should have known, as Herbert of the Colonial Office was able to divine because he was not prejudiced, that the lawyer signified his pleasure at the appointment by making the customary present. (It was traditional to give gold to someone leaving the country.) The determination of the Governor to humiliate the proctor – to have withdrawn the appointment would have had no other effect – shows how contemptuous Colonial Governors could be of persons they themselves had elevated to power. Eventually West Ridgeway was persuaded by the Secretary of State (Joseph Chamberlain) to ask the proctor to resign.

In theory the Colonial Office would not have objected strenuously to allowing the unofficial member greater voice in the business of the Legislative Council. Individual members on the permanent staff of the office were enlightened, but as the volume of work increased, routine and red tape hampered the best intentions. Precedents and parallels in other colonies had to be consulted; it became more and more difficult to dislodge the weight of custom on everything, and when in the twentieth-century Whitehall-trained officials went out to the colonies as Colonial Secretaries or Governors they moved easily from the control of one bureaucratic machine to another. Winston Churchill, who served for a time as Under-Secretary to the Colonial Office in the Campbell Bannerman administration, because he came to it fresh from prejudice felt that its procedures made good government difficult. Commenting on the attitude taken by the permanent staff to a dispatch from Ceylon (sent by the Officer Administering the Government, Hugh Clifford) on a manifesto of the recently formed Labour Union, he wrote:

I wish I could feel the same easy confidence about this document. It constitutes to my mind a serious and reasoned indictment of the Administration of Ceylon, of which I have been led to form, since my stay at the Colonial Office, no very high opinion. It is easy to dismiss these complaints with a gesture of impatience, to assume that officials are always right, and the population they rule always wrong. Such is the course sufficiently indicated in the minutes in this paper and in the dispatch. But in my opinion an earnest effort should be made to understand the point of view of the native population, to try to measure the weight of the burden they bear, to appreciate *their* feelings in being ruled by an alien administration. Then having assessed everything, having searched our hearts and found a clear strong justification, not only for the general basis of our authority, but for the special incidents enumerated in the protest, we should be entitled to describe it as unjust or untrue.

Churchill was disturbed that the permanent staff of the Colonial Office had agreed with Clifford that protests from the Ceylonese could be disregarded as being nothing but *Native Opinion*, a journal which colonial officials in Ceylon dismissed as scurrilous.[7]

It had been the declared aim of the Colonial Office, just before Torrington assumed the governorship, to make a start on municipal councils in its grand design of providing training in local government for persons of education and property from whom future municipal councillors would come. In 1866 the Municipal Councils of Colombo and Kandy were formally inaugurated. A year later Galle was given municipal status. But, once again, their presidents were the Government Agent or a senior civil servant, and a number of senior government officials or heads of departments served on them, so that they were little more than repetitions in miniature of the legislative assembly.

Members of Parliament were likely to pronounce enlightened ideas about free democratic institutions in the colonies, and, it should be noted, colonial officials, questioned by the Special Committee of the House of Commons inquiring into the disturbances of 1848, were convinced that such troubles would be less likely to occur if the intelligent native were much more definitely associated with the British Government. On the practical issue of how this was to be done – whether by election or nomination – Saunders, answering Joseph Hume, confessed to the difficulty of discovering any better method than nomination by the Governor: 'It must be left for some time to the Governor. The native members could not give up their time for so long a period as the session (of the Legislative Council) now lasts in Colombo. They should be paid, so as to render them independent, by a vote of the Council itself, and not by the government; but they must be paid.'[8]

The Colonial Office could be free from prejudice and be ready to go further than the Colonial Governor. This can be seen in Blackwood's minute on Governor Anderson's dispatch. He felt that changes 'would instead of producing the "Revolution" apprehended by the Governor, on the contrary avert one ... I cannot myself see that because Ceylon happens to be in the East, with a population of a million and a half of Natives, who are far from being a dull and stolid race, it is to be henceforward governed in the old-fashioned way which was probably suitable some years ago, but is not so now'.[9] But he agreed with the Governor that to agree to the claims made by the planters and businessmen would be wrong: 'There are only a few hundred Europeans in the island, and these in effect ask to govern and tax all the rest. It is just as if the Bengal indigo merchants and bankers asked to legislate for the Bengal Presidency.' Anderson thought 'the Council would not be the Council of the people, but chosen in the main from a few hundred Europeans whose interests are frequently in opposition to the interests of the people'. But in actual fact the memorial he sent the Colonial Office had been signed not by a few Europeans alone but by a large number of the people of the country.

The Governor therefore, left in the key position of arbiter, tended to see the world of Ceylon as a curiously contrived mechanism of weights, balances, checks and counterchecks, all of which could be maintained in operation only by his watchful overseeing eye. This was an eighteenth-century, possibly even a seventeenth-century, philosophy of government. It was a view not destined to last long, but while it lasted it gave a religious sanction to the authority of the Governor, who presided over the jar of conflicting claims in the adjustment of which to traditional order good government resided. It followed that there could be no change really, only the perpetual re-establishment of a balance which tended to be impaired.

When the demand for reform of the constitution was first publicly raised in the 1850s, the Governor could turn it down with the classical formula of maintaining the balance between conflicting interests: 'It is truly stated that these people in the mass, are not yet fitted for the management of their own public interests or affairs, but I know not that they would be better cared for – that their interests would be more impartially weighed by the Government carried on by a majority of the Legislative Council, as it is proposed to reconstitute it, than by the Government as now constituted, which has its eye over the interests of all, setting aside all class or class-interested considerations and views.'[10]

With this view the permanent staff of the Colonial Office were inclined to acquiesce, whatever the opinions of individual officials might have been, because the Secretary of State and the government at home were careful not to upset the Colonial Governor or to make the Colonial Government lose face. Reading the minutes of Colonial Office discussions of dispatches from Ceylon, one is often forced into the conclusion that only on important matters of change of policy would a Secretary of State have willingly overruled a Colonial Governor. One example given here of readiness to support him even to the extent of condoning injustice, has been selected only because the forthright views of the young Churchill were unable to win the day. The minute he would have liked to send Sir Henry Blake was never sent; instead his chief, Elgin, authorized a diluted compromise which would not have been a purge for the Colonial Governor.

The case was an unimportant matter of a railway official in Colombo accused of corrupt practices and tried before a court of law which exonerated him. A subsequent departmental inquiry on precisely the same issues raised in the courts found him guilty and he was dismissed from the service. Reading his petition to the Secretary of State for the Colonies (which Blake duly forwarded to the Colonial Office with the covering dispatch that the local hierarchy found the assistant station master unworthy of discharging his duties as a government official), Churchill objected in incisive language to the manifest injustice of trying a man twice for the same offence. His comments are a model of clear thinking and sharp expression:

> To try a man again upon the original charge, to renew without any of the safeguards of justice a case already decided in a court of law, to overthrow the acquittal pronounced by judge and jury and stolidly to attest upon departmental authority, that the man is guilty after all, is to commit almost every impropriety possible, and to commit them all in the stupidest way. The frequency with which this kind of irregularities appear to be committed in Ceylon renders action imperative. Draft a dispatch according to the minutes concluding with an order to the governor to re-employ Mr Serasinghe.

But as Elgin had the dispatch drafted, it stated that 'the question of re-employing Mr Serasinghe will have to be considered, but I defer my decision on this point until I receive your reply to this dispatch'. Churchill returned to the charge: 'This certainly does not as amended, express my view of what should be done. It practically leaves it open to the Ceylon Government to make a good case out against Mr Serasinghe on some other line. This I have no doubt that they will do: and this sort of scandal will recur to the endless inconvenience of all concerned.' But Elgin was not to be shifted from his position. He was convinced that the amended dispatch was a 'just compromise'.

The dispute dragged on. A. J. Harding's comment that the verdict of the court may have been arrived at by some weakness on the part of the prosecution evoked this rejoinder from Churchill:

> And what are we to say of the decisions of a Departmental Enquiry? They may have been reached only through official prejudice, or ignorance of legal matters, or dislike of the accused, or desire to please the governor or someone in authority, or the sweet and unrestrained caprice of the presiding officer. All human processes are liable to error, but a consensus of opinion has hitherto placed most confidence in regular and recognized Courts of Law and Justice . . . Mr Harding does not appear to recognize that English judicial procedure aims not only at securing the conviction of offenders, but also at protecting private persons against harsh action by Governments, their officers and agents. Further he is wrong in assuming that a Government may do to its servants whatever a private employer would do. Private employers may

often behave unjustly to their servants, but profit by their injustice or severity. Governments have a far higher interest in maintaining a high standard of justice, than in securing the conviction of any particular offender. Laws cannot prevent an employer from abusing his power and overriding the decision of a court by discharging his servant out of spite. But what should we say of a government which repudiated the decisions of *its own* courts! ... I do not find myself able to agree with the course taken by the governor.

Elgin after 'mature consideration', as he termed it, found himself very unwilling to differ from Mr Churchill, but he did not think that 'it is in the interest of the Public Service that he should have the option of compelling the Government to undertake a fresh trial'. All he was ready to do was to state that 'the case has been mismanaged'.[11] Mr Serasinghe was eventually dismissed.

Much more was involved here than a difference of opinion of matters of procedure arising out of a common-place accusation against a public officer. If a young and brilliant Under-Secretary of State with all his powers of mind and forcefulness of language could not make an impression on established routine, then it has to be concluded that a Colonial Governor, unless he was stupidly careless or contumacious, could count on having his own way.

If the agitation for reform was to succeed in wearing down the entrenched power of the Governor, it had to be waged on various fronts. The Colonial Office would have to be persuaded by activities outside the Council in Ceylon: the conventional modes of public meetings, petitions, personal interviews with the Secretary of State or some Junior Minister; through judicious questions in the House of Commons and articles in English newspapers, insisting that demands to which the Colonial Governor had turned a deaf ear had to be considered by Whitehall.

Agitation for constitutional reform resolved itself therefore by the end of the century into a long drawn-out duel between the Governor and the various leaders of the small group of the 'educated Ceylonese'. If they were in the Legislative Council they were supposed to represent some community, but they were not really chosen by anyone but the Governor, who invested them with all the power they had. The only representatives of groups were the two European nominated members who were chosen by the Planters' Association and the Chamber of Commerce.

The leaders of the educated Ceylonese were often graduates of English universities and felt more keenly than their compatriots the difference between the comparative freedom of England and the petty social and political discrimination against them in Ceylon. One of them, a double first of St John's College, Cambridge and a President of the Cambridge Union, made this quite clear in a letter to a relative from England: 'You cannot at all imagine the manner in which the greatest men treat us here. It is so totally different from what we get from Englishmen in Ceylon. Here the greatest man shakes hands with you, offers you a seat as high as his own, and talks with you most familiarly, as if you were his friend.'[12] Of course there were Europeans in Ceylon – missionaries, and others regarded as theosophists and cranks – who made no distinction between persons on account of their race, but officialdom too often succeeded in galling the educated Ceylonese by condescending to them.

There were, besides the Ceylon National Association, quite a few organizations which had taken up social reform and social service, like the Ceylon Social Reform Society and the various Temperance Societies already referred to. They, too, passed resolutions asking for some change in the constitution. These activities were kept going by people who never thought of themselves as professional politicians. That label would have offended their pride in their sincere and earnest attitude of amateurs brought into the political arena by their love of their country. There were, towards the end of the century, other activities on the fringe of theirs which for the first time came up against the depressed workers of the rapidly growing city of Colombo. There was as great a division between the gentlemen of the National Association, the Low Country Products Association, the Ceylon Reform League of 1917, and professional politicians as there were between Gentlemen and Players at Lord's. The gentlemen were no rabble-rousers; they were not slow to advise the worker on the value of thrift and sobriety; they could even put their hands into their pocket and satisfy the demands of a group of workers rather than have a horrid strike on their hands. They were taken up with their own struggle; once their own claims had been met there would be time enough to take up those of the poor. They were just as patronizing to the poor as officialdom was to them, and the label 'friend of the poor' was accepted as sufficient guarantee of the right degree of social conscience on the part of a number of those engaged in battling for reform of the constitution.

On occasion various members of the group would at their own expense travel to England to state their case for reforms before sympathetic Members of Parliament or the Secretary of State for the Colonies. There were deputations under the leadership of James Peiris, H. J. C. Pereira, E. W. Perera, D. B. Jayatilaka and P. Ramanathan. They met the Secretary of State or Junior Ministers, and interviewed Members of Parliament interested in Ceylon.

But all this in the end was to no purpose, since the opposition of the Colonial Governor would have to be dislodged. The personalities of these Governors in the first two decades of this century had a great deal to do with their unwillingness to be more sympathetic or more understanding. Besides they were a bit too ready to be alarmed at change in Ceylon which seemed to them dangerous in its propensities. Sir Henry Blake in 1906 expressed his nervousness about such episodes as the carters' strike in Colombo, which he diagnosed as a symptom of opposition to constituted authority: 'The movement seems to be rather a continuation of the wave of unrest that is felt at present all over the East, and that in Ceylon is encouraged by the *Ceylon Independent*, a morning paper largely read by the English-speaking natives.'[13]

Agitation of any kind of change in the constitution seemed to fit into the Colonial Governors' misgivings about giving the unofficial member either much more responsibility or more power. They were wary about conceding very much of either, because they felt uneasy at any curtailment of their own powers and responsibilities.

McCallum's attitude in 1909 to moves among the educated Ceylonese for change were typical of the old-style pro-consul. He distrusted the educated native and preferred to deal with 'the unsophisticated and uneducated villager', whom he claimed the European Government Agent was better able to understand and represent than any educated Ceylonese. His reply to the letter of James Peiris to the Under-Secretary of State for the Colonies on the subject of reform of the Legislative Council, together with memorials which he, as Governor, forwarded to the Secretary of State, was as adroit as he could make it. On no account was 'the class which has assimilated an education and training of a distinctively European type' to be trusted to be interested in anybody but themselves. He did not trouble to disguise his scorn of their pretensions; he was probably repeating what a number of officials in Ceylon at that time must have felt. (Many of the 'educated Ceylonese' thought that McCallum's dispatch had been drafted by the Colonial Secretary, Hugh Clifford.) The Governor refused to consider the need for any change whatsoever: either the natives were undeveloped and uneducated, or they had had an exotic education and had therefore 'ceased to be in any sense typical Orientals and thereby forfeited their right to speak with authority on behalf of the typical Orientals who form the immense bulk of their fellow-countrymen'.

McCallum's case against the Peiris letter was based on two dangerous half-truths: the Government Agents and their cronies – the native chiefs – could legitimately speak for the masses; and that the educated Ceylonese were quite out of touch with the people of the country. In addition, he was like all Governors at this time excessively confident in his ability to decide what was good for the country, and, though he was never explicit about it, he did not like the way events in Asia (in Japan and in India particularly) were moving.

Whatever the personal opinions of Crewe, the Secretary of State for the Colonies, might have been on the Peiris proposals, once again what weighed most heavily in the balance was the Colonial Governor's opposition to them and the suggestion that imperial interests could be safeguarded only by maintaining the *status quo*: that is, by ensuring an official majority in the Legislative Council. Only in a few details was McCallum not allowed to have his way. The changes brought about by Ordinance No. 13 of 1910 were certainly slight. The Secretary of State thought that two members were sufficient to represent European interests in the Legislative Council instead of the three already given them. These two would be elected by a European urban and a European rural electorate. The Burgher member was no longer to be nominated by the Governor, but elected by a Burgher electorate. McCallum had been ready to concede to the class he disliked – the 'educated Ceylonese' – the right of having one member nominated to the Legislative Council by himself. Crewe thought that this member should be elected too – by voters who had an income of not less than Rs 1,500 per annum, and had passed the Senior or Junior Cambridge Local examination or any other examination which the Governor should declare as being equivalent to either of them. No employee of the government could be elected as member representing this electorate. As the number of unofficial members was increased to ten, the Governor was empowered to increase the number of officials in the Council to eleven. This new official member was the Principal Civil Medical Officer.

The McCallum-Crewe 'reforms' were not a compromise, they were a snub to the persistent and loyal members of the reform societies and associations. The Governor had lost some of his power to nominate members to the Legislative Council; there were for the first time elected members in it, but the educated Ceylonese had achieved very little. Their first member was P. Ramanathan. Unfortunately the election revealed some strains in the identity of interest between educated Sinhalese and educated Tamils. The Governor was suspicious and on the defensive. In the towns there were unmistakable signs of discontent among the unrepresented on account of the rising cost of living. But within five years of the 1910 constitution the empire was at war. Ceylon was several thousand miles away from the front line, none the less it was involved in the consequences of the war, chiefly the reality of inflation and a shortage of food.

In 1915, when considerable disquiet about the turn of events in Europe had replaced the confidence of 1914 that 'the boys' would be back home before Christmas, a short and sharp episode of communal rioting in Ceylon showed the difficulty of maintaining the claims of the Colonial Government (like those of McCallum for instance) to represent the ordinary masses of the country. A new Governor had succeeded McCallum: Sir Robert Chalmers, an experienced Treasury official, with cultivated interests in Pali literature and the sacred lore of Buddhism. Of course he could not claim to know the country in the short time he had been in Ceylon. The Colonial Secretary was Reginald Stubbs, a Colonial Official rewarded for good service by his appointment to Ceylon.

The suddenness of the eruption of communal violence in Kandy and Gampola on the 28 May 1915, the day on which Vesak, the traditional anniversary of the Buddha's birth, was celebrated that year, is difficult to explain. So much legend formation has surrounded the events of 1915 that it is difficult now to separate what actually happened from what was honestly believed to have taken place. Rumour, the sense of which becomes second nature to people living in small communities (Tennent found it very well developed in European circles in Colombo and Kandy when he was Colonial Secretary), had as much to do with the spread of the disturbances as anything else. The Buddhists of Gampola and Kandy had been alarmed that their traditional procession with music would be prohibited from passing a mosque in Gampola built by a group of Moslem traders from the southern coast of India. The legal argument on the right of the Buddhists to conduct this procession in the traditional manner increased hostility towards these Moor traders whose prices, like those of everyone else, kept rising on account of real and fictitious shortages. A few professional agitators with their wild stories of what had occurred and what had been threatened in the Central Province on Vesak day – stories resembling that of the Russians with snow on their boots seen on various railway stations in England in 1915 – sent crowds on to the streets. Mobs in Colombo had been known, in the raised temperature of crowd hysteria, to run quickly through the gamut of catcalls, hooting, jeering, stone-throwing, rushing at the stalls of pavement vendors, furtive looting in the resultant confusion and a hasty retreat at the appearance of authority in the full panoply of power.

The situation in Kandy on the night of 28 May 1915 was more serious than on any of these previous occasions of mass excitement, because religious passions had been aroused. Unfortunately for the chances of the affair blowing over at the arrival of the police and/or troops, a combination of circumstances led to sporadic rioting at Kandy and elsewhere for three or four days. The Governor was at Nuwara Eliya; he had a few weeks previously lost his two sons on active service in Europe. Besides he seemed to have been incapable of making quick decisions. On 2 June as the disturbances had spread to various places in five provinces, he decided to declare martial law[14] and Brigadier-General Malcolm, the Officer Commanding the troops, was left in charge of a situation with which the civil administration seemed unable to cope. Malcolm, a survivor of the days of the Boer War, was not notable for his powers of speedy decision either. What orders were given to groups of the military (reinforced by a Punjabi regiment) were either not clear or misunderstood. The rioting and looting were soon brought under control, but martial law continued for three months. In this period another set of persons, as strongly moved by rumours of another kind, European planters and civilians, set about as Justices of the Peace trying the Sinhalese accused of complicity in the disturbances. Far too many Europeans were convinced that the riots were enemy inspired or were a deliberate threat to the war effort. It is true that the ranks of the European hierarchy responsible for the maintenance of law and order in the island had been depleted by the war. But that hardly excuses the panic of some of those on the spot. Sinhalese associated with the Temperance and nationalist movements were thrown into jail as their activities had earned them the suspicion of the government.

With the lifting of martial law the protests of the Sinhalese who considered themselves harshly and unjustly treated led to public meetings, telegrams to Whitehall and Westminster and the voyage of E. W. Perera to England to make representations on the need for a Royal Commission of Inquiry. Chalmers assured the Legislative Council and prominent Ceylonese leaders like Ramanathan that 'a revolt had been put down with rose water'. But public agitation and the scandal of court proceedings against those accused of complicity in the disturbances and appeals from those claiming compensation for wrongful arrest and imprisonment led to angry recriminations against the government.

In December 1915 Chalmers was asked by the Secretary of State to take up an important post in the Treasury to which his talents had clearly destined him. His departure and the attitude of his successor Sir John Anderson, another official from Whitehall, led to the myth, still current in Ceylon, that Chalmers had been recalled at the instance of Ceylonese leaders engaged in petitioning Westminster and Whitehall with their grievances. The cables offering Chalmers his new appointment were in no sense the stepping down of a Colonial Governor who had been found wanting. Nor did his subsequent career indicate that the home government had in any way punished him for any dereliction of duty in Ceylon. Chalmers was Under-Secretary for Ireland during the grave troubles of 1916. In 1924 as Baron Chalmers he became Master of Peterhouse, Cambridge.

It is possible that strong action at the time when the first signs of mob violence were manifested could have effectively prevented trouble spreading, for crowds in Ceylon, like undisciplined groups elsewhere, would either have fled or retired at the first sign of firmness. Of course no one then, or even now, could have been proved right that if the police had opened fire – over the heads of the crowd, or used blanks, or a few harmless pellets – the mob would have melted away. It is true, too, that it is easy now to write on what might have been done, or what should have been done, by the European officials in charge of law and order. According to W. T. Stace, the Police Magistrate of Kandy at the time:

On the first night of the outbreak I was called out by the Superintendent of Police, to take charge. The Government Agent was away on circuit. The District Judge, who was throughly enjoying himself on the streets as an onlooker who was not responsible for law and order and who when asked by me for advice whether to fire on the crowds, as the police were pressing me to give them orders to do, replied only with the memorable dictum: 'Why not pepper them on their rumps?' I did not order firing. Later when the Commission held its inquiry, Pagden asked Fraser, the schoolmaster (who was also an onlooker) 'what would have happened if Mr Stace had ordered firing?' he replied 'Stace would have been dismissed from the service' ... The crowd dispersed and reassembled in another street round a corner out of sight. Dispersed again, they reassembled elsewhere, and so on. On that first night we had so few police in Kandy that we could not be everywhere simultaneously so that a crowd could always disperse where we were and reassemble where we were not.[15]

Evidence from other scenes of trouble shows that the crowds were undoubtedly aggressive when they noted that the police had no firearms or that they were using blanks, but that the first live shot was sufficient to make them flee.[16] It is clear, too, that the appearance of someone in authority known to them did much to calm them.

Whatever the might-have-beens, what did take place – mob violence and the excesses of martial law – does suggest failure of some kind on the part of the government: a failure of communication perhaps, a failure of understanding, or an excusable failure of nerves. Some thought that the violence had been the work of criminal elements in the city of Colombo, but it has been pointed out that very few of those charged with damage to property and looting did belong to criminals on the police records. Rumour exaggerated the feelings of persons who, by themselves, would have been unlikely to resort to violence. There were trouble-makers who incensed the crowds with their accounts of what had never taken place. There were, too, those who profited from the breakdown of law and order to pay off old scores and to help themselves to what did not belong to them.

Once the mob got out of hand and the government lost its head the consequences were more or less inevitable: imprisoning the wrong people and the excesses of the courts martial. But were such measures as the appointment of military commissioners to assess the damages suffered by the Moors, forcing a few prominent Sinhalese to sign bonds making themselves responsible for the collective debts assigned to villages really necessary? And was it necessary to try civilians by courts martial while the ordinary courts of law were sitting?

The new Governor, Anderson, did not think so. As a result most members of his community felt that he was letting them down. For many years the responsibility for the riots and the way they were tackled were sore spots in Sinhalese-European relations. Hugh Clifford, who wrote the *Encyclopaedia Britannica* article on Ceylon in 1929 blamed the magnitude of the troubles on the inexperience of the Governor and the Colonial Secretary: 'Both the Governor and the Colonial Secretary were Home Civil Servants from Whitehall with no colonial experience. Instead of trusting to his trained Civil Servants and the Police the Governor abdicated in favour of the General.'[17]; It was well known, however, that Clifford was prejudiced and disliked Whitehall officials excessively. It should be noted, too, that the Governor 'abdicated' when it looked as if the situation had gone beyond the powers of the 'trained Civil Servants and the Police'.

When life in Ceylon returned to an uneasy normalcy the agitation for reform of the constitution was once more taken up by the 'educated Ceylonese', this time under the aegis of Ponnambalam

Arunachalam and the newly formed Ceylon Reform League of which he was elected the first President in 1917. Memorials to Sir John Anderson, who was himself reviewing the situation on behalf of the Secretary of State, followed. But before the Governor could complete his report he fell gravely ill in Ceylon and died on 24 March 1918. He had been welcomed in Ceylon as the Governor dispatched to the colony on the 'recall' of Chalmers with the express purpose of redressing the wrongs done the people of the country in 1915. The firmness with which he carried out his inquiries, his unpopularity with the European community and some details of little significance in the ceremony of his funeral led to the story (still widely believed) that European officialdom took the opportunity of revenging itself on the late Governor in the unceremonious way in which he was buried. Once again legend distorted into a morbid slight what was beyond the control of the officials concerned. Professor Stace, commenting on the incidents, writes: 'I recollect the cortège was trotted to the cemetery instead of being walked.' This was because neither horses (from the Ceylon Mounted Rifles) nor men had been trained in such an exercise, difficult enough for crack British regiments to perform. At the funeral of Queen Victoria the horses which drew the gun-carriage on which the coffin was placed at Windsor station got out of control. They had to be unharnessed and the carriage drawn by a detachment of the Royal Navy to St George's Chapel.[18] It is not surprising therefore that the hacks of a volunteer regiment in Ceylon were unequal to the unusual task of drawing the gun-carriage on which the coffin of a Colonial Governor reposed at a pace in keeping with the dignity of the occasion.

A public meeting in Colombo, organized by the usual 'Representative Committee', lauded Anderson's services to the country. A sum of Rs 200,000 was promised on the spot to provide a memorial to the dead Governor. Nothing came of this, as nothing had come much earlier of a similar public meeting and projected memorial to Dr Elliott. Having paid the conventional tribute to the dead, the living must have considered themselves absolved of any further claim upon the gratitude they expressed or their self-respect.

In its representations to the British Government the Reform

League returned to a theme touched on lightly before: when the Colebrooke Commission's report had inaugurated the Legislative Council, such an assembly had been unknown in India; but since that time India had gone ahead while Ceylon had remained stationary. In 1917 the Secretary of State for the Colonies was asked whether Edwin Montagu, the Secretary of State for India and on a visit there, could not receive a deputation of the Ceylon leaders. His Majesty's Government could not agree. All the Secretary of State for the Colonies would promise was that he would discuss the reform of the constitution with Anderson when he proceeded to England on leave in 1918. In the meantime the Reform League had prepared its own scheme which it addressed to the Secretary of State in December 1917. It pressed for 'the total abolition in the Legislative Council of the nomination of unofficial members by the Governor, and the provision for a large increase of the number of elected members and for an elected majority with an elected Speaker of the Legislative Assembly; and in the Executive Council a reduction in the number of official members and the introduction of an elected unofficial element'.[19]

A new Governor, Sir William Manning, arrived in Ceylon in September 1918. Some of his remarks in England had upset the Ceylonese leaders, but the omens seemed favourable and they hoped for constitutional changes in keeping with their demands. But the reforms, as presented to the House of Commons in 1919, disregarded the requests made by two deputations from Ceylon as well as the resolutions of various political organizations in the island. Milner told the second deputation from Ceylon that he wished them to give the new constitution 'a reasonable trial'. He would then be ready to 'consider any new proposals and should certainly rejoice if the degree of popular control now introduced were productive of such good results in practice as to justify its extension'.[20]

On the 11 December the newly-formed Ceylon National Congress (which absorbed the old Reform League and the National Association) met for the first time under the presidentship of Sir Ponnambalam Arunachalam. The Ceylonese leaders had never made specific what exactly they had meant by asking that the Ceylonese unofficials chosen by the Legislative Council to sit in the Executive Council 'should be made responsible for the administration of departments placed in their charge'. Nor were some of their other proposals less vague. Yet Congress was unanimous in rejecting the 1920 constitution as 'utterly inadequate and reactionary'.[21] The constitution added one nominated representative each from the British, Sinhalese and Tamil communities to the Executive Council. In the new Legislative Council of thirty-seven members there were to be twenty-three unofficials, eleven of whom were to be elected by territorial constituencies and eight by communal electorates.

Congress rejected the constitution, but was unwilling to come out in forthright non co-operation with the government, as a few of its more militant spirits suggested. The leaders, as James Peiris put it, did not wish to act 'like a sulky child who having asked for a cake gets only a slice and refuses to eat it because it has not received the whole'.[22]

Since this was the case and the Congress high command was clearly loth to let its fingers leave the cake, it was not difficult for the Governor and the Attorney General to persuade it to co-operate in working the constitution, on the understanding that certain amendments would later be made in it. The constitution was to be given a year's trial; after this period the Secretary of State would be asked to consider the promised amendments as well as Governor Manning's further recommendations.[23]

On these assurances Congress was ready to accept the 1920 constitution. But two things were clear: there were differences in the high command about the future, and among the rank and file about the wisdom of having anything to do with Milner's scheme. The identity of opinion which had plastered over the differences between the 'educated Ceylonese' no longer existed. By 1921 it was plain that the old unity had been flawed.

CHAPTER 8

THE FIRST CRACKS
1921-30

The old-time tug-of-war between Congress and Colonial Governor continued in the 1920s. Congress held meetings in the Public Hall, drew up memorials, sent deputations to England and interviewed Ministers and politicians in Westminster; Colonial Governors wrote innumerable dispatches, tried to follow instructions given them by Whitehall and to work the two constitutions of 1920 and 1924. Both sides – Congress and Governors – recoiled from going too far on any issue of real conflict.

Only one change in the probable result of the tussle is worth remarking. In 1924 for the first time a Labour government held office in England. Congress had already established good relations with some Labour parliamentarians, in particular with Colonel Josiah Wedgwood. He visited India in 1921 and went on to Ceylon, where he was enthusiastically received by the Congress leadership. So was Ramsay Macdonald in 1926, when Congress in honour of the Labour ex-Prime Minister turned the spotlight for a while on the relatively insignificant Labour Union of Ceylon. In a speech which he described as not being political, Macdonald spoke the same language as his audience on the future of Ceylon: 'The problem that we have got to solve with your co-operation, you sitting at the same table as ourselves, you thinking out the same problems as ourselves, you criticizing with us your own proposals; that problem of democracy has got to be solved in co-operation, in good-will, in fellowship, in communion one with another, but can never be solved otherwise.'[1]

Congress was sure of a new accession of strength at Westminster. Colonial Governors had always been nettled by questions in the House of Commons. Mrs Jayawardena quotes a significant confidential minute of the Inspector General of Police to McCallum in 1912: 'A successful prosecution (of Dharmapala) with a really deterrent sentence will be regarded as "cruel" at home, and even if the Secretary of State does not reduce it, the matter will never be allowed to die a natural death so long as Messrs Keir Hardie & Co can ask questions in the House'[2] With a Labour government in office in the 20s these were likely to be more than a source of irritation.

The fabric of British rule in Ceylon was beginning to show signs of 'settlement'. The ground on which it had been resting for more than a century had begun to shift and cracks were appearing in the walls. That an Inspector General of Police should have schooled himself to restraint was a portent of changed times.

Most significant of all the shifts in the foundations in the twenties was that caused by the upthrust of a new class – the urban workers – just emerging as individuals conscious of their rights and discovering that through combination with their fellows they could exert pressure on both government and employer. In the 20s Colombo was beginning to be a large town with a population of over 250,000. Concentrated in it were practically all the overseas trade and commerce of the island; it exported nearly all the country's agricultural produce; it handled all its imports; it was the hub of the railway system with the goods yards and engineering works needed to maintain the only effective system of transport in the island at the time. The few tools required for its plantation industry which could be manufactured locally were produced there. Its harbour was one of the largest in South Asia; it served South India and was an important coaling base for shipping between the United Kingdom, the Far East and Australia. Earlier writers describing the town – the largest in Ceylon as it had always been in British times – pull out all the stops of the picturesque in producing their tone poem. But by the 20s Colombo was treated in a more humdrum and prosaic key. The mass of its population was composed of the miscellaneous labourers in the yards and mills of export and import firms, dock workers, unskilled workers in its shops, bazaars, and business establishments, railway workers, among whom were to be found a small class of skilled craftsmen. They were all as yet unorganized; they had no voice in any of the political confabulations of their betters; they felt much more keenly than the latter the strain of making a living

1 Mihintale is one of the most ancient Buddhist sites of Ceylon. Here, according to the tradition, the son of the Indian emperor Asoka first preached Buddhism in Ceylon in the third century BC. The tablets in the photograph are of the tenth century AD.

2 The circular shrine or *Vatadage* at Mädirigiriya goes back to the seventh century A D. A beautiful example of Sinhalese elaboration of an Indian architectural mode.

3 A bronze of the goddess Parvati from the Siva Devale No. 5 in Polonnaruva. One of the remarkable pieces of sculpture of the Polonnaruva period (eleventh–thirteenth centuries AD). Now in the Colombo Museum.

4 This drawing of the Dalada Maligava, or Temple of the Sacred Tooth of the Buddha, in Kandy – the most eminent of Buddhist shrines in Ceylon – was made by Captain C. O'Brien in the 1840s. In Kandyan times the temple must have looked much as it did when O'Brien made his sketch.

5 Detail of wood-carving on the boss of a pillar at the Embekke devale in the Kandyan country. The rhythm of the design and the conventional modification of reality are noteworthy.

6 Sri Vikrama Rajasinha, the last reigning king of Kandy. He was of South Indian extraction and his reputation, like that of Richard III of England, is sadly in need of rehabilitation.

7 The Kandyan country as it looks today near one of the old royal domains at Hanguranketa: terraced rice-fields come down to meet coconut groves.

8 Coffee was first tried as a plantation crop by British planters in Gampola. Capt. O'Brien's sketch shows the plantation on Peacock Hill, now a tea estate. Gampola is in the background.

9 Ambegamuva was a district in which a number of Civil Servants and Government officials had invested in coffee plantations. O'Brien's drawing shows the clear markings of the industry which first transformed the hill country of Ceylon.

10 The harbour at Galle as seen from Closenberg (as it is called in English), in the days when sailing ships and the earliest steamships called with mails and passengers from England.

11 William Gregory, one of the ablest of the Colonial Governors of Ceylon, was knighted in the Audience Hall of the Kandyan Kings on the occasion of the visit of the Prince of Wales to Kandy in 1876. The drawing was made for the *Daily Graphic*.

12 The Arts Building of University College, Colombo. A typical example of colonial architecture.

13 The new University at Peradeniya. Its setting in the Kandyan hills was effectively used to provide an unusual landscape frame. The first students took up residence there in 1950.

14 Tea Taster – the possessor of a special skill which only assiduous training can develop, if, according to the initiated, the innate capacity is there.

15 Tea pluckers – in the highest part of what is known in Ceylon as Up-country. The women, adept at the work, are all of Indian Tamil origin.

16 Fishermen: all round the coasts of Ceylon the fisherman with his nets and lines and catamarans is at work.

17 Keerimalai – a fresh-water spring by the sea near Kankesanturai in the northern peninsula. No traveller in Ceylon who has dipped in its waters will ever forget it.

18 The cultivators of rice form numerically the largest group of workers in Ceylon. It is an ancient and honourable livelihood.

19 Kataragama is an ancient Hindu shrine in the jungle of the South East of Ceylon. Yearly in July thousands of pilgrims gather there to perform the vows they have made to the god.

20 Irrigating the tobacco field. The workers walk up and down the shaft on which the bucket is suspended into the deep well in the limestone soil of Jaffna.

21 In every Buddhist village men and women work at the lanterns which will hang outside their huts in honour and remembrance of the birth of the Buddha – the festival of Vesak: the full moon of the month of May.

22 Ananda Coomaraswamy, the son of Sir Muttu Coomaraswamy, left a deep impression on all those anxious to re-discover the traditional arts of Ceylon. Scholar, savant and sage, he spent only the early years of his working life in Ceylon.

23 The photo shows D.S. Senanayake in a characteristically relaxed, confident and happy mood. Beside him on the platform is S. W. R. D. Bandaranaike, at that time regarded as his lieutenant.

24 Dudley Senanayake addressing a political meeting in support of a UNP candidate in the provinces.

25 Sir Oliver Goonetilleke walking down the steps of the House of Representatives after the State opening of Parliament – an occasion reminiscent of the great days of Colonial power.

26 The short lived triumvirate of 1963: Philip Gunawardena, Dr S. A. Wickremasinghe and Dr N. M. Perera.

27 Mrs Sirimavo Bandaranaike conferring with the Chinese leader in 1965, when he spent a few days in Ceylon after his visit to Africa.

28 Where gods are made – the workshop in Jaffna of a master craftsman. The charcoal sketch on the wall shows the ease of the traditional line.

29 Temple Frescoes – another example of the strength of the indigenous tradition, this time of the painter who decks shrine rooms with scenes from Buddhist stories.

and raising a family. The cost of living had been rising steadily and relentlessly. Between 1907 and 1912 it had more than doubled. Prices and rents, once up during the war years, never dropped, and the slums of Colombo, euphemistically called 'gardens' (because there had been once upon a time a patch of green round which tenements had been built), were as overcrowded, malodorous and profitable to their owners as those of any metropolis.

The numbers of urban workers had been growing fast as a result of the great increase in government spending. The demand for labour, and the consequent influx of unskilled workers from South India to take up work which the drift from the villages into the capital city had not satisfied, caused as many divisions in the working-class of the metropolis as there were among the 'educated Ceylonese'.

The strikes of the 20s, caused by the rise in the cost of living while wages remained static, were very different in kind from earlier labour conflicts. They were larger in scale and more serious politically. It was their aggressive character which failed to enlist the patronizing interest or the sponsorship of the leaders of the 'educated Ceylonese'. The determination of the workers created a vacuum which was filled by outsiders on the fringe of the movement for constitutional reform, quick to see the possibilities of this important new factor in the political scene.

The attitude of the government and other employers to the very word 'strike' was no different from what it had been. Strikes were not to be tolerated and had to be beaten down. The first sporadic strikes in Ceylon took place among the labour force of European owned enterprises. They were unsuccessful, though they did attract newspaper attention of a faintly amused kind and the benevolent disapproval of political leaders of the time. It was obvious that the employers, helped by the police, were well able to deal with their uneducated and unorganized workers. There were, however, distinctions to be drawn, even in the earliest times, between the attitude of the large European commercial houses and Ceylonese employers to their workers. Mrs Jayawardena, in her able study of the labour movement in Ceylon, quotes a comment from one of the earliest social workers in Colombo interested in the condition of the working poor. Dr Lisboa Pinto writing in the *Ceylon Review* in October 1893 remarked that 'having had occasion to try to interest some of our wealthy labour employers on behalf of their men, and to enlist their sympathy in the cause of the hard-worked labourer in general, I found the Ceylon capitalist as much exacting and relentless as the Englishman, perhaps more'.[3]

Of course the Ceylon capitalist was likely to be 'more relentless' than the European. Working on smaller sources of credit and lacking the latter's experience of labour legislation elsewhere, he could not even count on the same uninhibited support of the authorities in any action taken against his workers. It was to be expected, too, that the hierarchy of the educated Ceylonese would resent trouble from an unknown sector of the populace, unpredictable in its behaviour and capable of queering the pitch for them in their peaceful campaign for constitutional advance.

Yet Congress was not entirely uninterested. There was a Ceylon Workers Welfare League and later a Ceylon Workers Federation with which Congress was associated. Resolutions urging social legislation had been dutifully passed, but little active work had been done. H. J. C. Pereira, President in 1923, recalled a strike thirty years previously, in order to assure his audience that Congress was not without interest in the working man:

He would tell them that there was no man, who was more in sympathy with the working class of this country than himself. Men of the middle and higher classes could well look after themselves. It was the poor working class that had to be looked after by others. He took upon himself to create the first Trade Union among the working classes, when he was young and the world was young. It was many years ago when a Printers' Strike took place caused by inordinate hours of work and poor pay . . . The strike ended fairly satisfactorily and the men got to a certain extent what they wanted and they returned to work and forgot all about the Union which lapsed into obscurity. That was the history of the first strike among the workmen in Ceylon.[4]

In spite of all this it was very clear that the poor working class and the Congress hierarchy had little in common. H. J. C. Pereira himself was, according to his contemporaries, a man of the highest professional skill, a wonderful charm of manner and of great humanity. But his attention (and that of his colleagues) was fixed on the way they had marked out towards their goal. It did not run through the dreary flats of working-class organization.

Indeed it was made perfectly plain by the end of the 20s that those in the forefront of the movement for constitutional reform would stand no nonsense from the organized working class. In 1929 D. R. Wijewardene, well on his way then to becoming a newspaper tycoon, reacted swiftly to a strike of linotype operators employed by the Associated Newspapers of Ceylon. Those who presented a petition asking for an increase of wages were instantly dismissed. Police protection was provided for those who did not join the strike and the importation of Indian lino operators broke it after a few weeks. Wijewardene had been – sixteen years previously – Secretary of the Ceylon National Association and he was closely identified with the movement for constitutional reform. After the strike he proposed a resolution at the Ceylon Employers Federation that it should refuse to recognize Trades Unions. It was lost and he showed his scorn for the Federation by promptly resigning from it. Since that time no unions have been tolerated in the large Associated Newspapers of Ceylon which Wijewardene built up as the biggest Ceylonese enterprise of the time.

The harbour strike of 1920, and the railway workers' strike of 1923 which led to the nearest equivalent of a general strike in Colombo before the 40s, were events on such a large scale that their size alone would have produced the leadership of which the workers stood in such need. According to Mrs Jayawardena's account, chance crowned A.E. Goonesinha king of Colombo's working class during the Railway Loco workers' strike in 1923. At the moment when the employers wanted someone to negotiate with he appeared.[5] The masses had to have a leader, they got more than they bargained for – a boss.

A.E. Goonesinha, a law student and teacher, interested in Youth League activities, was like many of his colleagues on the fringe of Congress. He was a person of little consequence, until the Railway Loco workers' strike began the first year of his reign. He was as good a king of the urban working class in the early days of the 20s as anyone else. The urban worker could not then, and could not for some time yet, produce out of its own ranks persons sufficiently educated in English to be able to shoulder the necessary tasks of standing up to the police, the government and the bosses, or even of being able to insist on their rights or to manage their own affairs. The role of working-class boss suited Goonesinha's talents, particularly his flair for the grandiose gesture and his belief in his role as leader. He held sway for close upon fifteen years. His amalgam of eclectic philosophy, personal rule and the subordination of Trade Union organization to power politics, together with the wave of successful strikes which first launched him, swept him ultimately up to a shelf of the establishment and finally left him there stranded. But in the early 20s he was a radical politician by virtue of his leadership of the urban workers in their demands for better wages and working conditions. To the police, the government and the employers he was an infuriating symbol of their own impotence in the face of a new menace. They were forced into the galling necessity of negotiating with him. His political significance was made clearer than ever during the successful harbour strike of 1927, when the crew of an Australian ship calling at Colombo refused to obey the employers' directive to help to unload its cargo and so beat the strike.

In the late 20s Goonesinha was at the height of his fame as leader of the workers. In 1929, during the riots caused by police treatment of pickets during the Tramway Company's strike, it was popularly believed that a bystander paid with his life for the distinction of bearing too close a resemblance to the Labour leader when the police opened fire on a crowd at Maradana.

But it was only for a decade that A. E. Goonesinha was the accepted leader of all the urban workers. Clear-sighted as he was in recognizing the powerful levering force of the working class which he first organized, he saw too, at a later stage, that he could provide a sharper edge to his organization by giving it a communal and racial character. In the early days of his activities he had been ready to speak for all urban workers; he was supported by a few Indian lawyers. He withdrew from that position however and in the early 30s repudiated any interest in, or concern for, the large group of Indian immigrants employed in industry. The working class associated with him, as he continued to represent it for some time yet, was not above a touch of national socialism with its contempt for lesser breeds. It would be unfair to write off Goonesinha's activities now as those of either a self-seeking politician or an exploiter of race hatreds. For a time he filled an important place in the working-class movement. It finally moved away from him. But while they were together he gave those he represented proof of their strength. In 1927 when he left the Congress he brought a Labour Party into being. It was not a political party;[6] it was much rather an umbrella lending dignity to the heterogeneous elements clustered under it. For those, like himself, not in the secret councils of Congress there was some advantage in their association with an imponderable factor in politics.

As for the ordinary worker on the land, he was as yet no one's concern. The educated *élite* in Colombo had been bothered in 1920 about the problem of who was going to represent the territorial electorates. But in them the villager had no vote. His living conditions varied from province to province. It would not be an exaggeration to state that the majority of those who had to make their living as cultivators continued to exist in that indefinable region between malnutrition and hopeless indigence. A Colonial Governor had this to say of them in 1907 when he was leaving Ceylon: 'The average villager has deplorable qualities of envy, hatred and malice. He is suspicious to an extraordinary degree, and, I am informed, adds to phenomenal cunning a bewildering disregard of truth.'[7] Sir Henry Blake did not know the villager and his informants were likely to have been government officials and the headmen the government placed over him. The Governor made a moral judgement, reinforcing it with a reminiscence of the Book of Common Prayer. The only fair comment would be Ampthill's on West Ridgeway: 'These governors are really hopeess.'[8] (Ironically enough Ampthill later became a governor himself.)

The other large group of workers on the land – those on the plantations – were immunized from any contact with other workers. Strict regulations warned off the enclave of the plantation all those whom their proprietors would have kept out. There were timid attempts made by some Indian lawyers to interest Head Kanganies in trying to persuade the coolies to organize, but naturally nothing came of them. In 1922 the Indian Government put its oar in and appointed its own Agent to deal with the Ceylon Government on the subject of recruiting and the working conditions of the plantation workers. In 1923 the Ceylon Government appointed its own Controller of Immigrant Labour. The small gains made on behalf of the immigrant workers in minimum wage agreements and medical benefits seemed to many Ceylonese politicians extraordinary generosity when contrasted with the living conditions of the villager in plantation districts. The politician continued to harp on this theme, not because he loved his fellow-countryman, but because he hated what he described as the Indian. His adulation of the Indian nationalist leaders on public occasions could, and did, exist side by side with suspicion of the plantation workers.

By the end of the 20s the educated Ceylonese realized that there were other problems besides that of their campaign for constitutional reform. But much more disquieting was the unpalatable fact that their ranks no longer marshalled all those who once could be counted upon to rally to the call of Congress. Discordant voices had been raised against the leadership. This was to be expected. Events were moving too fast for the old, and the young were beginning to be restive. Youth Leagues and new political groupings were apt to be critical, and though their criticism was accepted as legitimate democratic procedure, it sat heavy on the older stalwarts. Besides, death had taken its toll of the high command. By 1930 Arunachalam, H. J. C. Pereira, and F. R. Senanayake were dead.

These losses were inevitable; much more serious was the defection of a large section of its staunchest supporters. Arunachalam had withdrawn from Congress some time before his death. His brother, Ramanathan, never had been in Congress but was antipathetic to it. The first election for the Educated Ceylonese seat in the Legislative Council of 1910 had aroused so much communal bitterness that things could hardly be the same after it. Sir Hugh Clifford writing of it long after the event noted its consequences but misinterpreted its significance: 'The first election of a representative of the educated Ceylonese was fought purely on caste lines, a high caste Tamil being chosen with the aid of the high caste Sinhalese vote, caste prejudice thus proving to be a stronger passion than racial bias.'[9] The racial bias which the election aroused was overlaid by caste prejudice: that was all.

Communal tensions had been smoothed over and Ponnambalam

Ramanathan, who was elected to the educated Ceylonese seat, was acknowledged as one of their political leaders. He had been, during the disturbances of 1915, a champion of the Sinhalese cause. His brother Arunachalam, when he retired from government service, had naturally stepped into the position of elder statesman and philosopher of the educated Ceylonese. But communal fears which were never far from the surface were roused by the manœuvring and wrangling about the allocation of seats to the two communities in plans for constitutional reform. In the curious game of a seat for a seat in the mathematical computations of Sinhalese and Tamils, the suspicions of the latter that their interests had to suffer and that they would be reduced to the position of a poor minority were too strong for them.

Dissatisfaction over the Congress attitude to the provision of a special seat for Tamils in the Western Province led to the final breach. A large number of Tamils left the Ceylon National Congress, and in Jaffna the Tamil Mahajana Sabha was founded to work for adequate representation for the Tamil community. After 1923 there still were a number of Tamil lawyers associated with Congress, but it never recovered the old confidence that it and it alone spoke with authority for the *élite*. The few Burghers to be found in its ranks in the 20s moved out too. G. A. Wille, a useful committee man, stayed on till 1924, when the new constitution gave the Burghers a second communally elected seat. In his evidence before the Donoughmore Commission E. W. Perera made a good-humoured side swipe at the lost Burgher leader: 'We had Mr Wille for many years. They [the Burghers] were apprehensive of the extinction of their communal seats and after he was elected he left us.'[10]

Neither the manœuvres which led to the next change in the constitution nor the constitution itself were in the long run of great significance, for the situation was changing too fast for either the educated *élite*, divided as they were at the time, or for the Governor, dependent as he was on policy makers in Westminster. In any case the Secretary of State had made it plain that the new constitution was to be tried for a five year period, after which the British Government would review the whole field.

Congress, through James Peiris in the Legislative Council in 1921, submitted its proposals for further reform. Those out of

Congress and suspicious of it presented their own memorials to the Governor. Congress wanted control of the Legislative Council by territorially elected members on a slightly wider franchise with no communal electorates at all, and a radically changed Executive Council. The others urged communal representation in order to protect minority interests. The Governor, with his tradition of holding the balance between divergent and conflicting interests, had his own scheme for maintaining the equilibrium. As he saw it, the end to be aimed at was an arrangement by which 'no single community can impose its will upon the other communities'. He was ready to allow the Legislative Assembly to have 'a popularly elected majority' and a Vice-President elected by the members. He may have had his eye on the chance of securing in such an assembly a nucleus of supporters of the official point of view. The Secretary of State for the Colonies who had to decide, was not ready to allow much change in the Executive Council. The principle that the Colonial Governor had to be able to govern; that, in other words, he had to be assured of an official majority had been too long established as the cornerstone of Crown Colony government to be discarded now.

But change in the Legislative Council was not contested. The new constitution of 1924 gave the elected unofficial members a majority over the officials, but it retained communal electorates, because, as the Secretary of State saw it, 'so long as the several communities in Ceylon remain convinced, as they appear now to be, of the divergency of their interests in many important matters, so long must some provision be made for the maintenance of communal representation in the Legislative Council'.[11]

In a Legislative Council of forty-nine members, there were thirty-seven unofficial members to twelve officials, twenty-three of the former being returned by territorial electorates. Eleven communal electorates were to return three European, two Burgher, two Indian, three Moslem and one Western Province Ceylon Tamil. Three nominated members, representing the Sinhalese, Burgher and Ceylon Tamil communities, made up the tally of the non-official members.

The new constitution gave the Governor power to certify any measure on the ground of 'paramount importance', even though it had been rejected by the Legislative Council. Control of internal administration was assured through an enlarged but practically unchanged Executive Council.

Congress was once again disappointed that there had been no real change in the Executive Council. Even those unofficial members elevated to it from the Legislative Council had to give up their seats in the 'lower' house. Nor were any government departments, as Congress had suggested, assigned to the charge of territorially elected members. Yet the unofficial members of the Legislative Council had secured one important concession: though they could not initiate any motion involving taxation or the spending of money – such proposals as in the past originating only with the Governor – they could through their membership of the Finance Committee consult and question heads of departments responsible for the provisions of the budget. This was a congenial activity to those who in their desire for power over government departments and their expenditure were baulked of just this by the provisions of the new constitution. The most significant change made by the new constitution in the way things were done in the colony turned out to be the politician's tendency to interfere in the running of departments over which he had no control and for which he was not responsible. It would not be true to say that the territorially elected member became a permanent opposition without any hope of forming an alternative government. That prospect, as we shall see, seemed closer. What is important to observe is that the free rein given to the energies of members in the Finance Committee and the Public Works Advisory Board began the tradition of debates which were a joyous point-to-point, in which members frayed their energies and their tempers sometimes, in careering all over the fields of finance, government departments and their personnel.

Colonial Governors, through the Executive Council and their powers of patronage, still retained their control of power, but they had on their hands a Legislative Council which could be fractious and needed sensitive handling. Manning was too short a time in Ceylon after the constitution was introduced to gain much experience of its working. Clifford, who succeeded him, was explicit in his disapproval of it. He affected the attitude that since real power and financial control had now passed on to the members of the Legislative Council, any dissatisfaction with the government should be taken up with the elected representatives of the people. This practice of his was commented on by a member of Congress during its general sessions of 1925: 'He next referred to a remark of Sir Hugh Clifford who said that they controlled the finances of the Colony. He [the speaker] never fully understood that as he thought it was an empty statement to say that the unofficial members controlled the finances in the Finance Committee. The unofficials could only give their consent but never initiate expenditure. He would ask them to urge on Sir Hugh Clifford to fulfil that statement.'[12]

Sir Hugh, in the obvious pleasure with which he apparently made these remarks, was probably displacing his aggression against a stupid home government which had chosen to disregard the advice of experienced colonial administrators. In any case he preferred to spend his last years in the colonial service in the less troubled waters of Malaya. What he thought of the new constitution is briefly revealed in the article he wrote for the *Encyclopaedia Brittanica* not long after he left Ceylon:

During the governorship of Sir William Manning (1918–25) a series of legislative reforms were granted in rapid succession, the final instalment in 1924 definitely vesting all financial control in the hands of 36 unofficial members, three of whom only are Europeans and the majority of whom are elected, the officials upon the legislative council numbering only 12, and meetings being ordinarily presided over by an elected Ceylonese vice-president. In the meantime three unofficial Ceylonese (two Sinhalese and one Tamil) and one European had been added to the Executive Council. Responsibility for the good administration of the island continued, none the less, to be vested solely in the governor, who is unable to discharge it save by the good will of the unofficial majority of the legislative council or by the exercise of his power of veto, which can easily be countered by a refusal to vote supply – action which would necessitate the practical suspension of the constitution. An appreciation of the impracticability and of the dangers of this situation caused the present writer while serving as governor of Ceylon (Nov. 1925–June 1927), after a year of study to recommend the appointment of a commission to examine the situation and to report as to the measures that could be best taken to surmount the *impasse*.[13]

The inaccuracies of this statement are not as significant as the point of view responsible for them. The kindest inference is to put them down to the mental disease which had already begun to afflict a very keen-witted and intelligent Governor.

Sir Herbert Stanley, who succeeded Clifford, was a mild and forbearing man. Only once was the formula of 'paramount importance' invoked against the will of the Legislative Council. This was in 1929. But by this date the review which the Secretary of State had promised and which Clifford claimed he had initiated was already under weigh. A Commission under the chairmanship of the Earl of Donoughmore had visited Ceylon. Congress was certain that the pendulum of change was going to swing in its direction. The President – in September 1927 – had assured his audience that 'they were now not only within sight, but, in fact, on the very borders of the Promised Land. They might not find that land flowing with milk and honey, but it was their birthright and it had been promised them.'[14]

In two months of 'cold weather' in Anglo-Indian terminology – between the middle of November 1927 and the middle of January 1928 – the Earl of Donoughmore and the three Commissioners, appointed to examine the working of the 1924 Constitution and to consider any proposals for its revision, wandered about the island, listened patiently and courteously to innumerable deputations and gradually made up their minds. They presented their report to the Secretary of State in July 1928.

That they were in Ceylon to see for themselves and to decide how far the demands of the *élite* could be accepted by the British Government was, of course, clear to all those in Ceylon (and in the United Kingdom) who had been following with disquiet and impatience the trend of affairs in India. Ceylon compared with it was of little consequence to British interests, but what was happening in India under the pressure of the Congress movement of non-co-operation had stiffened Conservative and reactionary newspaper opinion in England into irritable watchfulness for the slightest sign of any betrayal of imperial interests. The majority of the British public whose minds are made up for them by the headlines in the evening papers may not have noticed any splash in them about what was 'threatening' in Ceylon, but the current mood in the United Kingdom was one of hostility to the claims of Asiatic peoples. This was shared by a number of Europeans in Ceylon.

The task before the Donoughmore Commissioners has been aptly described by a recent historian as how to give 'the leaders of the legislature representation in the executive without impairing imperial control and interests'.[15] What the Ceylonese leaders in the legislature had been asking for – self-government within the empire – they had made no secret about. This could, of course, place imperial interests in jeopardy, but on the other hand the resoluteness with which Congress in Ceylon had turned against the minority which bandied about expressions like 'independence' and 'Swaraj' showed that it offered no conscious threat to imperial control.

What the Donoughmore Commissioners finally decided was to hand out something to everyone, but not quite what they had been asking for. Their report was a thoroughly British document in its honest compromise. If a distinction may be drawn between their procedure and the act of giving, it can be said that they allowed certain things; they gave practically nothing. *Hactenus* might have been their watchword. In the fullness of time more might be hoped for, but this was as far as they were prepared to go. Their strategy resembled that of the strict father who, contrary to the opinion of other adults, is ready to make some concessions to the young, but not many. It follows that neither grown-ups nor young were exactly pleased. The old colonials thought that too much liberty had been conceded and that doomsday was at hand;[16] Congress was resentful that so many curbs remained. It had asked for a reformed Executive Council in which the unofficials would be in a majority; the new Constitution recommended by the Donoughmore Commission gave Ceylon an assembly with an unofficial majority which would perform both legislative and executive functions. But in it were to be three officers of state nominated by the Governor in charge of matters reserved for his control: the important fields of finance; external affairs and defence; the public service and the judiciary. Congress had asked for ministers in control of government departments; according to the recommendations of the Commission, the seven committees into which the new State Council would be divided would, in their executive capacity, elect chairmen who would be ministers presiding over departments except those reserved for the Governor's control. These seven ministers and the three officials nominated by the Governor were to form the Board of Ministers, whose responsibility would be the preparation of the annual budget.

The minorities had asked for the continuation of communal representation: this was refused, but under the Constitution the Governor was given the power to nominate up to twelve members from various communal groups, if he felt this was necessary to make the territorially elected Council better representative of the people of the country. The officials in the public service appointed by the Secretary of State – the majority of them Europeans – had made their own representations to the Commissioners. They had asked, remembering the criticism to which they had been subjected by the Legislative Council and nervous about changes in their conditions of service, for special protection. They could not, of course, hope for immunity from criticism by members of the State Council, but the public service was placed under the Governor and the officer responsible for it in the Council was to be the Chief Secretary (the old Colonial Secretary). Furthermore, no legislative enactment affecting its salaries, allowances or conditions of service could be introduced in the Council unless the Governor sanctioned it. Since the new constitution brought about a radical change in the conditions of employment of public servants appointed by the Secretary of State, they were given the privilege of retiring with compensation for loss of career and a generous increase in pension rights.

The Colonial Governor – previously the central authority for the functioning of all government departments – apparently had, as a result of the recommendations of the Commission, his spheres of influence curtailed too. The three Officers of State in the Council were responsible to him in those fields expressly reserved for them. 'His ten spheres of direct influence were reduced to three and, in the words of one of the country's earlier ministers, Ceylon had achieved seven-tenths of Swaraj.'[17] But in reality his powers, far from being reduced, were substantially increased. The Constitutions of 1920 and 1924 had given him the right to be the sole legislative authority in all matters of 'paramount importance'. Though, as has been noted, this power was very rarely used, its existence had been galling to the Ceylonese unofficials in the legislature as a reminder of the nature of colonial rule. It is not surprising therefore that a constitutional lawyer should have noted that for all its changes the character of colonial rule remained as clear as it had been heretofore. 'Step by step as more constitutional rights passed to the representatives of the people, the imperial government felt that it was necessary that there should be corresponding increase in the restrictive powers held in reserve by the governor.'[18] That rule did depend on the absolute nature of the power conferred on the representative of the rulers in the colony for use at his discretion. In all their public utterances previous Colonial Governors had been ready to acquiesce in the granting of wider powers to unofficial elected members. But the cardinal principle of the Colonial Office was that Colonial Governors had to govern.

These powers of certification, as they were called, in effect gave the Governor the power really to legislate by decree,[19] since he could, if the necessity arose, override any decision of the Council in its legislative capacity. That this did not lead to greater difficulties than those experienced during the sixteen years of the working of the Donoughmore constitution was due to the tactfulness of the Colonial Governors and the war situation after 1938 which put political development into cold storage. Very soon after the outbreak of war even Colonial Governors had their powers restricted by higher authorities yet.

Of all the Donoughmore Commissioners recommendations the most remarkable and far-reaching in its consequences was its only generous 'gift'. The ordinary man – in the street or in the village – had not appeared before them. He had therefore asked for nothing. He had stood by the wayside, pushed back by the officious police and gaped at the four Europeans in their strange garb with their grey tropical helmets *à la* Curzon during their excursions in the low-country and the north. From the four strangers the ordinary man received the boon of the vote – for some time to come yet a questionable benefit – the one notably generous action by which the Commission made itself memorable. Congress had made it clear to the Commissioners that it would not welcome any extension of the franchise. The existing qualifications of an income of Rs 50 a month and a literacy test by which just over 200,000 of the island's population of over four million had the right to vote were acceptable to them. E. W. Perera who put the

Congress case to the Commission did not wish to press for a change in the franchise:

> although it might be considered that the Congress wanted an oligarchy of small capitalists without extending the franchise. Their position was that Rs 50 represented practically the competent adult population who were fitted for the franchise. The sum was very low now considering that the country was booming in rubber. Wages had gone up considerably and so far as the Indian immigrant labour population was concerned, there would be a number of them who would have the vote. If they went to a grade lower than Rs 50 they might get a class of men, of whom a great proportion would not use responsibility in the exercise of the vote. He was sorry to say that the votes of many men might even be purchased. They did not want to wreck what had been achieved by them, by any precipitate and unnecessary reduction.[20]

But while the Commission had been in Ceylon there had been talk of manhood suffrage and a number of those previously hostile to the idea kept parroting the phrase as an enlightened slogan. It must be said of Congress that though it was opposed to manhood suffrage, its accredited spokesmen did not obstruct it when it was recommended by the Commission.

The Commission proposed that every male over the age of twenty-one and every female over the age of thirty, if they were permanent residents of the island, should be entitled to vote. In subsequent discussion in Ceylon women were spared the indignity of being required to mature nine years longer than men before arriving at the status of voters.

The recommendations of the Donoughmore Commission were the subject of debate in the Legislative Council in 1928 and 1929. Practically every one of their proposals was attacked at length and turned down. The debate continued even after the Secretary of State for the Colonies, on 15 November 1928, tried to apply the brakes on its interminable course by drawing the Legislative Council's attention to his point of view that 'the recommendations must be regarded as a whole, and while no doubt modifications in detail will be necessary when effect is being given to them, I should not be willing to accept any amendments in principle which would destroy the balance of the scheme. If it appears that a substantial majority of the inhabitants of Ceylon would not be willing to agree to a trial of the scheme as a whole, I might feel compelled to reopen the consideration of the whole question of any constitutional change.'[21] After such plain speaking it was clear that it was to be all or nothing.

Congress, nettled by its failure again to grasp power with both hands, had already reiterated its demand for full self-government. It was ready to accept the smaller measure of power given the elected representatives of the people on whatever pattern of government – the League of Nations or the London County Council – the Donoughmore Commissioners had based their scheme. Government by Committee, the divorce of administrative from legislative functions, the mode of election of ministers might all have been objectionable to Congress, but communal representation had gone, and it was to the credit of Congress that they had come out into the open against it with all the firmness in their power.

Although the debate in the Legislative Council, after the Secretary of State's ruling, seemed to be of academic interest, it showed which way the wind was blowing. The Vice-President of the Legislative Council, Sir James Peiris, saw that the subject of the franchise was of capital importance. On this subject the position of Congress, in the light of later events, was again unequivocal. It was determined that the franchise should be restricted to Ceylonese or those with a permanent interest in the island. Non-Ceylonese British subjects (in other words the large population described as Indian immigrants) should have the vote, only if they satisfied literacy and property or income qualifications not required of Ceylonese. Speaker after speaker in the Congress interest was explicit on this point. The member for Kegalle who moved the resolution was perfectly honest in his attitude: 'It has been said that this resolution of mine is brought in with the object of keeping out a large number of Indian voters. There is no use of any camouflage in this matter: I will boldly admit that that is so. We must not forget the feeling in the country at present in this matter.'[22] The class interest of this position was unconsciously underlined by the member for Tangalle:

I wish to make my position clear; what I fear most is the cooly on the estate, rather than the Indian who is living in Colombo . . . We are not against Indians who live in Ceylon and make Ceylon their home. There are so many Indians in Colombo who have bought tracts of land, sometimes thousands of acres. They live here and are becoming more like anyone of us Ceylonese. They are Ceylonese.[23]

The most able contribution to the debate came from the member for Negombo, D. S. Senanayake. By comparison with the tiresome verbosity and formlessness of the other speeches, his was a model of forthright competence in debate. He had no use for recriminations, flights of eloquence, or the trifling adornments of quotations from learned literature. He adroitly cut the ground from under the feet of his opponents by pointing out that those who were against 'differentiation' against Indians were themselves advocates of 'differentiation' in favour of communal interests. In the only reference to subjects outside Ceylon and India he had one telling point to make: 'We were told that if anyone of us went to England it would not be difficult for him to get the vote. But I wonder what the people of England will say if every year hundreds of thousands of people were recruited from abroad into England. They will have a different story to tell.'[24] The great virtue of D. S. Senanayake's speech was the firmness with which he nailed his colours to the mast:

We do not want to differentiate; we do not want to discriminate. We do not consider the Indians as aliens. We tell them 'Become part of ourselves, become Ceylonese, and then share in the government of the country.' That is our position, and I hope our communal friends will not, for their own purposes, misinterpret us, but will appreciate our real attitude in this matter.[25]

In this matter Congress, as one of the contestants for power, behaved normally and understandably. Those who seek more power for themselves must guard jealously the rights they have already gained. Suspicion of the plantation worker was linked with mistrust of the European superintendent, his lord and master. It was stated in the course of the debate that to give the Tamil estate worker the vote was to ensure that the nominee of the European estate superintendent would be elected.

In June 1929 the Governor, Sir Herbert Stanley, made his own observations on the proposed constitution to the Secretary of State. He was not averse from giving the 1924 constitution a further trial, since Legislative Council debates had shown that there was more hostility than good will towards the proposals of the Donoughmore Commissioners. He was ready, however, to recommend the new constitution offered Ceylon with some modifications. But before his dispatch could reach England,

There was a change of government in the United Kingdom, and a Labour administration took office, Mr Amery, who had presided for so long over the Colonial Office, and had set up the Donoughmore Commission, handed over the seals to Mr Sidney Webb; and the new Parliamentary Under-Secretary of State was none other than Dr Drummond Shiels, the Labour Party member of the Commission. It was only natural, then that the Colonial Office should have felt much less hesitation than the Governor about the advantages of the Commission's scheme.[26]

The Governor's dispatch was published and some modifications in the constitution were made. On 12 December 1929 the Legislative Council in Ceylon accepted the new Constitution by a majority of only two votes. It was 1931 before the old Legislative Council was dissolved and elections to the new State Council took place. It was to be, by the Order in Council of 20 March 1931, an assembly of fifty elected members, three Officers of State and not more than eight nominated members. Seven executive committees were to deal with the administration of the following functions of government: Home Affairs; Agriculture and Lands; Local Administration; Labour, Industry and Commerce; Education; Communication and Works. The Chairmen of these Committees were to be ministers and form, with the three Officers of State, the Board of Ministers whose views the Governor was asked to consider.

CHAPTER 9

REDECORATION
1931-47

Though the Donoughmore constitution increased the power of the elected representatives of the people, the structure of colonial rule remained essentially unaltered. Indeed the Colonial Governor's authority had to some extent grown; he was provided with more discretionary powers for use if occasion required. But after 1931 outside the council chamber things seemed different: to Britishers in Ceylon and in the United Kingdom the old edifice was crumbling; to the Ceylonese *élite*, on the other hand, everything within seemed refurbished and redecorated, there was more room to move about in and a freer air was streaming through the corridors.

Between the acceptance of the Donoughmore Commissioners' recommendations in 1929 and the elections to the new State Council in 1931 the ground had to be cleared in preparation for the new constitutional changes: legislative enactments, the registration of voters, the delimitation of constituencies, the arrangement of the new elections and planning for the administration of the new constitution, all took time. Before these plans were settled, the economic depression had begun to cast long shadows over the final shape of the projected State Council. In his dispatch to the Secretary of State on 2 June 1929, the Governor, Sir Herbert Stanley, was alarmed at the cost to the colony of administering the new constitution:

> One feature of the scheme which has caused me some hesitation is the increase in administrative expenditure which would be unavoidable. I am referring, not to those very desirable projects of social betterment which the Commissioners hope to see promoted by the advent of the more democratic institutions of the proposed new order but to the cost of the ordinary machinery of Government requisite for carrying on the basis of administration.[1]

These fears resulted in a pruning of the estimates. There were fewer seats in the new Council: fifty and not sixty-five constituencies were set up. Even so the new order seemed to the colonial administration a ruinously expensive luxury, since no group of Ceylonese was unanimous in welcoming it. The Tamil leaders in Jaffna, disappointed that their demands for safeguards and for communal electorates had been rejected, decided to boycott the elections. The younger men in the north, politically more advanced than their leaders, were not enthusiastic about the constitution either. The four Northern Province seats were therefore uncontested.

Before the country went to the polls attempts had been made to group some of the older politicians associated with the Ceylon National Congress into what was called the Liberal Party. The Donoughmore Commissioners were doubtful whether political parties would be brought into being by the new constitution. If they had, they certainly would have helped to orient individual members towards common points of view on important issues. In the end, with the exception of Goonesinha's Labour Party, the elections were contested by a number of candidates who could justifiably have been called Independents. Their only difference from the mass of ordinary voters was their proficiency in English. Proceedings in the State Council were to be conducted in that language. The Labour Party won two seats, Goonesinha being accompanied to the new Council by a retired Provincial Engineer whose sincerity of character and goodness of heart drew him to the only group which claimed to stand up for the common man. It was difficult to discover who, except E. W. Perera, belonged to the Liberal Party. Goonesinha referred mysteriously to arrangements about ministerial posts which had been sabotaged: 'There was an arrangement made by a certain party that certain ministerial posts should be filled by certain men. But what happened? There was absolutely no discipline with the result that each man voted for himself, and another party captured practically three or four seats.'[2] There probably was some substance in his gibe.

The elections themselves, despite numerous petitions alleging corrupt practice, provided few surprises. The voter, exercising his right to vote for the first time, respectfully indicated that those already recognized as his (her) superiors should continue to exercise power. This would not have surprised the Donoughmore Commissioners who noted that in the Ceylon setting with its feudal and patriarchal survivals 'no one has questioned the supreme right of one or few to dominate the lives of the multitude.'[3] Two Europeans sat in the new State Council as elected representatives of the people. The Bandarawela constituency, a tea-planting district with a number of plantation workers who had the vote, returned a Scots estate proprietor, and Anuradhapura its retired Government Agent who had already represented it in the Legislative Council. Ex-members of the legislature or of municipal or urban district councils benefited from the claims to public attention they had already staked. There was, as in previous elections to the legislative assembly, the usual crop of 'friends of the poor' seeking the suffrage of the voters.

The results showed that in practically all cases the vote went to those eminent for their social standing. The voter was aided in his (her) task by having no more to do than drop a card into a box of a colour corresponding to that selected by the candidate of his (her) choice. It was not felt to be a satisfactory solution of the difficulties of enabling the illiterate to vote without violating the secrecy of the ballot, as certain colours could have strong emotional and religious appeals.

The State Council assembled for the first time on 7 July 1931. On 10 July it proceeded to the important task of electing its seven Chairmen of Committees who would be Ministers under the new constitution. There were two unexpected results. Two territorially elected members of minority communities found themselves Ministers of Communication and Works, and Labour, Industry and Commerce. The rest of the Ministers were most of them Congress notabilities: D. B. (later Sir Baron) Jayatilaka, who had been elected Vice-President of the Legislative Council on the death of Sir James Peiris, became Minister for Home Affairs and Chairman of the Board of Ministers; D. S. Senanayake became Minister of Agriculture and C. W. W. Kannangara Minister of Education. The Speaker was another Congress stalwart, Francis Molamure.

That those who had moved up to the more important seats were on the whole gratified was evident in their reaction, as time went on, to the obstinacy with which E. W. Perera, now a spectre

at the feast, kept recalling their earlier objections to the same constitution. In the very first session of the new council (in which he
was a private member), he gave notice of seven resolutions
attacking the Donoughmore Constitution for what it had failed to
concede. He carried his old colleagues with him in his objections
in the first six of these resolutions, but when he kept on as the
stern unflinching man of principle, he became awkward to live
with. Nearly one year after the State Council had first met he
moved his resolution attacking the Committee system. By this
time those who were as Ministers stretching themselves out more
comfortably in their positions of power felt that the one time
President of Congress and their erstwhile leader was getting a bit
out of date. S. W. R. D. Bandaranaike, still a private member but
already marked for preferment, was ready to second the earlier
resolutions, but thought that the seventh was tiresome insistence
on pacing the beaten track. D.S. Senanayake was all in favour
of the Committee system and recommended it in terms which
showed the future trend of power politics in the State Council:
'We gain inside knowledge of the working of departments.
Besides that, there is another advantage: we get into touch with
officials who carry out the work and make them realize our point
of view. I think there is a great necessity for this in Ceylon.'[4]
The Board of Ministers clearly intended to control everything it
could.

It took up with the Governor the question of some restriction
on the powers reserved to him and on 21 April 1933 wanted the
method of electing Ministers changed. They suggested that the
Chief Minister should be elected by the whole Council, and that
he thereafter should nominate his colleagues. But the two Ministers from minority communities were against any change in the
mode of election, and neither the Governor nor the Secretary of
State considered that the time had come for recommending any
fundamental change in the constitution.

Though the Donoughmore Constitution did not give the *élite*
the passport to the promised land straightaway, it certainly placed
them on the slopes of Pisgah. They had wanted a reformed constitution which would give them, as elected representatives of
the people, more power. They had had a taste of this in 1924 and
had been able, even earlier, to secure a few of their demands. One,

always stressed by Sir Ponnambalam Arunachalam in the 20s, was the possibility of obtaining admission on easier terms to the higher grades of the government service. Those of the Ceylon civil service, the peak of ambition, were still the sanctuary of graduates from abroad, most of them from British universities. But in 1921 university education was inaugurated in Ceylon with the establishment of University College. Its students were prepared for the degree examinations of London University in the liberal arts and in science. Decades of agitation for a university in Ceylon had preceded the opening of University College. British universities had enabled students all over the empire to qualify for higher education. In Ceylon the Local Examinations Syndicate of Cambridge held their annual examinations, and as a result there was a fair-sized pool of candidates from whom undergraduates could be recruited for the new University College.

If it is true that 'University College did not measure up to the ideals of those who had expected it to contribute to a renewal of indigenous Ceylon culture any more than it did to the hope of those who wished it to become a centre of Western culture',[5] it should be noted that few human institutions reach the stature of the ideals of their founders. If they do enable a few to perceive how little they have fulfilled their high aspirations, then they have done much. Whatever University College failed to do, whatever it did wrong, it served an excellent practical purpose. It enabled an increasing number of young men and young women to provide themselves with the academic qualification necessary to man the higher posts in the bureaucracy. At the present time this may seem an insignificant, even a contemptible, achievement, but it should not be overlooked that academically the best products of University College Ceylon could be compared, not unfavourably, with those of the best universities in Britain, because the standards set by the new institution in Ceylon were high. It is true that University College made no great contribution to learning or research, but as the need at that time was for administrators and professional men, its earliest graduates had little opportunity for development as researchers in the subjects at which they showed promise.

University College did, however, provide something more than tuition for students preparing for the examinations of a foreign institution. This will probably be best appreciated by those in Ceylon who can remember some of the men first associated in the great task of the organization of university education: Marrs, very much the incarnation of conservative Oxford with his combination of administrative dignity and prowess on the playing fields; Leigh Smith with his caustic turn of phrase and his kindliness; Suntharalingam unrepentantly passionate in his enthusiasm for lost causes.

In addition, University College, as an educational institution modelled on British universities, made a difference to the political development and to the social configuration of the country. It brought a small student community into being, annoyingly vociferous at times, but out of whose ranks a fair number of men (and women later) graduated into politics. Co-education at University College did more than was at first perceived to bridge some of the awkward gaps which broke up the apparently smooth surface of *élite* circles in Colombo and in various provincial towns. The new young men and the young women of the Union and of the innumerable societies of University College were strange portents of the times. To their critics they may have been poor copies of Oxford and Cambridge originals, but they had a colour and liveliness of their own.

In 1929 the agitation for a university was taken a step further when a Commission under Sir Walter Buchanan-Riddell, the Principal of Hertford College, Oxford, decided that the projected university should be 'unitary and residential'. It was going to be another Oxford or Cambridge. A sharp and vexatious controversy about its site followed. It was decided that it was not going to be in Colombo, but in the hills near Kandy. The *élite* who fought these matters out among themselves would naturally have wanted something which corresponded to their estimate of the best. So would those who took no part in controversy or deliberations because they were outside these circles. It is difficult to be certain that they would have been content with something modelled on an indigenous institution if it had not been accepted as the best by all. One person with original private views about the form higher education should take at the time was C. Suntharalingam, the Professor of Mathematics at University College. He thought that the interest on the money voted for the university project should be used for sending a large number of students abroad to be trained technologically.[6] Perhaps they might have been more useful to the country than arts men. But the depression, and later the war, halted all schemes for the new university which had to wait twelve years after the visit of the Buchanan-Riddell Commission to be brought into being.

The depression was the preoccupation of a Council anxious to take up schemes once debated in the Legislative Council and shelved because of official lukewarmness. The economic frustrations of the depression sharpened the zest for constitutional reform. The two were closely related. It was natural that those who had now taken over greater political responsibility should have been 'increasingly anxious . . . to play a larger role in the economic life of the country'.[7] The depression had brought home once again to all Ceylonese in trade and agriculture the necessity of having credit facilities available to them.

The two major events in the history of the first State Council arose out of the effects of the economic crisis. In 1934 the State Mortgage Bank was set up in order to enable owners of land to obtain credit on the security of their land without having to pay the ruinous rates of interest charged by moneylenders. In the same year the State Council appointed a Commission under the chairmanship of the Parsee banker Sir Sorabji Pochkhanawala to report on all aspects of banking in Ceylon and particularly 'to make recommendations regarding the desirability of establishing a state-aided bank and sound local banks.' Its report published at the end of the year is an important sociological document revealing more about the background of the *élite* than any straightforward survey of their financial standing might have done. The Commission uncovered 'serious deficiencies in the structure of credit in the island'.[8] To deal with these it recommended the establishment of a state-aided bank which the State Council enthusiastically supported in 1935. But the Secretary of State was unimpressed and United Kingdom banking interests, whose expert advice was sought by him, were unenthusiastic too. For two years the Colonial Office passed the scheme from London committees to the Board of Ministers, until in 1939 the Bank of Ceylon, 'a far cry indeed from the bold and unorthodox proposals of the Banking Commission', opened its doors. Lack of sympathy and initiative had completely dismantled a project designed to help the country to build up its own sources of credit and to aid business development.

The depression must be reckoned partly responsible, too, for the catastrophe of the severe malaria epidemic of 1934–5. The rural population of Ceylon had been accustomed to living close to the edge of poverty and malnutrition. At all times malaria, endemic in the island, placed a severe physical strain on the constitution of the villager enfeebled by a diet 'sufficient to support a mean existence but definitely deficient in several constituents'.[9] The Donoughmore Commissioners did not take long to discover, in the two months they spent in the country, that in the dry zones 'measures are urgently needed to break the vicious circle in which the villagers of these parts live'.[10] The epidemic ravaged not only the dry zones, but also the better situated hinterland of the Western and North-Western Provinces.

The failure of the monsoon rains in 1934, followed by the drought of 1935, added to the hardships of the depression, caught the peasantry in a state and at a time when they were least able to stand up to their misfortune. A large number of deaths and the spectacle of poverty known to exist but generally overlooked stirred the country to action. The State Council set up an extensive programme of relief under a senior civil servant as Commissioner for Relief of Distress. His report, published as a Sessional Paper in 1936, is as important a sociological document of the plight of the peasantry as the Banking Commission's is of the economic predicament of the *élite*. The report elicited the following:

Of the twenty revenue districts nineteen suffered distress. Jaffna alone escaped. There is no accurate means of measuring distress but the following facts give some idea of the magnitude of the catastrophe. The epidemic area was 5,800 square miles in extent, rather less than a quarter of the area of Ceylon. It contained, however, over 3 million inhabitants out of the total population of Ceylon of about $5\frac{1}{2}$ millions. Among these 3 millions it was estimated that by the middle of December, 1934, there had been almost half a million cases of malaria, and by the end of April, 1935, nearly $1\frac{1}{2}$ million cases ... In the whole of Ceylon the total registered deaths during the fifteen months from September 1934 to December 1935, were 254,968 ... The mean figure (for the five previous similar periods of fifteen months) is 151,019 and on that basis an excess of 100,000 persons died during the distress, an increase of 68 per cent over the mean figure.[11]

The State Council had acted with commendable vigour and dispatch to deal with a situation which could only be relieved by as much government spending as could quickly be authorized. That this could have been done is a measure of the difference made by the Donoughmore Constitution to the political development of the country. The money could be voted without criticism on the grounds of financial imprudence, because the Council could use the financial powers given it without any procedural delay. Besides all this, an assembly into which the majority of members was voted by the common man could not afford to disregard his cry of distress. In the reaction of the State Council to the malaria epidemic is to be noted the first signal of the pressure of the ordinary voter on the country's chief legislative and executive assembly.

The longest shadow of all thrown by the depression was soon to darken the doors of the State Council so far as the *élite* were concerned. On 18 December 1935 the Lanka Sama Samaja Party (LSSP) was founded. Its founding members were a few young Ceylonese who were studying in the United Kingdom and the United States during the early years of the depression. Unemployment and the inability of private enterprise to deal with its financial and economic crises, raised the wind filling the sails of a young generation in the West for the first time discovering Marx and his myriad commentators. In the 30s many young men and women in the Anglo-Saxon countries (in Germany and in Central Europe this has happened very much earlier) passed through one passionate phase of their sentimental education. Even those – the large majority – who have since repudiated beliefs once held have testified to their importance by the vehemence of their recusancy. In the early 30s in Ceylon the young man returning from England ('England-returneds' as they used to be called) still had some social importance; but this alone will not account for the considerable influence to be wielded by this group of young men who addressed themselves to the political and economic problems of the country with minds trained in a

175

different school from the rest of the *élite* and benefiting from an experience very different from theirs.

They had already been active in political agitation, some of it cast in the old patterns of social reform. The most prominent members of the group were Philip Gunawardena, who had learnt his Marxism in the USA; N. M. Perera, a political scientist from the London School of Economics; Colvin de Silva, a historian and lawyer from London University, and Leslie Goonewardene, the product of an English public school. With their Marxist-oriented ideas they appealed straight to the urban worker. Their intervention in the Indian-owned Spinning and Weaving Mills strike in 1932 was actively resented by A. E. Goonesinha, who had the satisfaction of seeing his rivals worsted in their attempts to organize a large working-class element in Colombo. From this time onwards the increasing rancour of the Labour leader towards these intruders in the field betrayed his fear of the threat offered by younger and better trained minds to his monopoly of working-class agitation.

The recently published history of the LSSP shows that the attention of this revolutionary group was not focused exclusively on the urban worker.[12] It was the work done by it during the malarial epidemic in rural districts which laid the foundations for the entry of two of them to the State Council of 1936. By that date it was in existence as a party, with a discipline and programme which made up for its minimal representation in the Council.

It should not be forgotten that the leaders of the LSSP were all of them members of the English-speaking *élite*, to whom they were diametrically opposed in ethos and strategy. The dissatisfaction with the liberalism of the old Nationalist leaders of the Ceylon National Congress felt by the young in Colombo, now much more self-conscious and militant since the establishment of University College, gave the LSSP its first supporters. The new political movement was the objective correlative of all the emotional discontents of the intelligentsia. In the late 20s various Youth Leagues had reflected the criticism of the young (and the not so young) of the accredited political leaders of the country. The LSSP gave the expression of this opposition scope and direction and turned it into political action. Every occasion on which the Colonial Government and the leaders of the State

Council could be harried was made use of, for propaganda and for advertisement. These tactics could not fail to keep the new group before the public.

The Suriya Mal (the yellow flower of the tulip tree – *Thespesia populnea*) campaign was one shoot of minor irritation with the Colonial Government which later, on account of a change of leadership, blossomed into full blown political agitation. Originally it was an organization of Ceylonese ex-servicemen of the First World War dissatisfied with their treatment by a government allegedly collecting large sums of money on Poppy Day in Ceylon for distribution mainly overseas. It was transformed into a political movement during the heroic years of the Indian mass movement by the young, restive both at imperial government control and the tardiness of Ceylonese politicians to set themselves against it more effectively than they had done hitherto. The inspiration of the Suriya Mal movement, under the leadership of Doreen Wickramasinghe, the British wife of the member for Morawaka in the State Council Dr S. A. Wickramasinghe, was very strongly tinctured with ILP radicalism and identification with the movement for Indian and colonial freedom. The malaria epidemic took the Suriya Mal movement into the countryside where it did good work. It was soon led by the LSSP, but continued for some time on its own.

The general elections of 1936 at the end of the five-year period of the first State Council brought two members of the LSSP into the Council: Philip Gunawardena and Dr N. M. Perera. A third, Dr S. A. Wickramasinghe who recontested the Morawaka seat, lost. But much more important at the time than these results was the manœuvre by which the Sinhalese leaders of the Board of Ministers secured for themselves and their nominees the chairmanships of the seven committees. Sir Herbert Stanley had foreseen such a possibility in his comments on the report of the Donoughmore Commissioners:

A majority which might not possess sufficient cohesion to act together as a party for any length of time might nevertheless, especially if communal feeling happened to be running high, be prepared to co-operate at the beginning of the life of a Council to the extent of assuming the power of exercising effective control in every one of the committees and thus determining the selection of every chairman.[13]

Communal feeling was not running particularly high, but the manœuvre was successful on account of a mathematical formula attributed to the skill of the Tamil Professor of Mathematics at University College, Suntharalingam, at that time a firm believer in the nationalist cause as represented by the Sinhalese leaders. The intention of the Board of Ministers had been to show that it was unanimous in its demands for change in the constitution. As it claimed in its communication to the Governor, Sir Reginald Stubbs, 'the alleged disqualification (of lack of unanimity) hitherto urged against the Board of Ministers has been effectively and radically removed in the formation of the Board of Ministers in the present State Council'.[14]

It was known that the new Board of Ministers which now included S. W. R. D. Bandaranaike as Minister of Local Administration and G. C. S. Corea as Minister of Labour, Industry and Commerce, was preparing a new document on reform of the constitution and that the Leader of the House, Sir Baron Jayatilaka the Minister for Home Affairs, proceeding to London for the Coronation in 1937, wanted to see the Secretary of State on the same subject. In a series of debates on 'Political Representations by Coronation Delegates', these as yet unpublished documents were attacked by private members in the State Council.[15] Suspicion about the activities of the Board of Ministers had the effect of alarming the minorities, particularly the Tamils, and the demand of one section led by the member for Point Pedro, G. G. Ponnambalam, for a system of balanced representation by which the majority community, the Sinhalese, would not be able to dominate the rest, has been attributed to the 'defective psychology' of the manœuvre by which the Pan-Sinhalese Board of Ministers was brought into operation.[16]

The importance of these manœuvres lies in their indication of the nature of future negotiations between the Ceylonese leaders and the British Government and the preference of the Board of Ministers for private consultations. By 1936 it was obvious that what the Donoughmore Commissioners had set out to achieve – the future training of Ministers and others in the business of administration – had already been taken for granted. Whether the lesson had been well learnt or not, the Board of Ministers apparently felt that repeating it diligently was to no purpose. Undoubtedly the State Council was going over the old curriculum of the Legislative Council in the concern of its members with the details of running departments, particularly with appointments, terms of service and transfers. The debate on the Appropriation Bill, on which few members were ready to cast 'a silent vote', included practically everything under the sun.

The powers of the Board of Ministers and its position *vis-à-vis* government departments improved as more and more Ceylonese came to hold high office in them. Ministers gradually began to encroach on territory previously out of bounds. The civil servant and the Head of a Department, for their part, were ready to treat Ministerial decisions as binding on them, as Jennings and Thambiah point out.[17] The Public Service Commission, responsible to the Governor and controlled by the Chief Secretary, assured civil servant and Head of Department (in fact all officers appointed by the Secretary of State) of the inviolability of their terms of service, so that, except in flagrant cases of interference by a Minister, there was unlikely to be opposition by them to Board of Ministers' rule.

This rule tended to extend itself over all fields of administration except those reserved to the Officers of State. Nor were the latter intent on insisting on the letter of the law. In the Council private members, with a few notable exceptions, were content to leave the Board of Ministers to rule the country. The more energetic and ambitious members of the *élite* could hope at some time or another to be admitted to the powerful circle themselves. As time went on even the separation of the executive from the legislative sessions of the State Council had ceased, because Committees did not report, nor were they asked to do so, their decisions to the whole Council. In this atmosphere of let well alone friction could arise only if the Governor felt it was necessary to use his powers.

One bone of contention over which elected members and the Governor had quarrelled in Legislative Council days had been buried early in the life of the first State Council. The whole Council had taken up the question of the Ceylonization of the services and the opportunities of promotion in the higher grades of the public service open to Ceylonese. In the civil service, for instance, in 1928 there was not one Ceylonese in the three staff appointments of the service; only one in the twenty-two officers in the First Class, five in the twenty-seven in the Second Class, thirteen in the forty-three of the Third Class, and sixteen of the twenty-eight in the Fourth Class. Of the 123 civil servants in the island only thirty-five were Ceylonese.[18] It was well known that certain posts were closed to them. Stubbs, in the Colonial Office in 1907, had written the following minute on the case of Arunachalam, then the outstanding Ceylonese member of the civil service: 'It is difficult to resist the impression that Mr Arunachalam has not received the promotion which his abilities would have won for him if he had been a European.' Blake, the Governor, had to agree: 'In the position in which Arunachalam finds himself I consider that he has a claim to the appointment to Grade I Class I. The record of his service shows that he has never been permitted to acquire that experience, which was within the reach of every European member of the Civil Service.'[19]

In March 1932 it was agreed that the appointment of non-Ceylonese into the public service should be allowed only if in the circumstances no Ceylonese with the required qualifications was available. Such appointments could be made only by a resolution in the State Council – a 'March resolution' as it came to be known. A Ceylonese rose to the high office of Government Agent of a province for the first time only after the State Council came into being. But it was not until 1941 that the Chief Secretary was ready to give an assurance that the important agencies of the Central and Western Provinces would not be withheld from Ceylonese.

The chances of friction between Ministers and the Governor were much reduced therefore. There were, however, two *causes célèbres* in which the force of opinion outside the Council and in it pushed the Ministers into open opposition to the Governor. Both concerned the important department of the police, which the Donoughmore Commissioners had decided should be attached to the Department of Home Affairs, despite representations made 'by some witnesses that the police should be under the direct control of the Chief Secretary'. As the Commissioners realized, in a country with no real defence force the police played a decisive role. It had been placed on a semi-militarized footing by Sir Herbert Dowbiggin, and, though not exclusively, was effectively controlled by European officers.

Both excitements arose out of the activities of the LSSP in the country. The first, of more local than general significance, ended by establishing the rule of law against the most powerful organs of the state. The protagonist was Mark Antony Lyster Bracegirdle, a young Australian described by a police officer as 'looking like Rupert Brooke', who came to Ceylon to be trained as a tea planter on Relugas Estate, Madulkelle. At the end of his short planting career, he appeared on LSSP platforms to the embarrassment and annoyance of the European planting community, one of whom brought the matter to the notice of the Inspector General of Police, P. N. Banks, who saw the Home Minister and the Chief Secretary. The governor, using the provisions of an Order in Council of 1896 enabling him to deport in times of emergency all those whose presence was prejudicial to law and order, issued a deportation order on Bracegirdle who went into hiding. (The Chief Secretary, in the State Council debate on the constitutional propriety of the governor's order stated that the Inspector General of Police had informed the Minister for Home Affairs, Sir Baron Jayatilaka, of his action before the latter left for England, and that he himself had discussed it with the Minister. The Acting Minister said that he had no record in his papers of any police information. The Commission appointed by the Governor to inquire into the affair reported, with obvious reluctance: 'We are compelled to say that we must accept Mr Banks's version and reject Sir Baron's version'.[20])

Eleven days later, on 5 May 1937, Bracegirdle reappeared at a LSSP mass meeting and was arrested by the police. The LSSP issued a writ of Habeas Corpus on the police and the issue was decided by a Supreme Court of three judges, presided over by the Chief Justice, Sir Sidney Abrahams. The case aroused immense public interest; H. V. Perera, the ablest Counsel in the Ceylon bar, argued the application, offering his services free. The Board of Ministers, since the issues of constitutional liberties and the validity of police action without reference to the Minister were raised, came out strongly against the Governor. He defended his action in a confidential telegram to the Secretary of State on 12 May 1937 on the grounds that 'Bracegirdle went about the country making violent speeches, abusing Europeans and inciting labour to rise against planters. As ignorant coolies tend still to attach importance to speeches of white men, the Police and I have considered him a public danger.'[21] The Chief Justice and the two judges associated with him thought otherwise, and held that the government had no right to use emergency laws when there was no emergency. Bracegirdle left Ceylon shortly afterwards, his later career being apparently devoid of political excitement.

The affair gained the LSSP enormous publicity; it awoke both the government and the planting community to certain changes in the way things were managed in the country. The Board of Ministers, once the direction of public feeling against the use of special powers by the Governor was made clear, took up the public cause on its own with vigour. The Minister for Home Affairs came out of the affair with a somewhat tarnished reputation.

The second of these *causes célèbres*, though it belongs to wartime Ceylon, has to be taken up here, because it belongs naturally to the stage reached in the development of the working of the Donoughmore constitution by the Board of Ministers before the great difference made by Japan's entry into the war created another situation. In 1939 there was a wave of strikes on tea plantations in the Central Province and Uva. That on Mooloya, Hewaheta, was led by the All Ceylon Estate Workers Union organized by the LSSP. On 10 January 1940 the police opened fire on a band of workers, killing one of them. There was a demand for a Commission of Inquiry by the Executive Committee of Home Affairs which was supported by the whole Council. After some discussion with the Minister, Sir Baron Jayatilaka, the Governor, now Sir Andrew Caldecott, agreed to a Commission on 19 January. The strike on Mooloya Estate was settled on 22 January, but as there were some cases for unlawful assembly pending, the State Council expressed its opinion 'that steps should be taken to have all criminal proceedings instituted in connection with this incident postponed'.

On 25 January the Minister for Home Affairs requested the Inspector General of Police not to oppose any application for the postponement of three Mooloya cases pending before the Magistrate's Court at Kandy. The Inspector General claimed that he would be failing in his duty if these 'instructions' were carried out. This claim was reiterated on 30 January, in reply to another communication from the Minister: to have the cases postponed would have 'a disastrous effect on estate labour throughout Ceylon and on respect for the law generally throughout the country'. The Minister saw the Governor twice, but the latter held that the Inspector General was not guilty of insubordination, but was correctly discharging 'the statutory responsibilities given to the police under Sections 20 and 57 of the Police Ordinance'.

Once again public agitation outside the Council and criticism inside pushed the Ministers to make 'a grave constitutional crisis' out of the matter, as the Minister for Home Affairs wrote to the Governor on 13 February. On 27 February after a meeting of the Ministers with the Governor, D. S. Senanayake resigned. The others had really no option but to follow suit.

On 5 March after the adjournment had been moved in the Council to prevent any action being taken by private members, the ex-Minister for Home Affairs brought a two-part motion before the Council that 'this House condemns the action of the Governor in upholding the Inspector General of Police' and that it was not going to continue working the constitution. But already talks had begun between the Governor and his 'ex-Ministers' and by 13 February D.S. Senanayake made it clear in the State Council that the Ministers were ready to proceed with the first part of their motion (that condemning the Governor) but not the second (refusing to work the constitution). They had steamed into the tunnel of negotiations with pistons flashing, a scroll of smoke in the wind and the roar of mighty engines; they came out of it looking very much like a toy train. D. S. Senanayake moved the adjournment and the *status quo ante* was restored. The Governor was ready to appoint a Select Committee to investigate the whole field of procedure between Ministers and Heads of Departments. On 2 April a private member moved a vote of no confidence in the Minister for Home Affairs. It was defeated, but the Minister had less than half the house on his side, with a fair number of members abstaining. The Ministers had set proverbial lore at nought; they had both eaten their cake and had it.

Significant in the whole rumpus were neither the constitutional nor the legal technicalities involved, but the indication of the inextricable mixture of old and new in the way the country was being run. The police had acted with their customary highhandedness. The Inspector General, as it was pointed out in the State Council debate, could not allow a postponement of the Mooloya cases after the strike had been settled, though at the same time he allowed the postponement of similar cases against workers on another estate. The Governor chose to uphold the action of the head of an important department responsible for internal security. These were features of the old pattern. In the new pattern the Governor was involved too. Sir Andrew Caldecott had been appointed to Ceylon in 1937, after the excitements of the Bracegirdle affair. He succeeded two Governors who had been predominantly men with Whitehall experience. He had served in Malaya and Hong Kong and had the reputation of being sympathetic to the people of the country and easy to get on with. It is well to remember, too, that Colonial Governors in a colony like Ceylon who had to live with its unusual constitution were men at the end of their careers, with little to look forward to but a quiet retirement. To struggle on the strength of private views of theirs against the anomalies of the new dispensation, to try to reshape it (even if this had been countenanced by the State Council), were tasks for younger men. Caldecott was fresher and more enterprising than his predecessors. He could feel the pull of the current in the direction of more power for the representatives of the people, but he would have wished it to be less heady. His slogan of '*hemin, hemin*' – 'slowly, slowly' – was good-natured acquiescence in the trend.

He had, in addition, been instructed by the Secretary of State to examine the working of the constitution and to report on it. This he did in a dispatch to the Secretary of State on 13 June 1938. As he saw the trend of things in Ceylon, he realized that it was 'outside the pale of practical politics' to try to reverse its direction by restricting the franchise, conceding anything to communal representation or imposing conditions on membership of the State Council. He was certain that 'the functions of both, i.e. the Executive Committees and the Board of Ministers, could then be entrusted to a cabinet of a normal type. In such a cabinet, however, the Officers of State could find no place. . . . A Cabinet system is necessary in order to fix and develop government responsibility.'[22]

The Ministers who were weaving the texture of the new pattern would have been glad of these aids, but set up in their own way. In actual fact the Donoughmore Constitution was manifestly not functioning as it should have done. Sir Baron Jayatilaka, during the debate on the Mooloya affair, claimed that 'in actual practice, to a very large extent we have reduced Article 45 (of the Order in Council) to a dead letter of the law. I have issued instructions on behalf of my Ministry thousands of times without any reference to this Council, without getting the prior ratification of the governor. I believe it is the same case with my fellow ex-Ministers.'[23] The head of steam generated by the Ministers over the incident was built up by their irritation that now, unaccountably, objection had been taken by the Governor to the routine they had established.

It was obvious by the time of the Mooloya affair that the strongest conscientious objector to any opposition to the Ministers' way was D. S. Senanayake. He was too clever a politician to allow the public to receive the impression that the Ministers were impotent; on the other hand he was unwilling that they should relinquish their hold on power. His resignation was the gesture of an experienced politician. As a private member put it: 'Once the member for Minuwangoda (D. S. Senananyake) resigned too, other Ministers had simply to follow. I do not think there was any doubt about it. So then, all this talk of a Constitutional crisis was, I may say, mere eyewash.'[24]

The new pattern, now that the Board of Ministers had proved that they held all the trumps in the State Council, was going to involve arrangements and discussions by the Board over the heads of private members. The country was going to be ruled by the Board – or by those who turned out to be the strongest in that body – provided nothing was done to upset or ruffle the Colonial Governor who had the power to rule on his own. Those who saw what was happening and were hostile to this development felt that it was not going to be government by the State Council, but government by a caucus. (As Sir Ponnambalam Ramanathan described the word in 1928 to the Legislative Council, 'caucus is said to be an Indian term which came to be used by the Americans ... The Indian term especially among Tamils for "caucus" is kusu-kusu-kuttam. It means in English "whisper-whisper-meeting".')[25] It was this term which was used by its critics of the way the Board of Ministers tended to arrange and decide things.

Had the war not intervened and the life of the State Council not been extended by the British Government, then it is likely that the right of the Board of Ministers to do things their own way would have been contested. So far as the *élite* in Ceylon were concerned, the outbreak of war in Europe was unlikely to alter the political situation in the country radically. Hitler's systematic attack on the Versailles settlement, Nazism, and the integrity of Poland did not unduly excite or exercise their minds. On the afternoon of 5 September 1939, the Governor addressed the State Council and informed its members that they were 'on the threshold of a war in which our Island will bear her part shoulder to shoulder with all her fellows in the British Commonwealth of Nations; a fight for right against might, for freedom against force'.[26] On decisions of this kind naturally he did not have to inform the Board of Ministers or anyone else of the action he would have to take.

The same afternoon the Leader of the House moved that the State Council 'at the time of this crisis assures His Majesty the King and the British Government of their whole-hearted support in the prosecution of the war'. The two members of the LSSP abstained from voting on the motion of the Leader of the House. They were joined, surprisingly, by Dudley Senanayake, who deplored 'violence as a means of achieving one's ideals and violence as a political technique'.[27]

The Council went on to vote large sums of money for improving the island's defences and for initiating schemes of rationing and control necessary to meet the war situation. In June 1940, when Hitler's armies had overrun Western Europe and threatened England, the State Council voted Rs 5 million as Ceylon's contribution to the war effort.

As long as the struggle seemed to be not only remote but frozen into unreality after the quick end to the German campaign in Poland, it receded even further than before in the minds of those who kept up to date by reading their newspapers and listening to radio programmes. There was some *Schadenfreude* at British reverses in the spring of 1940. An amending order extended the life of the State Council for a period not exceeding two years.

There was therefore no general election in 1941. In effect the war preserved the political *status quo* and without any contrivance on their part the Ministers continued to govern the country.

To the LSSP, the only active political party in the field, the war made a profound difference. (There was, of course, the Labour Party in the field too, but it was becoming a one-man band performing intermittently for the benefit of a rapidly dwindling audience.) The LSSP went through the first of those fissions typical of a political group sensitive to the reality of political change. The Moscow Trials and the Ribbentrop-Molotov pact brought out into the open a conflict of principle within the party. The majority of the LSSP condemned the action of the Third International. Soon after, Dr S. A. Wickramasinghe, who had sat as an Independent in the first State Council before he joined the LSSP, and some others were expelled. Thereafter the LSSP was openly a Trotskyist group, later affiliated to the Fourth International. The expelled Stalinists formed themselves into the United Socialist Party, and in 1943 organized themselves into the Communist Party of Ceylon. The group had in 1941 come out openly in support of the war once the Soviet 'fatherland' was attacked, and appeared on the same platform as the Board of Ministers.

The government could afford to ignore the LSSP during the period of the 'phoney war', but with the crisis of the fall of France and the threat of the invasion of England it proceeded against its leaders: Dr N. M. Perera, Philip Gunawardena and Colvin de Silva were arrested and detained, Leslie Goonewardene evaded arrest and went into hiding. A year later the LSSP was declared an illegal organization.

When Japan entered the war in December 1941 after the spectacular success of the attack on the American fleet at Pearl Harbor, there were people in Ceylon (and in Malaya too for that matter) who could still feel that they had nothing to do with these things. During the first four months of 1942 they awoke sharply to the reality of the advance of the Japanese forces down the Malay peninsula and the growing threat to Ceylon.

In December 1942 the Governor appointed a Civil Defence Commissioner and named the Auditor General, O. E. Goonetilleke, for the post. He was unquestionably the ablest Ceylonese of his time, a man of varied attainments, and great skill as a conciliator and diplomat. He was also the very loyal and close personal friend of D. S. Senanayake. On 5 March 1942 Admiral Sir Geoffrey Layton arrived in Ceylon as Commander-in-Chief. He was given powers wide enough to brook no opposition from anyone. He was placed in command not only of all naval, military and air forces, but also of all civil authorities in the island, including the Governor, whose emergency powers he could, as Commander-in-Chief, use to any extent he wanted.

Only service chiefs and His Majesty's Government could know the seriousness of the situation, with its probability that the already strained and inadequate resources of the navy might fail to prevent Ceylon from going the way of Malaya. The Malayan campaign had been over too quickly to allow any of its lessons to be digested, but one thing stood out clearly in its sorry mess: the complete unreadiness of the civilian population to stand up to the situation, because neither the civil authority nor the military had reckoned it a factor in the war. In the directive to Sir Geoffrey Layton which was tabled at a meeting of the State Council on 24 March 1942, he was instructed to 'have regard to the importance and value of maintenance of the services of the civil population as long as they can operate efficiently in the prevailing conditions'.[28] He established a War Council consisting of representatives of the Navy, Army and Air Force, the Governor, the Board of Ministers and the Civil Defence Commissioner, over which he presided.

Sir Geoffrey Layton had the forthrightness of manner and picturesqueness of phrase of a naval man accustomed to command. It does not appear that he had to use either frequently, since to whatever he did there could be no opposition. The Board of Ministers acquiesced in a situation which asked little of them, either as individuals or as a Board, but to continue as they had been doing in the State Council before. His Majesty's Government had no reason to doubt their loyal co-operation. D. S. Senanayake's statement in the State Council on 8 April 1943 showed that there had been some heartburning, but the Ministers accepted the position. He referred to 'a resolution in which Council in which we ourselves declared war. Although we were entitled to be consulted, although we were not consulted, we were in sympathy with the attitude of England and were willing to fight on the side of England.'[29]

In the language of propaganda Ceylon had become 'a bastion of freedom'; strategically it had reverted to its position in 1795 as the key to the defence of India, as long as it was unknown where the enemy blow to the Indian Empire would be launched; politically the Ceylonese leaders gradually awakened to the fact that they were in a better bargaining position than they had been for many a long day.

The island had its taste of direct enemy action on two days only – both in April 1942. On 5 April, Easter Sunday, Vice-Admiral Nagumo's task force made a light air-raid on Colombo. On 9 April carrier-based planes of Admiral Ozawa's force attacked the harbour of Trincomalee, presumably in search of the British navy which it failed to locate. Both attacks – the small-scale raid on Colombo and the large one in the Bay of Bengal – repeated the lesson the Japanese had learned from Admiral Boyd's successful carrier-based raid on the Italian fleet at Taranto in 1940, which completely altered the balance of naval power in the Mediterranean. Though the raid on Colombo did little damage, as many of the civilian population as had not already fled to the hills and inland streamed out of the city in panic. But the administration – the European hierarchy in particular – carried on. The slight anti-aircraft defence and the four fighter squadrons did much better than could have been expected. For two months more Colombo and the coastal towns were deserted, then life slowly flowed back to them as there were no further raids and the defences of Ceylon were being built up by men and materials arriving too late for action in Malaya. By the last quarter of 1942 it was clear that the threat of invasion had faded. It finally disappeared with the American naval victories of the Coral Sea and Midway.

Strategically Ceylon continued to be of importance because Burma, Malaya and the Dutch East Indies had gone and the north-east frontier of India was under Japanese attack. The island was to be the vast aircraft carrier from which the attack on the Japanese was being mounted under the South East Asia Command. In 1942 Lord Mountbatten set up his headquarters in Peradeniya. Special consideration continued to be given to Ceylon in the light of its importance as a supply line via the Persian Gulf to the USSR, and of plans for the destruction of the whole of the Japanese sphere of influence in South East Asia.

To His Majesty's Government Ceylon was the Board of Ministers. The State Council, elected in 1936, continued to 'represent' the people of the country. In the council itself there was no government or opposition. Private members and Ministers voted as they pleased, owing apparently no allegiance to anything but the point of view they happened to be presenting at the moment. Since the beginning of the war, however, the Board of Ministers had been developing an identity of its own. It had been upgraded by the Colonial Government and given a wider range of responsibility. Before the outbreak of war, on 10 November 1938, Malcolm Macdonald, the Secretary of State, had found himself in agreement with Caldecott's conclusion that the future development should be towards the ideal of cabinet government. In November 1940 the Board of Ministers was entrusted with duties which had, up to that time, been regarded as the sphere of the Chief Secretary under the designation of External Affairs. D. S. Senanayake, S. W. R. D. Bandaranaike and G. C. S. Corea, together with the Financial Secretary, Huxham, formed the Ceylon Government delegation to New Delhi to discuss with the Indian Government the question of the franchise for plantation workers deemed to be Indian. Nothing came of this exchange of views, nor of the visit the next year of Sir Girja Bajpai leading an Indian delegation to Ceylon on the same mission. But by 1941 the Board of Ministers had been given the right to speak for the country on this topic of external affairs.

By 1942 the Board, on its own, had begun to move towards the great cohesion of a cabinet. It was at any rate going to be a more tightly knit body. Sir Baron Jayatilaka, now deadwood on the vigorously sprouting growth of Ministerial influence, was shed and D. S. Senanayake became Vice-Chairman of the Board and Leader of the House. A member of the Board, whose own version of the appointment of Sir Baron as Ceylon's representative at New Delhi was published in 1956, claimed that the Commander-in-Chief favoured the move.[30] It certainly gained the Board a valuable recruit – a Tamil, Arunachalam Mahadeva, the son of Sir Ponnambalam – since it broadened its base and became less vulnerable to the reproach of being a Pan-Sinhalese group. Though there was as a result of these changes greater control at the top, there was not as yet unanimity of opinion.

There were other groups in the country besides the Board of Ministers which His Majesty's Government might have consulted, had it wished to do so, after 1941. There was the Ceylon National Congress. It is true that the high command was controlled by the Board of Ministers, but there were younger politicians who were at the time airing progressive views. In addition since 1943 the Communist Party had been affiliated to it. But Congress was not destined to live long; it went into a decline in 1945, when D. S. Senanayake refused to have any truck with it because of the presence of Communists in its ranks. There was the Sinhala Maha Sabha, led by S. W. R. D. Bandaranaike, with a number of members of the State Council pledged to support it and an even larger number of provincial associations linked with it. There was also the All Ceylon Tamil Congress, whose general was G. G. Ponnambalam, the member for Point Pedro in the State Council. It could count on strong support in the north for its 'fifty-fifty' slogan of 'balanced representation'. There was, of course, the Labour Party.

If His Majesty's Government had not wished to consult any, or all, of these groups, it could, if it had wanted to test the reaction of the whole country to any of its proposals, have dissolved the State Council and held a general election. Of course it was clear that a general election in Ceylon would hardly have been fought on any political issues, but on the personalities of the candidates. On these grounds the ex-Speaker of the State Council in 1945 exonerated the Secretary of State from blame for not having taken this step.

Whatever His Majesty's Government might have done, what it did was probably what it preferred to do. It conducted negotiations with a Board of Ministers apparently only too willing to negotiate. It must not be imagined that the activities of the Board were approved of by the rest of the Council, or indeed that the Council knew exactly what was taking place. On 8 June 1943 the member for Udugama asked the Leader of the House: 'Is the Board of Ministers acting on behalf of the State Council?' To which the Leader of the House replied: 'I believe the Board of

Ministers have been selected by the State Council.' When the member for Udugama went on: 'There seems to be a separate identity established now itself, that the Board of Ministers are acting on their own behalf and not on behalf of the State Council', the member for Matale ironically commented, 'They are the government.'[31]

In the same debate the member for Matale referred to the way in which the Board had been treating private members about their negotiations with the British Government: 'All that the Ministers have done is that they have taken the House into their confidence and stated "We are sending this letter to the Secretary of State and we inform you of it", because the grievance of the House has very often been that they have written letters to each others as though they were sweethearts and they never let us know.'[32] Throughout this period there was dissatisfaction in the State Council over the reticence of the Board of Ministers on the subject of their negotiations.

A tabulation of the sequence of expressions of views and of significant dates in the parleys will be useful. More important stages in the exchanges were as follows:

1941

1 September. His Majesty's Government declares that the position in Ceylon will be examined by a Commission or Conference after the termination of hostilities.

1942

24 March. A private member gives notice of a motion demanding Dominion Status for Ceylon after the war. The Board of Ministers' request that Sir Stafford Cripps should extend his visit to Ceylon is refused, because 'his present visit must be confined to Indian problems'.

1943

19 January. D. S. Senanayake states in the State Council that 'correspondence is being carried on between the Secretary of State and the Board of Ministers with regard to the reform of the Constitution, but there have not been any memoranda sent'.[33]
26 May. His Majesty's Government declares that post-war re-examination of Ceylon's constitution will be directed 'towards the

grant to Ceylon by Order of His Majesty in Council of full responsible government under the Crown in all matters of internal civil administration'. His Majesty's Government reiterates that it will proceed 'to examine by suitable Commission or Conference such detailed proposals as the Ministers may in the meantime have been able to formulate in the way of a complete constitutional scheme'.[34] His Majesty's Government in their consideration of the problem 'have very fully appreciated and valued the contribution Ceylon has made and is making to the war effort of the British Commonwealth of Nations and the United Nations'.

The Council does not debate the tabling of these papers. The Board of Ministers, according to the Leader of the House, is negotiating for Dominion status.[35]

1944

February. The Ministers' draft of the Constitution is ready. (Sir Ivor Jennings, Vice-Chancellor of the University of Ceylon, who undoubtedly had a hand in drafting the Constitution, stated that the draft which Mr Senanayake 'submitted to his colleagues was the fourth'.)[36]

5 July. The Secretary of State for the Colonies announces in the House of Commons that His Majesty's Government has decided to appoint a Commission to visit Ceylon 'to examine and discuss any proposals for constitutional reform in the Island which have the object of giving effect to the Declaration of His Majesty's Government on the subject dated 26 May 1943; and after consultation with various interests in the Island, including minority communities, concerned with the subject of constitutional reform, to advise His Majesty's Government on all measures necessary to attain that object'.[37]

The Board of Ministers reacts by refusing to co-operate with the Commission, since the 1943 Declaration spoke of examining by Commission or Conference only the Ministers' proposals.

Sir Oliver Goonetilleke goes to London ostensibly to 'discuss problems of food supply with the Ministry of Food'.[38]

September. The Ministers' draft Constitution is published as S.P. XIV of 1944. This is formally withdrawn by the Board of Ministers as a basis for discussion. Sir A. Caldecott retires as Governor of Ceylon and is succeeded by Sir Henry Moore.

22 December. The Soulbury Commission arrives in Ceylon: Lord Soulbury, its Chairman; Mr (later Sir) Frederick Rees, Vice-Chancellor of the University of Wales; and Mr (later Sir) Frederick Burrows, associated with him.

1945

The Board of Ministers refuses to give evidence before the Soulbury Commission, but 'their refusal to give evidence proved to be an advantage. On the one hand, it was clear enough that any scheme which did not approximate to that of the Ministers would inevitably be defeated by a large majority; on the other hand, the Ministers were spared the *necessity of a public controversy with their opponents.* Their opponents had their "day in court", and indeed it stretched into weeks, but in the end the Commission approved the Ministers' scheme with minor amendments and the addition of a weak Second Chamber.'[39]

19 January. S. W. R. D. Bandaranaike moves in the State Council that the Bill 'intituled "An Ordinance to provide a new Constitution for Ceylon" be now read the first time'.[40] This bill is later taken through all its stages in the Council. In the end forty vote for it, seven against. The Minister for Home Affairs, A. Mahadeva, declines to vote.

7 April. The Soulbury Commission leaves Ceylon *July.* The Soulbury Commission presents its report to the Secretary of State.

D. S. Senanayake flies to London and is shown the Soulbury Commission's report in proof.[41]

August. Mr Senanayake presents his draft of the constitution he wanted within a few days of being asked to provide one by the new (Labour) Secretary of State for the Colonies.[42]

September. The Soulbury Commission Report is published: Cmd. 6767.

31 October. His Majesty's Government publishes a White Paper, offering a constitution on the lines proposed by the Soulbury Commission, with certain emergency powers reserved for the Governor for use if necessary. His Majesty's Government hopes 'that the new constitution will be accepted by the people of Ceylon with a determination to work it that in a comparatively short space of time such Dominion status will be evolved.'[43]

8 November. D.S. Senanayake in the State Council moves the acceptance of His Majesty's Government's offer although it does not go as far as his draft [of August] had suggested, because 'we have a specific promise of Dominion Status'. He goes on to state that 'Secondly, limitation of self-government to matters of internal civil administration has been removed.

'Thirdly, the dyarchy implicit in the Governor-General's powers of legislation is swept away.

'Fourthly, the Imperial control over defence and external affairs can be made effective only by Order in Council and by reservation of Bills.

'Fifthly, the Imperial control does not extend to immigration, franchise, tariffs or shipping.

'Sixthly, we have gained a power of amending our own Constitution, though subject to reservations. Of these, the first four and partly the fifth were due to my visit to London. The fifth and sixth were claimed by the Ministers and accepted by the Soulbury Commission.'[44]

On the personal assurances given by Mr Senanayake to the minorities his motion of acceptance is carried by a majority of fifty-one votes to three. The two Indian members and the member for Bibile (W. Dahanayake) voted against.

1946

17 May. Ceylon (Constitution) Order in Council.
December. His Majesty's Government offers Burma full independence within or outside the Commonwealth. Mr Senanayake, through Sir Oliver Goonetilleke, repeats his request for full Dominion Status.

1947

D. S. Senanayake organizes the United National Party (UNP).
18 June. His Majesty's Government agrees to 'fully responsible Status'.
(August–September Elections to the new House of Representatives on Soulbury Constitution).
24 September. D.S. Senanayake Prime Minister.
11 November. Agreements on Defence, External Affairs and Public Officers signed between His Majesty's Government and the Prime Minister of Ceylon, D.S. Senanayake.

21 November. Ceylon Independence Act is passed in the House of Commons.

3 December. The Independence Bill is passed by the House of Representatives in Ceylon by a majority of fifty-nine to eleven.

10 December. Royal Assent is given to the Bill, with 4 February 1948 named as the 'appointed day' on which Ceylon would be formally independent.

The briefest review of the stages in the process towards independence reveals the existence of three determining factors in the background: in the first place the weight given by His Majesty's Government to the importance of maintaining harmonious relations with Ceylon (or the Board of Ministers) in the interests of the successful prosecution of the war[45] and the impossibility of denying to Ceylon, after its successful termination, what had been conceded to India and Burma; the preference throughout for informal or private discussions; the emergence of D. S. Senanayake, ably seconded by Sir Oliver Goonetilleke, as the key figures in these exchanges.

The result of the negotiations was undoubtedly a personal triumph for D. S. Senanayake. His Majesty's Government was persuaded into accepting a constitution which, as described by an authority in constitutional law, was produced 'by Mr Senanayake'. The same authority goes on to comment: 'The belief that the Soulbury Commission produced the Constitution is due partly to the fact that people doubted whether Mr Senanayake had the capacity to produce a Constitution.'[46] Whether or not most people in Ceylon knew that the new constitution was actually produced by D.S. Senanayake, it was in fact so much bound up with his management of negotiations with His Majesty's Government, that for his opponents the fully responsible status, or independence, it bestowed on the country had the same questionable reputation of being an artifact of his own too.

His success should not obscure the awkward fact that the Soulbury Commissioners did not think, for reasons very concisely stated in their report, that though Ceylon was ready for a constitution on the British model it was poised to reach the goal of Dominion Status 'in a single step'.[47] The Commissioners felt unable to resolve the paradox of the political situation in Ceylon, where the majority community had justifiably to govern and the minorities with equal justification to feel themselves adequately represented in the government. They stated the paradox but left its resolution to the passage of time.

Perhaps the crystallization of the political situation into such a figure as that used by the Soulbury Commission was the defect of its terms of reference. Consultation with 'various interests in the island, including minority communities, concerned with constitutional reform' could scarcely have permitted any other conclusion. Left to itself their political wisdom might have discovered other conclusions and different recommendations. During their three months in Ceylon, in their twenty public sessions in Colombo, their various excursions in the country and their private conversations with Mr Senanayake, they did see that they met only the politically vocal, and among them only those interested in the special theme of the reform of the constitution. Besides, as the wisest of the Commissioners himself remarked, some part of what they were shown in Ceylon smacked a little bit of Potemkin.[48]

They were definite that there had to be some advance on the Donoughmore Constitution. Manhood suffrage, responsible for the considerable advance in social legislation in the fourteen years of the working of that constitution, had to be retained. They went on to recommend Cabinet government on the lines proposed in the Ministers' Draft; reservation to the Governor of external affairs, defence and the amendment of the constitution; and a Second Chamber on the lines of the House of Lords, composed of persons of eminence in the community or with a record of distinguished public service. The minorities were not forgotten: a Delimitation Commission was to redraw constituencies in order to give weightage to them.

The difference between this Constitution and that produced by D. S. Senanayake was not great. The Board of Ministers had not taken kindly to a Second Chamber, but this feature was included in the Senanayake constitution of 1946. What is significant is not the similarity between the two constitutions, but the notable success of the Leader of the House in securing the approval of the Secretary of State for his.

Despite this remarkable success there were, even in the Board of Ministers in 1945, signs that the Ministers were not all in agreement on what had been obtained and what should have been gained. The seconder of the motion on 8 November 1945, when D. S. Senanayake gained the approval of the State Council for his acceptance of the White Paper proposals, was S. W. R. D. Bandaranaike. He saw several defects in the proposals which the Leader of the House was ready to accept. He particularized: 'Admitting these defects, admitting even the defects which the Honourable Member for Bibile pointed out, but which I could point out to this House much more adequately if I went into the details of those defects, what are we to do?' The hint was significant, as it came from one who described himself in the following terms: 'The party to which I have the honour to belong – the Sinhala Maha Sabha – happens to be the largest party in this House today and on the attitude of that Party, to a great extent, would have rested the final decision on this very important question.'[49] It was clear that an important member of the Board of Ministers had reservations of his own, close enough to those made by one of those who voted against the motion.

His was not the only hint of objection. The LSSP was not represented in the House since 1942. Then there was the All Ceylon Tamil Congress whose leader, Ponnambalam, was out of the island when the motion was debated. He had some influence with an important minority group and would have to be reckoned with. The two Indian members in the Council had asked D. S. Senanayake for pledges resembling those he had been ready to give to the European nominated member, but he remained firm. They, too, remained a group which would have to be squared.

In May 1945 the State Council had moved a resolution asking for the unconditional release of the political detenus. On 24 June they were set free, and the following year those who were in hiding in India returned to Ceylon. The LSSP emerged after the war as two parties – the group in Ceylon under the leadership of Philip Gunawardena and N. M. Perera which kept the designation of LSSP, and the Bolshevik Leninist Party of India grouped round Colvin de Silva and Leslie Goonewardene.

The political activities of both could now be resumed in the open. Seven years of war with inflation and an acute housing shortage had transformed a once placid element of the *élite* – the lower grades of the clerical and commercial services – into a discontented mass, agitated not by the need for constitutional reform but the practical question of maintaining an adequate standard of living on fixed incomes which had depreciated. Just below them were the urban workers in a similar predicament, while in rural districts the withdrawal of money spent by the armed forces which had guaranteed full employment for the past four years was beginning to be felt as a very sharp pinch.

Once the Japanese threat to Ceylon was over, for everyone except the salaried on fixed incomes the war had been a good thing. The forces were spending on their establishments all over the island, in the remotest districts where camps and airstrips were cleared in the jungle, sums much larger than the government of the country could ever have expended. For all those with anything to sell to the forces the war was a golden opportunity. A host of 'contractors' of all kinds profited from the chance of making much more money than they had ever dreamt of acquiring in several avatars. More timber than the forests of Ceylon ever possessed at any one time was sold to His Majesty's Forces. Fortunes were made by purveyors of entertainment, food and drink. Those of the *élite* with rubber and graphite to sell were assured of prices which they had not obtained for two decades and more. With the elimination of the Dutch East Indies and Malaya as sources of supply, Ceylon became the largest rubber producing area for Britain and her allies. In order to meet war demands large acreages were slaughter-tapped – the maximum quantities of latex being obtained even though the trees' capabilities were destroyed.

An official cost of living index, in relation to which war allowances were paid to state and commercial firm employees, limped haltingly behind the real rise in prices. In Colombo, where there was the largest concentration of workers, the situation in 1946 was tense. A number of unions had been organized and there was some rivalry between opposing groups. The Communist Party had entered the trade union field in the war years and had founded the Ceylon Trade Union Federation. There was also the Ceylon Federation of Labour which placed itself under the leadership of N. M. Perera on his release from detention.

During the war years emergency regulations and the formation of an Essential Services Labour Corps had practically outlawed strikes. The militant LSSP leaders were in prison or in hiding and the CP urged its workers to support 'the Peoples' War'. With the collapse of the Germans and the Japanese this pattern of industrial inactivity began to change. Large-scale retrenchment and the withdrawal of the Forces' establishments from Ceylon caused grave hardship during a period of steadily increasing prices. Strikes among industrial and transport workers in the three years between 1945 and 1947 were a symptom of the desperation of thousands suddenly deprived of their livelihood. In addition clerical workers in the government service were agitating for trade union rights and protesting against the meagre increases awarded them by the Salaries Committee of 1945. They were led by T. B. Ilangaratne.

Faced by a threatened general strike the Board of Ministers reacted with a hesitancy which was later criticized by the Governor, Sir Henry Moore. His account of events ran as follows:

In 1946 an attempt was made by the Clerical Service to engineer a general strike in preparation for the general elections to be held under the Soulbury Constitution after the demarcation of the constituencies which was being done by a Commission under the chairmanship of Mr L. M. D. de Silva, Q.C. It illustrated the unwillingness of the Board of Ministers to face up to their responsibilities. Despite the threatening situation they were conspicuous by their absence. I was in Kandy at the time and Mr George de Silva urged me to take immediate action. I went to Colombo and met the Ministers who all urged me to declare a state of emergency and exercise dictatorial powers. I then pointed out to them that they had full powers to pass legislation of the same character in the State Council and that if they considered the time had come to take such action it was their plain duty and responsibility to take the necessary legislative action themselves. If they did so I would of course support them in every possible way and they could base their legislation on the draft in my possession. Eventually they did so, and indeed provided more severe penalties than in the original draft. It was quite obviously an attempt to leave me holding the baby if such strong action was criticized.[50]

Interesting as these comments are, the Governor's memory or his information on the reasons for the strike seem to have been at fault. The threat of a general strike had nothing to do either with the elections or with the Government Clerical Service.

The action taken by the Ministers included the use of the military against the strikers. Later, while the Governor was on leave, the Acting Governor agreed to meet a deputation of the Government Workers Trade Union Federation led by N. M. Perera. He was arrested by the police on his way to the meeting, but was released and the strikes were settled.

The Chief Secretary, in his comments after the strike on trade unionism in Ceylon, stated that 'it is the politicians and not the workers who have created the unions and it is the politicians and not the workers who run them.'[51] It is only fair to point out that no display of political militancy on the part of a few leaders would have been able to rouse the masses had they not been provided with the incentive to action by the strong compulsion of their economic plight. The Ceylon worker had benefitted from Forces' spending during the war years, but his conditions of work, of which he found himself redundant, made most of his gains of little consequence.

Again in 1947, in a situation which had hardly altered for the better so far as the lower grades of state employees were concerned, there were large-scale strikes. It was just before the General Election under the new Soulbury Constitution. The daily paid government servants and clerical workers determined to gain recognition of the trade union rights promised them in the settlement of 1946. They struck despite government warnings on 23 May that state employees did not have the right to strike. A great deal of political opposition to the Board of Ministers was injected into the series of strikes which followed. The government, stronger now after its experience of the previous year, threw all the weight of its command of the police and influence with the Press against the strikers. In addition, a detachment of Royal Marines from HMS *Glasgow* marched through the streets of Colombo. On 5 June the police opened fire on a crowd of strikers near Kolonnawa, killing one of them, a government clerk by the name of Kandasamy. By this time the strike was beaten. It had neither the organization nor the propaganda to stand up to the forces arrayed against it. The newspapers, which were solidly behind the government as could be expected, maintained an efficient campaign of misrepresentation of the aims of the strike and the backing it had received. Shortly after the shooting incident there was a gradual return to work. It had ended in a com-plete defeat of that section of the *élite* which had dared to oppose the Board of Ministers. The official history of the LSSP called it 'not only a defeat, it was a smash-up. Thousands of government clerks, government workers and workers in private employment were victimized. A Public Security Bill giving the government various repressive powers, had also been rushed through the State Council in the latter days of the strike.'[52] Among those summarily dismissed for his part in the strike was T. B. Ilangaratne.

Though they failed, the strikes drew attention to the changed economic situation which was responsible for the militancy of a section of the *élite* (and the working population) hitherto deemed the great toe of the assembly, whose subordination to its leader-ship could no longer be taken for granted. The *élite* was once assumed to be homogeneous, not only by those who belonged to it in Ceylon but also by intelligent observers in England. Beatrice Webb made the remark in her Diary on 13 August 1928 that

> One of the difficulties in granting what is called 'self-government' is that it means that the Legislative Council is engaged in criticism and re-fusing supplies but not itself administering anything. The right to criticize and reject without the right to construct and administer seems a demoralizing form of activity and inevitably tends to dull and inert governments. In the new constitution which is to be granted to Ceylon (said to be the work of Drummond Shiels) the representative Council is to administer as well as legislate on the model of a County Council. *But then the population of Ceylon is more homogeneous than that of Kenya, Cyprus and Palestine.*[53]

The population of Ceylon was never homogeneous; the *élite* may have seemed to be so. But this was no longer true.

CHAPTER 10

THE NEW FAÇADE
1948-56

In the acclamation with which His Majesty's Government's award of 'fully responsible status' to Ceylon was received by the majority of the *élite* in the island, D. S. Senanayake was hailed as 'the architect of freedom'. He had had conscientious lieutenants and it was generally known that powerful support for the line taken by him had come from D. R. Wijewardene and the house he had built up in the newspaper world of Ceylon. Sir Andrew Caldecott and Sir Geoffrey had had the benefit of the newspaper magnate's views and the Chairman of the Soulbury Commission acknowledged his indebtedness to his 'invaluable advice and assistance.'[1]

Both the Soulbury Commission and His Majesty's Government would probably have arrived at their decisions without any prompting, or much persuasion, from anyone in Ceylon. There was indeed little choice before them. The Soulbury Commission, consulting opinion in Ceylon and having before it the recommendations of previous Governors, was ready to go all the way in recommending more power for the *élite* with safeguards for imperial interests and for minorities. For its part His Majesty's Government was already committed – the Labour government in 1945 more specifically than the wartime Coalition – to a new deal in Asia. It was a matter of deciding in 1946 how much could be given and where. India, Burma and Ceylon were given political independence, Malaya was not. The calculations on which these awards were based have not as yet been revealed.

S. W. R. D. Bandaranaike, when he resigned from the UNP Government in 1951, regarded the gift of freedom as no extraordinary event. Of course he was in opposition then and was not disposed to make overmuch of the UNP's advertised political achievement:

Then came freedom. But how did freedom come? It came not after a fight upon definite principled policies and programmes, but it really came in the normal course of events, that is, attempts to persuade Commissions sent from England to grant this little bit or that little bit extra, and, finally, in the wake of freedom that was granted to countries like India, Pakistan and Burma, our Soulbury Constitution was altered to extend to us the same type of Dominion Status. There was no fight for that freedom which involved a fight for principles, policies and programmes which could not be carried out unless that freedom was obtained. No. It just came overnight. We just woke up one day and we were told, 'You are a Dominion now'.[2]

Whether there was much opposition to be overcome before Ceylon was granted political independence, or whether His Majesty's Government was only too pleased to concede what was asked for, the representative making demands for Ceylon was D. S. Senanayake. He therefore was, to repeat the figure of speech so frequently used then, the architect of Ceylon's freedom. What he built, what he was responsible for constructing on behalf of the *élite* whom he represented remarkably well, was a new façade with a burnished brass plate on the door: Free Ceylon. It was the outward and visible sign of all the *élite* had been pressing for since 1910. The structure raised by the British remained intact; inside there was some rearrangement. A number of Ceylonese previously relegated to rooms without a view moved higher up; they could stride the corridors of power with more confidence and even peer out of the commanding heights of the structure. The new façade was impressive; it delighted those who filed in and out of the building as the new VIPs. The Donoughmore Constitution had provoked the first Minister of Health to remark that Ceylon now had seven-tenths freedom (since they had seven ministries of the ten in the State Council). The Ministers in the Cabinet of 1947 could feel that they were no longer seven, but that they had all they wanted and more.

The Associated Newspapers of Ceylon hailed the appointed day – 4 February 1948 – on which the island ceased to be a colony as a transfiguring process: 'The pealing of temple and church bells, and the sound of joyful drums awakened the people of Ceylon in the first hours of 4 February 1948 from their "slumber of servitude" into the unfamiliar consciousness of a free people.'[3] It was pardonable hyperbole on the part of a powerful financial group which had taken under its wing the new freedom, its champion, and the group organized by him – the UNP – to contest the elections of the previous year. The alliance between the UNP and the Associated Newspapers of Ceylon has continued ever since. Opponents of their point of view had for some time before 1947 dubbed them 'the Senanayake Press'. The member for Bibile in the last two and a half years of the State Council – W. Dahanayake – as a rumbustious critic of the Board of Ministers was given to exaggeration, but when he gave the Associated Newspapers of Ceylon this label,[4] he was only expressing what had often been felt about the identity of views shared by the Board of Ministers and this newspaper group.

Whatever action freedom might have had on the people of the country, for the *élite* the official celebrations marked the hopeful beginning of a new era. On 4 February 1948 the last Colonial Governor, Sir Henry Moore, was sworn in as the first Governor-General of independent Ceylon. The comings and goings of the great were watched by large crowds on the streets, as the day had been declared a public holiday. On 10 February, another holiday, the Duke of Gloucester, representing his brother King George vi, formally opened the first session of the Parliament of independent Ceylon. The ceremony, from which the Marxist opposition absented itself, took place in a large hangar imaginatively decorated in the traditional Sinhalese style with strips of tender coconut leaves and festoons of paper. Once again large crowds in the neighbourhood of Torrington Square, where the ceremony took place, and along the road to it watched the full panoply of a State occasion. On 4 February, all over the country, in provincial towns and large villages official meetings of the administrative hierarchy and Police parades drew attention to the significance of the day.

The General Election of 1947, which provided the new Parliament with its ninety-five territorially elected members, differed little in its preliminaries and the features of its polling days from that of 1936 to the old State Council. Of the old parties contesting seats there were the two groups of the LSSP and the Labour Party. There was the new UNP, an *ad hoc* formation brought into being to realize the need for a cabinet on party lines.[5] Sir Ivor

Jennings thought that 'the UNP had no very positive policy to offer, nor was it well organized'.[6] The Treasurer of the new group was J. L. Kotelawala; its funds were believed to have come from business interests, foreign and indigenous, supporting the old Board of Ministers, and from party members themselves. The Tamil Congress ran a number of candidates in the Northern Provinces, so did the Ceylon-Indian Congress in constituencies in planting districts where the plantation worker still had a vote. For the first time the Communist Party of Ceylon (CP) had a number of candidates too. The presence of a large number of Independents – no less than 181 – was the surest indication that to the majority of people in the country there were no political issues at stake, but, as constituencies had been delimited, those with a fair chance of securing a bloc of caste votes appeared on the hustings, postponing the decision to make any political decision until it was clear who was likely to be in power and how some profit was to be gained from taking sides. The political development of the country can be traced in the gradual elimination of Independents. One or two still survive as communal busybodies with more metamorphoses than the Vicar of Bray than as figures to be taken seriously.

Politically the elections resolved themselves into a conflict between the old Board of Ministers and the left parties. UNP propaganda made a great deal of the threat to religion offered by the LSSP, and, *bhikkhus* were paraded in support of some UNP candidates. The Roman Catholic priesthood too took a hand in the election, coming out very strongly, in their advice to their flock on the side of the UNP. The LSSP campaign was one of opposition to a constitutional change by which the nationalist *bourgeoisie* had now been entrusted by the colonial power with the task of ruling in their place. The votes cast for them did not depend on political understanding of this claim. Support for them, too, depended on the personalities of the candidates, but as a group the left was identified with advocacy of the cause of the working man and the peasant. To that extent the political implication of the work of the Sama Samajists in the country was clear.

The mass of voters did not go to the polls. Only 49 per cent of the total electorate voted. The UNP secured the largest number

of seats, but had no absolute majority. The three left parties –
the two Sama Samajist groups and the Communists – had eighteen
seats; the Tamil Congress seven and the Ceylon-Indian Congress
six. The momentum of his past activities carried A. E. Goonesinha into the House of Representatives, but once there he transferred his allegiance to the UNP and was later made Minister
without Portfolio and Chief Government Whip. One unexpected result was the election of a Burgher as third member for the
Colombo Central seat – P. G. B. Keuneman, a well-known member
of the CP. His success was a tribute to the impression made
by his personality rather than to the voters' approbation of the
programme of his party. He was then, and still probably is, the
strongest card in the C P pack. He had had a remarkable career at
Cambridge in the mid-thirties, had been Editor of *Granta* and
President of the Union.

It was with the support of the Independents (twenty-one of
whom had been returned to the House) and of the six nominated
members – four Europeans and two Burghers – that D. S. Senanayake formed his government. It was a coalition government which
the Prime Minister had to discipline both in the Cabinet and in the
House, if it was going to last. Sir Andrew Caldecott had been
justified in his forecast nearly ten years earlier that 'for years to
come parties might be many and some of them wear a communal
complexion, so that Cabinets would probably be coalition
Cabinets'.[7]

The new Cabinet took over exactly where the old Board of
Ministers had left off. If 'inevitably the electors thought of the
first House of Representatives as a larger and more important
version of the State Council'[8], they might have been excused, for
the Cabinet was the Board with its numbers increased. There was,
however, under the pressure exerted by the Prime Minister some
feeling for collective responsibility in spite of the jealousies and
squabbles from which no Cabinet is free. But in its attitudes to the
tasks confronting a new government, there was only the slightest
evidence of any development or advance from those of the State
Council.

The thirteen new Ministers of the Senanayake Government
were the old Board of Ministers at nearly twice its strength.
Four of the Board – more than half its number – found key posts

in the new Cabinet. The new recruits were either related to the Prime Minister: his son Dudley became Minister of Agriculture and Lands, his nephew by marriage, J. R. Jayawardene, was the new Minister of Finance; or tried supporters of the Board; or linchpins, because of their communal affiliations, in the new party. The gibe that the UNP was really the 'Uncle-Nephews Party' was an irrelevant jest. It is typical of all oligarchies that they tend to rely on a small core of persons related by blood or marriage to the leader. Harold Wilson's opening remarks in the 1964–5 session of the House of Commons: 'There are no relatives of mine in the government. There are none of my wife's relatives in the government', seem needlessly severe. In the setting of Ceylon an experenced Colonial Governor had ventured the opinion that 'there is indeed nothing intrinsically immoral about nepotism'.[9]

There were two able men in the Cabinet. As member for Kelaniya in the State Council, the new Minister of Finance had been a useful co-adjutor of the Board of Ministers, particularly in the support he had given the Police Amendment Bill and the Public Security Bill in 1947. That he should have been given a key Ministry was no surprise. Dudley Senanayake was intelligent and could express unconventional opinions in debate. Of the old Ministers S. W. R. D. Bandaranaike kept his portfolio of Local Government, in which was included Health. He had had to relinquish all claim to maintaining the Sinhala Maha Sabha as a party in its own right. The Prime Minister was strong enough to insist on this. Like other groups it could continue as an organization affiliated to the new party of the UNP.

The task of giving effect administratively, both at home and abroad, to the changed status of the island had to be taken in hand. Sir Charles Jeffries[10] describes how the process of both the transfer of power and the obligations and responsibilities from the United Kingdom to the new Dominion was undertaken by the Colonial Office and the Commonwealth Relations Office. In Ceylon six new ministries and expanding government departments resulted in the creation of a new type of superlative civil servant: the Permanent Secretary to a Minister, through whom all his dealings with the administration were supposed to be channelled. These new officers were, by force of circumstances and by ministerial pressure, hard put to it to resist becoming agents of political influence. Those who relished the opportunities offered were going to be powerful determinants of policy.

The numerous officers needed to man new departments were fortunately provided by the old University College transformed into the University of Ceylon in 1942 by Sir Ivor Jennings. Sir Ivor would have left his mark on wartime and postwar Ceylon even if he had not been associated with the constitutions in which he had a hand.[11] His remarkable source of energy *motu proprio* made a university materialize. When he arrived in Ceylon in 1940, the site and the character of the university had long been decided, but the formidable task of levering government departments into a speed resembling his own had yet to be taken in hand. Once again the backing of D. S. Senanayake made the difference. The University of Ceylon was created in 1942. During the war years the university site in Peradeniya was SEAC Headquarters. In 1951 the first students of the Faculty of Law took up residence on the 3,000 acre site planned as a complex of Halls of Residence and Park for 3,500 students by Sir Patrick Abercrombie and Clifford Holliday. Their plans were carried out by the university architect, Shirley D'Alwis. Sir Ivor secured the university its autonomy, and the special interest of the Prime Minister and a government requiring personnel for the new tasks of the administration. Above all, he gave it a new organization and the freedom of developing as a university and not a government department. It will have to be judged by what his successors make of it.

The Cabinet had been formed in 1947 before the change in the constitutional status of the country was decided. Its continuation of the character of the previous Board is therefore understandable. As Leader of the House, looking back over fifteen years of the State Council, D. S. Senanayake summarized the achievements of the Board in terms of the money spent by various Ministries. It could stand as a valediction forbidding mourning for the old as well as the exordium of the new dispensation: 'Before the Ministers came into office, the government spent Rs 9,000,000 on agriculture. That was in the year 1931. Today we are spending Rs 47,000,000 or almost 48,000,000 on agriculture . . .' Similarly the Minister for Local Administration spent Rs 3,500,000. 'Today it is almost Rs 10,000,000 . . . The expenditure on the health services has gone up to Rs 26,800,000 . . .' And so on. The Leader of the House asserted: 'Our record from 1931 onwards is one of which any Board of Ministers can be proud.'[12]

Fair enough; in arithmetical terms it did, and does, seem impressive. On the other hand it is difficult not to conclude that the new Cabinet did little in their handling of the problems of postwar Ceylon than spend more money on the time-honoured projects of the Board of Ministers.

The money was there. In 1948 the Ceylon Government had Rs 1,260,000,000 in sterling balances representing the money owed to it on account of His Majesty's forces' spending in the island. This was not available on demand, but agreement was reached by the two governments on the release of funds. The Ministers in the new Cabinet had more money to spend, but schemes for spending it – as envisaged by the First Six Year Plan for 1947/8–1953/4 – were little more than a congeries of proposals by Heads of Departments into which the numinous word 'plan' had been spatchcocked.

Wartime restrictions and shortages had generated an artificial climate of supply, in which even amateurish schemes of Heads of Departments long out of touch with their specialized academic subjects of study could flourish. A number of these had succeeded in satisfying the demands of the local market for such articles as plywood for tea-chests. In the Administration Report of the Director of Industries for 1946–7 it was stated that the government factories had been able to show a net profit of Rs 412,000 at the end of 1946. But the factories themselves were never intended to 'last beyond 1947 at the latest (excepting the Plywood and Glass factories)'.[13]

As soon as the wartime emergency came to an end these hopeful projects were seized with the cramp. In 1951 an investigating committee was appointed to look into the state industrial projects. By that time the only successful state enterprise was the cement factory at Kankesanturai in the Northern Province. Planned before the war it had come into production in 1946, but still had to work at its rated capacity. The hydro-electric scheme, for which funds had been appropriated in 1924, showed a history of dilatoriness. The Industries Commission of 1916 had stated the obvious in its comment that the provision of cheap power should precede industrial development. Though the scheme had been initiated in 1924, it took twenty-six years for any hydro-electric power to be developed. Even so most of it was used not industrially, but for household and mercantile consumption. The only difference between prewar and postwar planning was numerical. Each Minister felt free to promote on paper as many schemes as he had 'experts' to provide him with reports. This designation, at a time when the Great Powers after the war were determined to develop the old markets and open out new ones, soon became a term of dubious validity. Some of these 'experts' were pensioners who owed their selection to their influence with their governments; there were so many commercial travellers in disguise among them that the highly qualified specialists were lost in the crowd. The first UNP Six Year Plan could hardly be a serious attempt at any planning or development. A member of the Cabinet described it later as follows: 'No greater joke has been foisted on this country.'[14] Of course he was in the opposition then and he should have remembered that he was a party to the practical joke himself. Still his comment is revelatory.

The only serious planning of postwar years was a continuation of the work of D. S. Senanayake as Minister of Agriculture and Lands in the State Council. He had turned his attention to restoring old irrigation channels and tanks and so increasing the country's rice production. Agriculture was the kingpin of the Six Year Plan, its object being to achieve self-sufficiency in food. The opening up of the Dry Zone by the government for the benefit of colonists and the introduction of modern techniques of food production was the *leitmotiv* of planning in agriculture. Colonial Governors like Ward and Gregory had plans for restoring old tanks, but there was no money for them as the interest of the colonial power was primarily in the development of the plantation industry. There had been private attempts at colonization of the Dry Zone and a number of professional men in Colombo had put money and energy into schemes like that at Hatamune near Minneriya. But the lack of large-scale irrigation schemes and the scourge of malaria were too great handicaps for private energies to carry. The use of DDT by Allied forces during the war years, when jungle air-strips and camps were built all over the Dry Zone, brought malaria under control and practically eradicated it. The work done by various government departments under the stimulus of the Minister of Agriculture in the 30s and 40s could therefore pay returns.

The most spectacular of the government's agricultural projects was that in the Gal Oya Valley in the Eastern Province. A long dam across the Gal Oya River was expected to bring into production 150,000 acres of irrigable land, of which 120,000 acres were to be in rice and 27,000 in sugar. Hydro-electric power was to be developed for industrial purposes. The Prime Minister officially inaugurated the project on 29 August 1949; but according to a statement made by the Minister of Finance in 1955 the original target had not yet been hit.

That there was a short fall in the acreage developed is not a realistic criticism of the project. Nor is it fair to turn on it as offering no solution to the problems of land utilization in the island. Land reform, the problems of the landlessness of the peasant and of assuring the cultivator of security of tenure, had to wait till after 1956 to be taken up. D. S. Senanayake did not intend to deal with any of these things directly in his Gal Oya project. He was chiefly interested in bringing into cultivation areas once known for their productivity in the days of the Sinhalese kingdom. These schemes – particularly in Minneriya and Polonnaruwa – had the edge over any schemes for industrialization or the solution of the contemporary problem of the peasantry, because they appealed to nationalist Sinhalese sentiment.

Criticism of the large multipurpose project of Gal Oya, that in spite of its technological equipment it seemed to ensure the cultivator's persistence in age-old methods of tilling the soil, overlooks the innate conservatism of the peasant. More serious criticism might be levelled at the cost of settling the peasant on the land and of the choice of recruits for peasant colonies. Too often the colonist was the nominee of a politician whose man he was and whom he was ready to support. Extensive state aid, in addition, introduced an element of artificiality into colonization schemes, because the cultivator settled on them enjoyed the best of both worlds: he was both landowner insisting on his privileges and tenant of the state which owed him a living.

The political character of these colonization schemes – particularly the possibilities of carving out dependable seats in the House through the colonists settled in them – was not lost on either the Sinhalese or the Tamil politician. To the latter, colonization schemes were a threat to the communal composition of areas for some time populated mainly by Tamils. It is an illuminating side-light on the political programme of the Federal Party (formed in 1949) that the only Ceylon of which it could apparently think was a country divided as it had been in the eighteenth century into Sinhalese and Tamil areas. On the other hand, to the Sinhalese nationalists of the UNP (and later the Sri Lanka Freedom Party), Ceylon could be the country of the Sinhalese alone – as it never had been in ancient times. Kipling, writing of the various racial elements out of which England came to be composed nearly a thousand years before, described the process as 'England is being hammered into shape'. If the Sinhalese nationalist of the 1950s had similar notions about Ceylon, certainly it was the Tamils who were going to get the hammering.

However, these policies of agricultural development did enable less rice to be imported during a period when population grew rapidly: 'Against the import of 11·6 million cwt of rice in 1939, the quantity for 1963 was 7·9 million cwt. During this period the population increased from 6·5 million to 10·6 million. The very fact that rice imports have declined appreciably while the population increased by 63 per cent is an indication of the increase in local rice production.'[15] This was achieved not only by expen-sive colonization schemes but also by increasing yields all over the country. It may yet be that a rise in the productivity of the agricultural worker could make possible an acceleration of indus-trial development.

Since World War II the government had become the sole importer of rice, flour, and sugar, which it was providing to the consumer on a strictly rationed basis at controlled prices. It is to the credit of the administration that food rationing worked fairly well. During the war years a marked change was noticeable in the people's eating habits. Wheat flour baked in bread crept more and more into the diet of the rural population. The govern-ment, as sole importer, could use the profits made on some of its imports (sugar in particular) to offset the losses on rice. But with the end of the war and the rise in the world prices of food the subsidy on rice began to weigh on the budget. The first Minister of Food and Co-operative Undertakings in the UNP Government put the case graphically in the House on 28 January 1948: 'Honourable Members must realize that when a constituent of theirs, say in distant Beliatta, goes and buys a measure of rice, he buys it at 36 cents when the government has paid as much as 62 cents, which means a subsidy of 26 cents per measure.'[16] The government's intervention in the import of food had prevented the possibility of famine in wartime, and its food subsidy cushioned the voter against some of the hard realities of inflation. Not only was the price of imported rice subsidized, the home grower was – in order to stimulate production – paid a price for his grain which needed government subsidy too. These subsidies had been built into the fabric of life in the country and had to be taken into account as part of the welfare services provided by the state. They were taken for granted by the majority of voters accustomed to a semi-feudal way of life which guaranteed the tenant his lord's protection.

The better part of the island's industrial development during these years was concentrated in the work done in its commercial crop industry. The three Research Institutes – for tea, rubber and coconut, sponsored by the state in the 1920s – had done more efficient work in the application of scientific skill to production than had been planned in any of the parts of the First Six Year Plan.

In the old State Council chamber, now the overcrowded House of Representatives, procedure continued on the English model, with one important change. Members could address the House in Sinhalese and Tamil too. A recent commentator, who writes from experience of membership of the House, remarks that 'there was a genuine desire that things should be done "decently and in order" and on the whole this was generally observed. Some years later a party of Ceylon M.Ps visited the British House of Commons, and one of them remarked to the author on coming out that in his opinion the Ceylon House of Representatives was rather better behaved! This has, regrettably, ceased to be the case.'[17]

The Senate never realized the hopes of the Soulbury Commissioners, but became, by and large, common land on which party hacks were loosed to graze, or a club for those who delighted in collecting baubles of distinction and honours. As fifteen of its thirty members were elected by votes of members of the lower House, there was, as one of the latter confessed, 'heavy competition for "first preferences" – somewhat embarrassing to some members of the House of Representatives'.[18] As an upper house the Senate provided the mode by which those who did not contest an election could hold office in a government – like Sir Oliver Goonetilleke, Minister for Home Affairs in the first UNP Government, and Mrs Sirimavo Bandaranaike, Prime Minister in 1960.

As the UNP was still a collection of sub-political aggregates, D. S. Senanayake had to take on himself tasks which should have been shared by others in the Parliamentary group. He looked after Defence and External Affairs and had the additional burdens of keeping both Cabinet and party together.

In the House the full tide of speech flowed at all times, covering all subjects with such a surge of words that it seemed that the greater part of these sessions of talk (there seldom were real debates and debaters could have been counted on the fingers of one hand) justified the doubts of the Donoughmore Commissioners whether British Parliamentary institutions were either worth imitating or even worth having. They wondered (in 1928) whether this system which seemed at that time obsolescent should be foisted on a country where it lacked even the excuse of being a traditional anomaly.[19] S. A. Pakeman, who sat in the House of Representatives as an European nominated member, thought that British Parliamentary procedure 'worked quite well' in Ceylon, 'despite the fact that it was never possible to have anything like a two-party system'.[20] A two-party system on the British model was indeed well beyond Ceylon's means. It would seem that it can only be afforded by wealthy nations, where power is already so well established outside Parliament that two groups in it with little to distinguish one from the other can debate issues with no great difference made, whichever happens to form the government.

Despite the danger that proceedings in the House could insulate the ordinary member from what the country and his constituents were really thinking and feeling, he was a figure of considerable importance on whom constant calls were made for the exertion of his influence. Ordinary members could express their opinions of the qualifications of candidates for posts in the government service, although in theory a Public Service Commission consisting of three persons, appointed by the Governor-General, i.e. the Prime Minister, took charge of functions previously discharged by the Chief Secretary. The power of Ministers grew and that of the civil servant lost something of its lustre. The prestige of the service, once almost completely European at the top levels, still stood high, but heavy recruitment in postwar years reduced the scarcity value of these bright products of secondary school and university.

In the House the Prime Minister had to defend the agreements signed with the British Government the previous year. The Leader of the Opposition was Dr N. M. Perera, a skilled parliamentarian who took his responsibilities very seriously. The opposition launched its attack against what were supposed to be secret clauses in the Defence Agreements. D. S. Senanayake insisted that they were Gentlemen's Agreements which either party could abrogate if it wished. So they turned out to be, when they were examined by S. W. R. D. Bandaranaike nearly ten years after they were signed.

The Prime Minister had the satisfaction in 1949 of persuading Lord Soulbury to accept the office of Governor-General. In the five years he spent in Ceylon Lord Soulbury interested himself very greatly in the arts. His influence brought the Arts Council of Ceylon into being. Whatever this institution is likely to achieve, the initiative of the Governor-General in organizing it must be commended. He saw quite clearly that both the traditional arts of old Ceylon and the newer modes which centuries of cultural contact with Europe had brought into being were in need of stronger support from above than small groups, however dedicated, could provide. He saw, too, that in a hierarchical society the vigour of the arts depended to a great extent on the social position of their patron. Colonial Governors had lent the prestige of the presence and their patronage to various groups and societies interested in the arts. But the indigenous arts of the country did not rank high in these circles, nor could such notice as a Governor, with more important concerns on his mind, take of them make up for the languishing of the old sources of energy: particularly religious institutions and the feudal nobility, both of them displaced by the new political and economic structure.

Ceylon had developed an artistic heritage with traditions and conventions of its own. Such forms as the Kandyan dance, temple frescoes, ornaments in stone and on lacquered wood, related though they may have been to Indian prototypes, had a sophistication and character which distinguished them from the Indian. Besides, the rich stores of Buddhist legend and the yearly round of obligation owed to temple, *bhikkhu* and feudal overlord, kept alive in the village arts typically Sinhalese in their form and expression. As change intruded into this way of life, the traditional arts declined. Skills which village craftsmen had once brought to a level of elegance and dignity – the work of blacksmiths, of workers in brass, and wood-carvers – deteriorated. But even in their decline they showed strong traces of their earlier excellence – like the village potter's clay figures of animals, birds and gods with their pleasing design and colour. The old festivals and fairs, to which vendors of the work of village craftsmen crowded, lost their importance. Itinerant artists whose virtuosity of patter, skill in repartee and range of song were an index of the dramatic and mimetic talent of their audiences all but disappeared. Figures like these in the older way of life were as little able to stand up against the incursion of the economy of the machine as their counterparts in Europe.

Sinhalese scholarship and its literary tradition survived despite change in the way of life, as a result of the work of a number of learned *bhikkhus* who founded *pirivenas* or institutions of higher learning. The most erudite of these scholars was Hikkaduve Sri Sumangala (1826–1911) who was responsible for the establishment of the Vidyodya Pirivena. This institution, as well as the equally well-known Vidyalankara Pirivena, are now universities. The Tamil language and its literature were in a different position, contact could be maintained with South India and its centres of Hindu learning.

The activities of Colonial Governors in such institutions as the Royal Asiatic Society and the English Association, remote though they were from the life of the people of the country, are not, however, to be scorned. Nor were the interests they were really concerned with promoting – those patterned on the institutions of their homeland – to be undervalued as being forced, unnatural or unrelated to the emotional needs and the background of the people

217

over whom they ruled. The astonishing resilience of the human mind should not be forgotten. More than a few people in Ceylon could derive genuine sustenance from the literature or the music or the philosophy of Europe. It has to be admitted that the culture of the Britisher in Ceylon, as well as that of the Ceylonese *élite* who modelled themselves upon it, produced its own anomalies and absurdities. The fairest criticism to be made of this culture was that where it might have helped it did not go far enough, nor did it ever penetrate deep enough. It provided only the very few with a chance of acclimatizing themselves to the new. Those who could do this did benefit from what they had accustomed themselves to, and their standards were neither trivial nor negligible. It would have been surprising indeed if this minority should have proved unable to appreciate (even inadequately) the old cultural tradition of the country in which they lived.

The interest of this minority in the older culture and their dissatisfaction with the taste of their time led to the beginnings of a revival of interest in the indigenous arts of the island. Ananda Coomaraswamy was an important figure in this early twentieth-century movement. His education had been entirely Western. He was an excellent specimen of the English-educated *élite*, unusual though his talents and interests were. His was a seminal influence on all those anxious to rescue traditional arts fallen into neglect and decay. The Ceylon National Reform Society owed a great deal to his example. It was founded in order 'to encourage and initiate reform in social customs amongst the Ceylonese, and to discourage the thoughtless imitation of unsuitable European habits and customs'.

The ideals of the Indian nationalist movement and the work and personality of Tagore later exerted a strong influence on one section of the *élite* in Ceylon. It would have been strange if they had not, for India has always left traces of its cultural trends on its island neighbour. The work of the Buddhist revival and of Buddhist secondary schools has already been referred to. These were all *élite*-led developments and were the counterpart in Ceylon of the discontent felt in Europe with the values and the character of the new industrial civilization.

The enthusiasm of these groups could not recall the traditional arts to the vigorous life they had once led. But the balance, unfairly weighted against them, could be redressed by the influence of gifted artists like Lionel Wendt, to take only one example. Wendt was a remarkable figure: a concert pianist of great distinction at a time when piano playing, as it dutifully echoed in a hundred households of the *élite* in Colombo, could be little more than a sign of the insipidity of imitation of the West. Yet he was keenly interested in Kandyan dance forms; he was a photographer whose eye revealed unknown aspects of Ceylon to those who, living in the country, had scarcely seen it, and he was the patron of painters, musicians and writers. The work of the '43 Group, for the organization of which he was largely responsible in 1943, showed that the attention of the Western-trained artist could profit imaginatively from contact with the artistic traditions of the country in which he lived.

Of course such contacts were to prove fruitful. European models had left their imprint on writers in Sinhalese, notably on Martin Wickramasinghe, whose novels (a new form in Sinhalese) used the resources of a living language freshly and originally as a result of his sensitive reading of Western literature. The impetus given to studies in Sinhalese and Tamil in the university, and the experiments of university musical and dramatic societies showed that there were new possibilities to be explored. In recent years the emergence of new writers in Sinhalese – both novelists and poets – and the exploitation of a rich vein of folk tradition in drama by E. R. Sarathchandra were striking of the transformation of the old by the new.

As in the political movement, the radical impulse in the rehabilitation of the indigenous culture came from the English-educated *élite*. Its results have been none the worse for this. By the time Lord Soulbury had interested the government of the time in the creation of an Arts Council there was a fair-sized field ready for cultivation.

It had been made clear by D. S. Senanayake, in his remarks on the subject of the franchise on 8 November 1945, that it would be restricted to those deemed to be citizens of the country. The plantation worker would be excluded. In spite of delegations and deputations to and from India, the question of the status of this group of persons of Indian origin had been left unsettled. In 1939, soon after the Ceylon Government had decided to retire compulsorily a large number of Indian workers from the government and municipal services, Nehru himself visited Ceylon to discuss the problem with the Ceylon Government. The only outcome of his visit seems to have been a stiffening of opinion on both sides. Apparently more interested in mobilizing support for the Congress struggle for *swaraj* in India than in anything else, he advised the plantation workers in Ceylon to join the Trade Unions just being organized by the Ceylon Indian Congress, an association of big Indian business men and a fair sprinkling of Head Kanganies, most of whom had done very well for themselves. Nehru's advice had the effect of cutting the plantation worker off from the working-class movement in the country.

The status of the plantation worker of Indian origin became a political issue in Ceylon in the 1920s, not only because it was clear by then that more political power was in the process of being transferred to the Ceylonese, but also because of the Indian Government's reaction to the treatment of its emigrants in other parts of the world – notably in South Africa. So far as Ceylon was concerned, Ceylon National Congress leaders in the 1920s and the 1930s asserted that the majority of plantation workers were, by reason of their ties and contacts with their homeland, not a Ceylonese but an Indian population. In 1946, according to census figures there were no less than 665,853 persons classified as Indian Tamils working on plantations.

It is not surprising that the Indian Government and the Ceylonese leaders should have maintained totally opposed points of view, for both were involved in a problem created by a larger entity to which they were subordinated: the British Empire. The migration of Indian peoples all over the world came about as a result of the poverty of the Indian masses and the demand for cheap labour on plantations in various parts of the empire. Both of them were a function of imperial rule. Mrs Knowles stated the case dramatically nearly forty years ago:

Most people are aware of the emigration from the U K which gave an English impress to parts of three continents. Few people, however, seem to realize how important a part both Indian and Chinese emigrants have played in the development of the Empire, although the King rules over a miniature Chinese empire in Malaya and a miniature

Indian Empire in the West Indies. There have been, in fact, in the past century three mother countries of the British Empire, i.e. the U K, India and China.[21]

At the time that British statesmen were engaged in divesting themselves of political control of overseas territories, they were, whether they realized it or not, washing their hands publicly of responsibility for decisions they should have made. Indian migration had assumed the size of a world problem on account of the development of British imperial interests. Those who had created the problem should surely have played a more vigorous part at least in sorting out its difficulties. Left to themselves, the representatives of India and Ceylon could merely confront each other over a no-man's-land of disagreement and negation.

This situation was already reached in the late 1930s before imperial control had been lifted. There was a half-hearted attempt made by the State Council in 1938 to determine whether the Indian immigrant had deprived the Ceylonese worker of employment and how many could be regarded as having made Ceylon their permanent home. The conclusions of the Commission set up under the chairmanship of Sir Edward Jackson were published as Sessional Paper No. III of 1938. The Commission working on samplings made by the Planters' Association concluded that 'If an estimate of 60 per cent is taken for purposes of illustration, it will be seen that at the end of 1936 there were in the island approximately 400,000 Indian estate workers who had become part of the permanent population of the Island.'[22] But the figures were based only on samplings of ninety-five estates, and 'permanent' was equated with residence of not less than five years in the country.

Throughout the 1930s, in spite of the professed agitation of the Board of Ministers about unemployment in the country and the threat of the Indian plantation population to the Sinhalese villager, recruiting licences for Immigrant Labour were being used to provide workers for the plantations. In the State Council in 1937 Dr N. M. Perera made the position of his party perfectly plain. He was against the continued immigration of indentured labour from India: 'I would emphasize that it is our bounden duty to find work for indigenous labour wherever possible. We know very well that there is unemployment and underemployment in Ceylon. Our duty is to provide employment for those people before we agree to labour being brought into Ceylon from outside it.'[23] Those already in the country as workers should enjoy the rights and privileges of workers, but no further immigration should be allowed because the country had its own problems of finding work for its nationals. The debate provoked a paradoxical reaction from the Minister of Communications and Works, then engaged in his campaign to fire all Indian workers in government employ: 'If we are going to replace the Indian coolie with Sinhalese labour, I say "God help Ceylon". It will be worse than allowing Indian coolies to come in. Once the Sinhalese come in as coolies, they will lose the desire for land, they will lose their culture and self-respect and they will be a wandering set of people in Ceylon.'[24] This implied that for certain kinds of work stigmatized as inferior an inferior type of non-citizen should be available. In other words the plantation worker of Indian origin was to be the nigger in the Southern States. Huck Finn's Pap would have put it more racily and eloquently, but he could not have put the case more succinctly.

In spite of its fears of the inundation of Kandyan districts by Indian workers, the Board of Ministers during the war again raised no objection to workers being recruited from India for work in the country, not only on the plantations. In 1943 the Member for Point Pedro used the opportunity to accuse the Board of having kept the Council in the dark about this influx: 'It would appear – and it is perfectly clear that under the guise of an increased war effort, this government and the Board of Ministers have been agreeable, if they can catch the other government napping, to bring into this country a number of labourers upon the indentured system.'[25]

The UNP Government's Citizenship Act No. 18 of 1948 was the first move in denying citizenship to nearly one tenth of the population. It limited the status of national of Ceylon to those who could claim it by descent or by registration on certain conditions, which in the next year the Indian and Pakistani Residents (Citizenship) Act No. 3 defined. Proof of continuous residence since 1946, and before that of residence for seven years (if married) or ten years (if unmarried), was much less difficult for the worker to provide than legally valid documentation of his parents' and grandparents' marriage. To have asked the illiterate worker to furnish such proofs was equivalent to disqualifying him in advance. The Ceylon (Parliamentary Elections) Amendment Act No. 48 of 1949 gave the worker of Indian origin the *coup de grace*. He was denied the right to vote. Whatever long-term policies and principles were involved, the Acts had the immediate effect they were intended to have. Six constituencies in the Central Province where the plantation worker was in a majority and in 1947 had returned members belonging to the Ceylon-Indian Congress (Nuwara Eliya, Talavakelle, Kotagala, Navalapitiya and Maskeliya) lost the great majority of their voters. In the next General Election five UNP candidates and one Labour Party member who supported the UNP were returned by these electorates. The fall in the number of registered voters in these electorates – the greatest drop was at Talavakelle, from 19,298 to 2,912– completely altered the balances of forces in the country.[26] The Sinhalese rural voter was on his way to becoming the centre of gravity in the political world of Ceylon.

The UNP Government's move was a cynical abandonment of the ostentatiously altruistic motives which led to the Delimitation Commission's care, in 1946, to demarcate constituencies in such a way as to provide representation for interests otherwise likely to be unrepresented. One of the constituencies so created was Kotagala.

The opposition of the Left to the disfranchisement of the plantation worker was, immediately and in the long term, another political advantage to the UNP. The LSSP, in particular, could be branded as unpatriotic and lacking in loyalty to the nation on account of its opposition to the Citizenship Bills.

Finally, the 'Indian question' as it was called could always be used to generate emotional racial feeling whenever it was convenient. Racial feeling was known in Ceylon, the Citizenship Bills gave it the sanction of political respectability. In the House of Representatives later, members nominated to represent Indian interests kept complaining about the slowness of government departments in dealing with the applications of those seeking to have themselves registered under the provisions of the Act of 1949. Undoubtedly it did not require much insight on the part of administrative officers to discover that it was government policy to place as much difficulty as possible in the way of these applicants. By 1963 some 100,000 had been registered. The rest remain stateless and have been the subject of periodical argument between every Prime Minister of Ceylon and his counterpart in New Delhi.

The UNP Government's disfranchisement of the plantation worker led to the resignation of one of its Ministers, C. Suntharalingam. A remarkably intelligent Tamil, a close personal friend of the Prime Minister, he never had any use for communal agitation. His defection was only a personal disappointment to the Prime Minister. The government recouped itself for any loss of support it might have suffered by persuading the Tamil Congress to join forces with it. Its leader, G. G. Ponnambalam, found himself on the government front bench, but the party he led lost an important section of its following which regrouped itself under S. J. V. Chelvanayakam as the Federal Party (FP), with a programme of securing justice for the Tamil minority through a Federal form of government. Chelvanayakam, a Christian and an able lawyer, became a passionate advocate of his Federal scheme which was never as clear to others as to himself. Increasing racial tension made his party the spokesman for the Ceylon Tamil minority in the *élite*.

The first two and a half years of UNP rule were years of extravagance by the government and their flashy supporters all over the country. After nine years of wartime shortages those who had made money proceeded to throw it about. Bus tycoons in their high-powered limousines; war profiteers on the lookout for honours for themselves and for anything else they could buy; contact men who were ready to fix anything for a price – the blatancy of these persons in the foreground of the political scene led to comments like that of an American observer, not unsympathetic to UNP politics, who described its nine years of power as being characterized by 'a generous "bonanza" of cabinet posts to reward the faithful and to enlist additional support among key groups of voters'.[27]

Very little of the volume of government spending went into financing essential imports or into capital expansion. Imports were steadily rising in 1947 and 1948. In the latter year the island's external assets had dropped to Rs.m 997.9. In the House of Representatives the Minister of Food wailed: 'We are rapidly finishing our sterling balances; we are rapidly finishing our cash balances. A time will come when we will have no money at all to pay for even the rice we buy.'[28]

The government was saved, not by any action of its own but by a turn in world affairs. Walter Lipmann has been credited with the invention of the phrase 'the Cold War'. He used it to describe the attempt to persuade, or to press, the Soviet Union into withdrawing its armies from Central Europe. Since then, as used by the great powers, it has betokened a callous indifference to the miseries they have wreaked on small nations by their power politics. It was clear then, it is clearer than ever now, that this phrase of understatement is the clue to the development of the political situation in South East Asia and in the Indian Ocean no less than in Europe. That Ceylon should have benefited temporarily from a turn of events in Cold War politics was only a happy accident, which cannot alter their harsh reality. The Korean war situation boosted the price of rubber. In 1950 it was being sold at Rs 3-25 a pound – a level it had not reached since 1912. In 1951 the government was able to reduce the price of rationed rice to twenty-five cents a measure and to increase the guaranteed price paid to the producer of paddy to Rs 9 a bushel.

The windfall of the Korean War temporarily rescued the government from its predicament. But it was impossible to budget on the prospect of such lucky chances. It was unfortunate, too, that few people in the government could see or understand how the future of the country was involved in the Cold War, however distant were the regions in which the heat had been turned on. With the cessation of hostilities and the end of stockpiling by the USA the boom was over. What remained so far as the whole of Asia was concerned was the emergence of China as a great Asian power. World strategy in the Indian Ocean, as the USA and the UK saw it, was shortly to wear a new look.

The strategy of Cold War politics was not the expressed concern of the Conference of Foreign Ministers which met in Colombo on 9 January 1950 with D. S. Senanayake as Chairman. It concluded its sittings on 13 January with its decision to give aid to the underdeveloped countries of South East Asia. This was the beginning of the Colombo Plan. Whoever was inspired to suggest aid to South East Asian countries, it could well be imagined that the capitalist world, with Marshall Plan aid as it had worked in Europe in mind, must have welcomed an opportunity in this way of penetrating the economies of aid-receiving countries.[29]

The meeting of the Commonwealth Foreign Ministers, in Colombo, with the United Kingdom represented by Ernest Bevin and India by Nehru, conferred enormous prestige on the Ceylon Prime Minister. A later meeting in Australia in 1950 worked out the details of the organization, and in 1951 the founding fathers of the Plan – Ceylon, Canada, Australia, India, New Zealand, Pakistan and the United Kingdom – met again in Colombo together with representatives from Burma, Laos, Cambodia, Thailand and Vietnam. The USA had expressed interest in the Plan and the desire to participate. Better organization of requests for aid from Ceylon had to be undertaken and a Planning Secretariat was set up by the government in Colombo in 1951.

It was in the high tide of the years of power at a time when the prestige of the Prime Minister was at its peak and the country's financial prospects were brighter than they had been for some time, that the UNP hit its first snag. It had been evident that there had been more than the usual bickering in the Cabinet. S. W. R. D. Bandaranaike was Leader of the House, but apparently could never feel that he belonged to the inner circle round the Prime Minister. Though officially he occupied a position of importance in the Cabinet and the party, he was out of the real centre of power. On 12 July 1951 he took the honourable course of resigning from the Cabinet and the party. Whatever reasons weighed with him in making his decision, the statement he made in the House that day showed that he clearly realized its consequences: 'I am only too well aware of the forces that may be arrayed against me. Pride and power, influence, money and even misrepresentation and distortion are all weapons that might be used against me.'[30]

Whether he confidently expected a number of his colleagues in the UNP to follow him or not, he must have felt that in the country, apart from the respect in which the Prime Minister personally was held, there were definite signs of dissatisfaction with the evolution of free and independent Ceylon. Concerns which had lain, and still lay, heavy on the minds of top rankers in the UNP – such things as the failure of the country to be admitted into the United Nations because of the Soviet veto; diplomatic representation abroad; the innumerable conferences to which party members were travelling all over the world – failed to trouble the ordinary man in the country. The majority of people expecting some radical change after the much vaunted process of independence were disappointed with the obstinate way in which there seemed to be hardly any change at all, except for the stridency of one section of the people. As S. W. R. D. Bandaranaike put it: 'It may be true that from the tourist point of view Ceylon is a pleasanter land than most countries of South East Asia, but from the point of view of the people of the country, there is a growing sense of frustration and disappointment.'[31]

He made himself the political spokesman of this sense of frustration. The Sinhala Maha Sabha became the Sri Lanka Freedom Party (SLFP), the English title combined with the old Sanskritic name for Ceylon emphasizing that the leader of the party insisted on realizing through the new freedom the idealized blessedness of the country's ancient past.

In the House, after the first reaction of anxiety on the part of the UNP, business went on as before. The Prime Minister took over for the time being the portfolios of Health and Local Government. With the support of the Tamil Congress the government was assured of a comfortable working majority. But the Six Year Plan was in the doldrums and the government decided to apply to the International Bank of Reconstruction and Development to investigate. Its mission was headed by Sir Sidney Caine. But before its report on its study of the economy was received in the country the UNP suffered its second setback: D. S. Senanayake was thrown while exercising his horse on Galle Face Green in Colombo on 21 March 1952, and died the next day. He was sixty-eight years old, but in spite of the strenuous life he had been leading and diabetes which would have taxed a younger man severely, he was vigorous and active.

His death removed an outstanding figure from the political scene. Shortly after – more rarely now – those who came to praise him buried the man everybody knew in the sticky periods of their eulogies. To try to decide whether he was a great man is to obscure his real quality. It has to be said of him first of all that he was not, as he was made out to be in the well-established myth about the three Senanayake brothers in Ceylon, the lad from the country who lacked brains but had energy. As 'Jungle John' he used to be contrasted with his eldest brother, F. R. Senanayake, who had been up at Cambridge and knew many English notabilities of his time. Nor was he at all points the apotheosis of the *élite* of the country whom he successfully represented. He had their solid virtues, their extrovert loyalty to friends, their assurance, quite sincerely held, that they were the rightful rulers of the country. But he lacked their arrogance. He had, in addition, an innate modesty. Of the tributes paid to him in the House of Representatives the most perceptive came from C. Suntharalingham, who was right to stress his humility and to remember the man he knew as friend and colleague in the days before he became Ceylon's first Prime Minister.

While his body lay in state in the House of Representatives, the high command of the UNP was engaged in intrigue about the succession. The lying in state and the state funeral, when his body was cremated at Independence Square (the Torrington Square of colonial Ceylon) on 29 March, were occasions of public tribute. He had been the UNP since 1947. His connection with it was to dominate the political scene for some time yet.

Only one account is available so far of the secret history of the events which followed the death of the Prime Minister.[32] An anonymous and scurrilous pamphlet, 'The Premier Stakes', in circulation at the time, purported to push the door of the thieves' kitchen ajar. Its authorship is not as important as its plausible revelation of the disunity among top-ranking members of the Cabinet. The Governor-General, Lord Soulbury, was out of Ceylon at the time of D. S. Senanayake's death. He returned immediately. After two days it was announced that Dudley Senanayake, the late Prime Minister's eldest son, was ready to become Prime Minister. The presence of rival candidates with claims which seemed to him stronger than his may have contributed to his hesitation in accepting office, for his career has shown how often and how suddenly he has found himself restrained by his private judgement from accepting the advice of his friends. His reluctance to take over the political responsibilities of the pre-miership was significant. He had, somewhat surprisingly after the completely unpolitical interests of his undergraduate days at Cambridge, come into politics. Both in the State Council and the House of Representatives, he had a reputation for making the intelligent comment, even if it did not suit the political line of his group. He had an enviable reputation in the country, and of all the figures eligible to lead the UNP he certainly stood highest in the estimation of everyone. No sooner was he pressed into accepting the office of Prime Minister than he decided, quite unexpectedly, on dissolving Parliament and going to the country.

The country went to the polls on four days in May 1952. The UNP won fifty-four seats, which gave it with the four TC members and a number of Independents (eight-five contested, of whom eleven won their seats), an overall majority.

The opposition was routed: the SLFP, the two Trotskyite groups and the CP obtained twenty-three seats. The FP secured two. Completely taken aback by these results, the opposition accused the government of having been a party to sharp practice in the conduct of the election. The victory of the UNP must be ascribed first of all to the effect of its emotional appeal: a son approached the voters soon after the 'tragic' death of his father, the suddenness of which illustrated the truth of the Buddhist belief in the transitory nature of all things and the illusoriness therefore of mortal life. If the party had been led by anyone else but Dudley Senanayake, the UNP may still have won, because it was the party in power, the party with most money, and it had been the party of D. S. Senanayake. No political issues deflected the straightforward appeal of the UNP to the voter to return it into power because it was the organization of the 'great man' who had just died. The old attacks on the Left opposition by religious groups, and the greenness of the organization of the SLFP effectively deprived them of any chance of doing better. The posi-tion taken up by the SLFP on the rightful place of the languages of the country (Swabasha) could not, in the suddenness with which the dissolution of Parliament was announced, be worked up into an issue more compelling emotionally than that on which UNP propaganda was based. With or without the foreign aid which was popularly believed to have helped its campaign, the UNP would have won the election of May 1952 because it was led by the son of the late Prime Minister.[33]

Much was expected of the new Prime Minister. In the House he had the reputation of not flinching from the awkward truth. His comment on the announcement that Ceylon was at war with Germany in 1939 has already been referred to. In the State Council in 1943 he declared himself sceptical of the ideals the United Nations were professing; 'I should like to ask honourable Members what it is that the United Nations are fighting for. What is this freedom that they talk so much about?'[34] On another occasion he reminded the House 'that even the best brains even in the most die-hard capitalist countries have admitted that profit as the sole motivating factor in our social dynamics is a bad thing'.[35]

Those who expected an overhaul of the party or the Cabinet were, however, fated to be disappointed. The breach between the Prime Minister and the powerful Minister of Transport, Sir John Kotelawala, who had, out of chagrin at being passed over for the Prime Ministership, resigned, was closed through the intervention of the President of the Senate, Sir Nicholas Attygalle, an extremely influential member of the *élite*. The Minister who was reconciled with his cousin gave as good a reason as any for the pressure in the UNP for their reconciliation – he was the party treasurer and controlled its funds.

The new Cabinet was a reshuffle of the old familiar figures, the former Minister of Education in the State Council becoming Minister for Local Administration. Among the new members of the Cabinet was R. G. Senanayake, the first cousin of the Prime Minister, who became the new Minister of Commerce. He had opinions of his own and had shown restiveness under the tutelage of older personages in the party. The new government, again a coalition between the UNP and the TC (though the UNP had no need of any support), presented the appearance of a broad front which stressed the first element in its name. It should be noted, however, that whereas four UNP candidates had contested seats in the predominantly Tamil Northern Province in the 1947 election, only one faced the electors in 1952.

The failure, or the inability, of the new Prime Minister to make any radical change in the personnel of the government, in spite of the public desire for change, seems again to suggest the reluctance of a person with one irksome decision on his conscience – that of accepting the Premiership – to add to its burdens. What was involved was more than loyalty to one's friends, it was loyalty to one's father's friends.

The government's victory at the polls had made no difference to its economic difficulties. The country was back again at the state it had been before the Korean War. The price of rubber was lower than it had been and rice had become more expensive on the world market. Some change in the established pattern of trade, if not in the economy, had to be made if difficulties were to be tided over. In 1950 China had taken 1,168 tons of rubber from Ceylon and had increased its purchases to 12,416 tons in 1951. Some attention was given to the remarkable fact, early in 1952, that China had become Ceylon's best customer in the rubber trade, in spite of the American and NATO ban on the supply of 'strategic materials' to Communist countries. It was in this atmosphere, somewhat thickened by the known hostility of elements in the Cabinet to trade with the Communist bloc, that the Minister of Commerce set out at the invitation of Peking on a trade mission to China. It was clear that the USA were unwilling to offer Ceylon anything more than the low world market price for her rubber, or to sell rice to the country except through the open market. The result of the Ceylon trade mission to China was the signing of a pact by which the two countries agreed to a barter arrangement at terms favourable to both. Ceylon contracted to supply China with 50,000 tons of sheet rubber for five years at a price higher than the world price. In return it was to receive 80,000 tons of rice at a price somewhat lower than the world price. Prices of both commodities were to be negotiated each year.

The rights and wrongs, the advantages and risks, of this deal were hotly debated in the English Press. In the House the Pact, with its clear implications that trade between the two countries would reach an annual volume of Rs 250 million of exports on each side, was welcomed by the opposition. R. G. Senanayake, who signed for Ceylon, represented it as an advantageous deal to which the country had no option but to agree. The colour of the contracting party made no difference to its value.

The Pact was revolutionary in the large inroads it made into the accepted pattern of Ceylon's trade. Once preliminary contacts had been made between China and Ceylon, obviously much more trade could be expected to follow. It had been assumed by most supporters of the UNP that the USA would come to the rescue of a country which would, if it were unaided, have to form trading links with a Communist power. But neither the US Government nor its trading interests were ready to make any concessions. To the majority of people in the country who were directly affected by it, the signing of the Pact brought neither marked change of sympathies nor notable political consequences. The Pact enabled the government to meet the demands made of it with regard to the subsidies on rationed rice and the guaranteed price paid for paddy, rights of long standing which in its election manifesto it had underwritten. One immediate consequence of the Pact was the stabilization of the rubber price. Crisis had been postponed for at least a year.

Not the Pact but the government's precipitate action produced a state of crisis in 1953. The price of sugar was raised by fifteen cents a pound and the rice ration was reduced by a quarter. The free midday meal for older schoolchildren was withdrawn and milk-feeding centres were closed down. All this because the government was disturbed about the financial position. The increase in the price of sugar led to the resignation of the Parliamentary Secretary to the Ministry of Home Affairs, the member from the rural constituency of Medawachchiya, M. Senanayake, no relative of the Prime Minister. The government could, however, still assert that one of its election slogans, 'So long as this government lasts, a measure of rice will be 25 cents', was still valid.

The Report of the Mission from the International Bank for Reconstruction and Development, published in July 1952, had taken up the annual theme on which the Central Bank of Ceylon had dilated: 'It would be sound policy to abandon the system of subsidies and allow food prices to find their expression in wages and costs of production. Therefore the Mission concurs in the view of the Central Bank that food subsidies should now be reduced.'[36] In 1953 the report of the Central Bank once again urged a reduction in the food subsidies. The Prime Minister conscientiously decided to follow this mounting volume of advice. The subsidies were reduced and on 20 July 1953 the price of rice rose from twenty-five to seventy cents a measure. The Left decided to mark its opposition to this change of policy by an island-wide *hartal* or stoppage of work. Despite formidable government warnings about the consequences of such action – the dismissals of workers failing to report for work – the *hartal* called for 12 August took place.

On the western coast, in Colombo in particular, the workers rallied to the call of the Left parties. Transport was paralysed. The strikers moved from passive to active resistance and saw to it that no buses could run, despite the propaganda of the bus tycoons that traffic would be normal. There were several incidents in Colombo, particularly on the High Level Road leading out towards Avisawella. The police opened fire, killing a number of people. The government called out the military, imposed a curfew and declared a state of emergency. Police shooting and intimidation continued.

All this was too much for the conscience of the Prime Minister who had publicly avowed his horror of violence. Despite the repeated pleas of influential friends anxious that he should continue in office and alarmed at the consequences to the country if he did not, the Prime Minister was adamant and resigned in October 1953. The new Prime Minister was the Leader of the House, Sir John Kotelawala. The food subsidies were partially restored soon after.

The *hartal* was political transformation of mass feeling which, but for the leadership and organization provided by the Left, might have wasted itself. The LSSP, with its Youth Leagues in particular, contained and gave a head to a volume of emotional pressure which ended by blowing a Prime Minister out of office. The ordinary man and woman felt themselves humiliated by the UNP Government. As they dramatized their plight in a telling Sinhalese phrase, the government had callously kicked the starving poor in their stomachs. It was probably an exaggeration, but this was how the action of the government in removing the subsidies was seen. Some of the *bhikkhus* who fasted on the morning of 12 August in the Colombo Town Hall may have been obeying the call of the Left to action. It is more likely that they in their own way, as honoured persons in the community, were involved in direct action similar to that taken by the crowds in the streets. (In

233

the *hartal* and the demonstrations following it the SLFP took no part.)

However they are evaluated, the events of 12 August 1953 showed how decidedly the mood of the country was expressing itself against the party in power. Had a general election followed, it is difficult to believe that the UNP under its new leader would have obtained a fresh mandate.

The new Prime Minister described himself as having been 'coaxed into politics' by the late D. S. Senanayake.[37] Sir John Kotelawala had been twenty-five years in active politics; he had been a Minister since 1936 and Leader of the House since 1951. He had very strongly developed in him one quality of the *élite* to which he belonged: its loyalty to its friends – an outlay of feeling which can often provide its investor with the comforting return of compensation for his own demission of responsibility. Had there been in the background of the new Prime Minister's immediate circle a friend with the qualities of experience of the late D. S. Senanayake, then perhaps his tenure of office might at least have been uneventful.

Unfortunately there was not. In addition, the mainstay of the UNP, Dudley Senanayake, retired temporarily from politics, leaving a Cabinet in which the removal of his restraint caused personal rifts to open wider between Ministers. The Minister of Commerce, R. G. Senanayake, left the Cabinet and the UNP not long after. The new Prime Minister was taken up by the Lake House Press, and, with the occasional reproof which guarantees the impartiality of the sponsor, was launched into a figure of world prominence whose immediate sphere of activity was South East Asia. 'For Alisander he was a trifle o'erparted', might well have been any observer's comment on the metamorphosis. The consequences of the Prime Minister's dedication of himself to the new role were fateful, for the country had only just before furnished unmistakable proof of its mood. The only role the head of the government at the time could have played should have been confined to domestic drama.

But tea prices were rising. They began to recover in 1953, and 1954 'saw the beginning of the best boom in the history of tea. The average price of tea rose from Rs 1/73 in 1952 to Rs 2/56 in 1954.'[38] The China Pact had stabilized the price of rubber at profitable rates to the producer. The vulnerability of the country's economic position had been stressed by the Commonwealth Consultative Committee.[39] Its correlate – its illusory buoyancy if export income went up even by 5 per cent – gave the UNP a feeling of security.

The Prime Minister therefore could accept the role cast for him and, as his own account of his performance shows, his two years and ten months of office were played against a backdrop of international concerns. In 1954 a Conference of South East Asia powers met in Colombo at his invitation when the French were engaged in the losing battle in Indo-China. It was the year, too, of the American-inspired South East Asia Treaty Organization. The meeting of Asian nations on the pattern on two previous conferences called by Nehru, served the useful purpose of drawing the attention of the Great Powers to the alarm they could cause by their continued intervention in Asian politics. Little, however came out of this 1954 meeting.[40]

In the same year the Prime Minister met Nehru in Delhi on the perennial topic of status of the plantation workers. The Indian Government was ready to accept as Indian citizens those who wished to register as such. But no real difference was made to the position of the plantation worker as a result of the talks.

Her Majesty the Queen and the Duke of Edinburgh visited Ceylon in April 1954. As Queen of England and also Queen of Ceylon she was received with great public enthusiasm and curiosity by the large crowds which lined streets, the railway track and villages during the events of her crowded programme in the tropical heat. While she was in Ceylon, she announced that on the termination of Lord Soulbury's fifth year as Governor-General Sir Oliver Goonetilleke would succeed him.

In 1955 twenty-nine nations, including Communist China, met at Bandung in Indonesia. On this occasion the Prime Minister attempted to steal the limelight with his condemnation of 'the new colonialism' of the Communist Powers. In the same year Ceylon was admitted to the United Nations Organization – the result of a package deal between the Soviet Union and the Western Powers.

But these excitements and displays had little to do with the immediate concerns of people in the country. The SLFP had already launched its campaign to make Sinhalese the official language of the country, and Buddhist leaders on the eve of *Buddha Jayanti* – the official celebration in 1956 of 2,500 years of Buddhism in the world – were agitating for adequate recognition of the claims of the religion after centuries of colonial rule. The activities of the Prime Minister and the UNP seemed to be rotating further and further on an axis of their own away from the centre of the country's strongest emotional interests. The spirit of life in *élite* circles in these years, with its unashamed revelling in corruption and the exhibitionism of its socialites, was caught remarkably well by H. C. N. de Lanerolle in his *Ralahamy* plays.[41]

In the end, with shows and circuses becoming more prominent as in the Marx Brothers film, orchestra and conductor drifted farther and farther on the lake where their raft had been moored. The conductor in desperation changed the score, but both orchestra and himself were lost in the distant horizon as events panned out to the General Election of April 1956 which routed the UNP and marked the end of nine years of its rule.

CHAPTER 11

A RECENT CONVERSION
1956-65

The events which preceded and followed the General Election of 1956 merit special attention, because they were at the time, and have been since then, regarded as the prelude to, and the consummation of, a social revolution in the country. An eminent historian's recent verdict repeats this opinion: 'The English-educated class which until 1956 exercised most influence had been overthrown and the Sinhalese-educated class had taken their place.'[1] To acknowledge the unexpectedness of the result of the General Election, unexpected no less by its victors than by the ruling party in power, is, however, not to grant that the change in the structure of power in the country was revolutionary. The new rulers did not belong to the masses who put them in power; those who were out – the UNP – still had, if heads were counted, a substantial following. Nor was the house built by the British pulled down and a new edifice put up in its stead. Had this followed, it would have been time to speak of the revolution.

What happened was, in the extended metaphor in which the politico-economic structure of Ceylon has been described in these pages, that as a result of demands made by the supporters of the new government an internal conversion of the old structure was carried out in the course of time. Some of the older features were modernized, in the way a stockbroker's Victorian mansion in Metroland can be turned into a set of flats without in any way altering the basic foundations, the four walls which enclose the old structure or the turrets which cap it. The lodge at the gates was put to other uses, but the house itself still presented the same face as of old, but for the disarray of the washing hanging out to dry from some of the windows, unthinkable in the august old days. Those who remembered its former dignity may well have shaken their heads at changes they lamented, but these did not add up to a revolution.

It was no revolution, whatever the joyous delirium which greeted the defeat of the UNP may have proclaimed. Those who travelled on the main roads of the western and southern parts of the country on the four nights of the elections will find it hard to forget the spontaneous joy – a folk pleasure as it seemed in its expression – with which every result announcing a fresh UNP reverse was received by voters round the radio of some wayside shop. Yet it was only the calendar of the feelings which made it a social revolution. The calendar of facts pointed to quite another day. Rarely does the one correspond with the other.

Those who believed that the General Election of 1956 heralded a social revolution must have swallowed unwittingly the hard lump of the UNP results which, properly chewed, should have made them cautious of accepting the opinion of contemporary sociologists that the mess was indeed a revolution. The UNP lost nearly 300,000 votes and forty-six seats; yet it very nearly maintained the voting strength of the party in 1947 and received more than half the votes cast in a General Election which brought out more voters than either of the two previous General Elections. Its apparatus of support in the country, despite the unfeigned joy of its opponents, remained more or less intact. The majority of the *élite*, business men in town and country, the landed gentry (Sinhalese- and English-speaking), the small shopkeepers and all their men, making up a fair mass following, were temporarily dashed, but soon were to recover their spirits.

Even if the demonstration of the strength of the UNP had not been so clear numerically, one look at the members of the coalition in power would have shown that most of them came from the class which had since 1931 provided the State Council and the House of Representatives with its members. The leader of the victorious group, S. W. R. D. Bandaranaike, was by family connection and upbringing an unusually distinguished member of the *élite*. His father, grandfather and ancestors for several generations had held high office under the Dutch and the British. He himself was the godson of a Colonial Governor. But he had become a Buddhist, had discarded the Western dress of the *élite* and was the founder of the Sinhala Maha Sabha. The greatest number of those returned as members of the House of Representatives belonged to the *élite* too. I. D. S. Weerawardana who made a special study of the General Election wrote: 'At least 75 per cent of the candidates had attended what are popularly called English-medium collegiate schools . . . from the point of view of education and occupation the preponderant majority of the candidates came from the middle-middle and upper-middle classes. Parliamentary leadership continues to remain in the hands of this class.'[2] The dress worn by most of the members of the ruling coalition and the preference of some of them for Sinhalese in debates may have given the impression that most of them came into the House from a social stratum as yet unrepresented there. Some of the rank and file of the MEP (the new coalition) belonged to the rural intelligentsia: 'many M.P.s had come to Parliament straight from the villages, often with no previous experience of politics. Their very dress and speech transformed the parliamentary scene.'[3]

But the Ministers in the new government were all of them from the *élite*. The Minister of Finance, who sported a monocle, would have impressed the Tailors and Cutters' Guide with the correctness of his clothes.

The defeat of the UNP, which polled 700,000 votes but won only eight seats, was facilitated by the electoral no-contest agreement between various parties opposed to it. Personal feelings between the leaders of the two groups of the LSSP prevented any pact between Philip Gunawardena's and Dr N. M. Perera's groups. The Tamils were occupied in fighting out the problem of politics in the North: which group – the old supporters of the UNP the Tamil Congress, or the FP – should represent the Tamil *élite*.

The atmosphere was so heavy with rumours and uncertainties in the pre-election period that the SLFP lost to the UNP one of its most important figures: Bernard Aluvihare, who had been member for Matale. Had he remained with the Bandaranaike group he would undoubtedly have been Leader of the House. Another figure lost to the UNP was P. de S. Kularatne, a prominent Buddhist educationist, who most certainly would have been the Minister of Education. These defections are indicative of the fluid state of party loyalties even on the eve of a General Election. They deprived the SLFP of dependable and experienced supporters who certainly would have exercised a moderating influence on passions which agitated the empty-headed members of the party.

The General Election of 1956 proved that the opponents of the UNP had heeded the lesson of 1952 – the necessity of understanding the strategic value of offering the voter the fewest possible choices in matters involving even the most rudimentary political principles and of appealing to him emotionally. The majority of those who fought the election against the UNP were ready to consent to a truce in order to defeat it. It was literally a popular front, but only for one specific battle – the General Election. With another leader the UNP might perhaps have fared better, but whether it would have been able to stand up to the violence of the sortie against it is doubtful.

When S. W. R. D. Bandaranaike resigned from the UNP in 1951 he placed himself at the disposal of those uncommitted by predilection or by receipt of favour to the party of the English-educated *élite*. His manifesto in the 1952 General Election differed from that of the ruling group in the emphasis on the place to be given to *Swabasha* (the country's own languages) and the promise of state aid for the development of Buddhism and to *Ayurveda* (the indigenous systems of medicine). At that time very little pressure apparently could have been generated out of these appeals to the voter. Four years later so strong was their force that they altered completely an important item in the programme of the SLFP, for by that time they had become the potent emotionalism of nationalism against which nothing could prevail. Even if the conduct of the high command of the UNP had not been offensive to the rural voter – as it undoubtedly was in the years between 1953 and 1956 – national feeling would have yet blown up a storm against it. The great achievement of the UNP – the new freedom of 1947 – could not generate any enthusiasm, not really even among the *élite*. It left completely cold all those who did not belong to the *élite*, particularly those who in the upper levels of the Sinhalese-speaking intelligentsia were reckoned persons of consequence: the *bhikkhu*, the village teacher and the Ayurvedic physician. To the *élite* these personages were lightweights in the economic and cultural scale and were dumped into a frowsy backroom of the structure of power. The *bhikkhu* had a long history of political activity in Ceylon during the Sinhalese kingdoms. The UNP had brought a few selected representatives into active politics in 1947 and had assumed that once they had performed what was expected of them they would retire into the backroom. This was not to happen. The few *bhikkhus* who came out against the UNP in 1947 stayed on right through the late 40s and early 50s as political activists. Their lead made it easier for the younger *bhikkhus* to become partisans of nationalist politics on a large scale. The village teacher and that large body of young men who had their education in Sinhalese, with or without the benefit of the Senior School Certificate to mark the end of their schooling, took political agitation much further. They could attend to all the chores the *bhikkhu* had to abstain from because of his traditional discipline.

The recommendation of the UNP as the party pledged to maintain and develop the new freedom gained in 1948 assumed the existence of a nation. The feeling worked up in the Sinhalese parts of the country in 1955 and 1956 claimed that both the nation and the religion had been scandalously neglected, almost bartered away in exchange for a way of life against which the opponents of the UNP revolted. As the passions of race and religion had been unloosed, there was a tendency to restrict identification with the nation to Sinhalese Buddhists alone.

In the absence of any documentation of the secret history of the political manœuvres of the time, it is impossible to say who was responsible for the decision that the slogan of the groups forming the Buddhist opposition to the UNP should be the salvation of the religion and the language. A University don, a highly placed civil servant and an important *bhikkhu* have at various times been credited with it.

Several Buddhist groups were already in the field. The *Eksath Bhikkshu Peramuna* (United Front of the *Bhikkhus*) was inaugurated deliberately on 4 February 1956, the anniversary of Independence Day, in order to signify its opposition to the ideals it attributed to the leaders of the newly independent country. There was the *Bhasa Peramuna* – a Language Front – and an association of Sinhalese school teachers. Both these groups and others were canvassing with vigour against the UNP. By the time the SLFP was invited to place itself at their head its leader had to give up his original programme for the country's languages. Only one language, and not two, could now be thought of as the official language of the country. This is clear from Weerawardana's account, which was apparently based on intimate knowledge of the formation of the new groups. He noted that 'the Executive Committee of the SLFP also bowed to the language storm in the country and decided that its language policy would be to make Sinhalese the official language with provision for the reasonable use of Tamil'.[4] He pointed out, too, that 'the S.L.F.P was not unaware of the criticism that its leader had once supported a motion which amounted to parity. It was argued that Mr Bandaranaike acquiesced in such a motion chiefly because in 1944 the issue was really between English and Swabasha.'[5] If the Executive Committee of the SLFP 'bowed to the language storm', its leader, S. W. R. D. Bandaranaike must have felt that with his formula of Sinhalese as official language and 'the reasonable use of Tamil' he could 'ride the whirlwind and control the storm'. He was not a racialist.

Early in 1956 a Buddhist commission, set up in 1954 by a number of Buddhist societies, presented its report. It had been compiled after numerous sittings in Colombo and the major provincial towns of Buddhist Ceylon over a period of two years by laymen belonging to the *élite*, who intended to bring pressure to bear on the UNP government to make radical changes in its political support to Buddhism in the year of the celebration of *Buddha Jayanti*. Its value lay in its recapitulation, with a show of authority, of the opposition throughout four centuries of the Christian rulers of Ceylon to Buddhism and its institutions. Whether it was intended as a political weapon or not, it became that in the emotional situation of the early months of 1956. Its resentment fed the flames of political feeling against a government which, in spite of all it claimed it had done for Buddhism and all it hoped to do, was now pilloried by Buddhist opinion in the country.

On 21 February 1956 the *Mahajana Eksath Peramuna* (Peoples' United Front), a coalition of the SLFP with various groups campaigning on religious and language issues and the one-time Trotskyist group of Philip Gunawardena, was formed. Only a few days before – on 17 and 18 February – the UNP at its Annual Sessions went back on the pledges given its Tamil members, and repeated by Sir John Kotelawala on his visit to Jaffna four months previously, and decided to make 'Sinhalese only' the main plank of its programme. On 18 February Parliament was dissolved and the General Election fixed for April. The UNP had trimmed its sails to the prevailing winds and hoped to ride out the storm. The LSSP, though it was officially for parity for both languages, had made an electoral agreement with the SLFP earlier; so had the CP.

The UNP switch-over from its official position of support for both languages lost it all its Tamil membership. In the North the Federal Party benefited from the alarm of the Tamils at the fierceness of the feeling roused in the South about the language issue. Attempts at patching up some electoral agreement between the major Tamil groups failed and the FP took the field as the party regarded as being dedicated to the Tamil cause with no compromise. No UNP or SLFP candidates contested any seats in the Northern Province, though there were some LSSP and CP candidates. The language agitation was beginning to split the country effectively into two.

The General Election of April 1956 destroyed the UNP as a parliamentary group, but left it as a major party in the country, with its new colours of Sinhala Only rather bedraggled but none the less firmly nailed to the mast. It could still count on a large element of Moslem support in the south and the northwest where most Moslems spoke Sinhalese. The MEP with its fifty-one seats, helped by the usual readiness of most Independents (some sixty-four contested the election) to jump on the bandwagon, had an absolute majority and formed the new government. Now that the no-contest pact was no longer valid, the LSSP with its fourteen seats was the largest group in the opposition and Dr N. M. Perera became Leader of the Opposition. The FP won ten seats and the CP three. The swing against the UNP can be gauged by results in Dambadeniya and Kelaniya, where R. G. Senanayake, one of its stalwarts now standing as an Independent, won both, defeating his cousin J. R. Jayawardena, the UNP member for Kelaniya. He continued to represent both constitutencies in the House.

The clue to the sequence of events in the MEP Government of 1956–9 can be unravelled out of the tangled skein of the election campaign and the character of the coalition S.W. R. D. Bandaranaike came to lead. First of all the nationalist emotion wound into it was going to give the strongest twist to the ultimate fabric. Whatever the benevolent professions of manifestos, the aggressiveness marking the campaign could not have existed and continued without an object on which it could be discharged. In addition, the UNP though defeated was not to be outdone by any of the victorious groups and made its own violent contribution to racial and religious intolerance. It is a banality that institutionalized religion bears little resemblance to the teaching of its founders. The hostility of *bhikkhus* and Buddhist leaders to Tamils, Roman Catholics, and all others who drew their fire, was more reminiscent of the fanaticism of Tertullian or Torquemada than of anything which might have been culled out of the *suttas*.

How to control this aggressiveness was the new Prime Minister's first difficulty. His second was that the electoral agreement which guaranteed the MEP its victory at the polls gave him neither a unified cabinet nor any respite from the resumption of party warfare once the armistice was over. The MEP had been scorned by the UNP as being a kind of dog's breakfast of all sorts of unsavoury bits and pieces from everywhere. The elements which composed it, except for the SLFP, owed loyalty not to the Prime Minister but to various pressure groups. They now put in their claims for services rendered and had to be rewarded with Ministries for their nominees. The MEP was not a party. It had no funds. Its campaign was financed by various private persons, among whom were *bhikkhus*, and a rank and file who dipped into their own pockets. It was a do-it-yourself structure by contrast with a party organization. It has been remarked of the peasant in Ceylon that he is more interested in the distributive side of production than in any other. So indeed are most human beings who tend to demand a quick return to any investment they have made. In the country there were a medley of people waiting to cash in on the accession to power of the friends whom they had backed. No scruples were going to restrain them in the demands they made or in means they used to press them.

The new Cabinet, composed of SLFP stalwarts whose connections with the party went back to *Sinhala Maha Sabha* days, a small Marxist group led by Philip Gunawardena, and the nominees of pressure groups, gave the Prime Minister a divided following. Its only dependable section, that of the SLFP, lacked any figure of more than average ability. The two Marxist Ministers were clear about the objectives they pursued. The rest, with the exception of the Prime Minister, were unfortunately given more to the exercise of self-publicity than to any other activity. Divisions in his Cabinet and the mediocrity of its talents forced the Prime Minister into a monotony of tropological language in the House and in public for which he was continually criticized. In truth he was trying to spin out of his own severely taxed resources threads with which his Cabinet Ministers should have provided him.

The three years of the Bandaranaike Government resolved itself accordingly into a series of crises, each sharper and more exhausting than the last to the body politic. The first arose out of the vehemence of the language campaign. In his incredulous scorn for the excuses made by the previous government the new Prime Minister had promised that once in power he would make Sinhalese the official language of the country within twenty-four hours. His government was therefore pressed into precipitate action to implement this part of his election programme. In June 1956 the Sinhala Only Bill was introduced in Parliament and the Tamil members of the House protested against it by a peaceful *satyagraha* (passive resistance). This was the signal for ugly scenes on Galle Face Green in Colombo, where the Tamil members staged their sit-down 'strike', and in the Gal Oya Valley where Tamil colonists were beaten up by Sinhalese. The situation in Gal Oya which threatened to become catastrophic was saved by the personal courage of the Sinhalese Deputy Inspector General of Police.

The *Swabasha* campaign – for the rightful place of both languages of the country – had everything to recommend it. It aimed at putting an end to economic and social discrimination against the majority of the country's citizens. English, the language of the administration and of the secondary schools which provided most of its employees, was spoken by less than 5 per cent of the population. It meant, in fact, that the common man could not be understood in all government offices, in hospitals, police stations, in all but the rural courts, except through the medium of interpreters. As a second language some English had been available in government schools from the beginning of the century, but this could not replace the mother tongue for the villager and for the working-class townsman, whether Sinhalese or Tamil. As a result of its economic value and its prestige as the language of the rulers, English forced a language like Sinhalese, spoken only by eight million people in Ceylon and nowhere else in the world, into an inferior position and made it suffer from desuetude. Though Tamil, the language of two million people in Ceylon (if the stateless plantation workers are included) was the spoken language of thirty millions in India, its inferior position in Ceylon was no different from that of Sinhalese in relation to everyday life. Its greater use in South India in no way compensated for its degraded position in Ceylon. Danger of South Indian domination was the product of Sinhalese fears of Tamil reactions to the suppression of their language by a Sinhala Only policy. It was more the result of Sinhalese feelings of guilt than any Tamil policy.

Sinhala Only, without regard for other language groups in the island, could not but be resisted by the Ceylon Tamils – a minority of nearly one million persons who were citizens of Ceylon.[6] Its sharp edge was in its economic point. If there was a larger number of Tamils in the service of the state than in proportion to their numbers in the country, this was due to their greater industry and thrift. British rule, which had made Ceylon one after the lapse of several centuries, had permitted all those who had reached a certain level of proficiency in English to enter the administration. The effect of Sinhala Only, had it been implemented immediately as its most enthusiastic propagandists were demanding, would have inflicted severe hardship on those who could not be expected to satisfy the new language demands. The Prime Minister, anxious to be responsible neither for the partition of the country – as the FP demand for a federal form of government was interpreted – nor for deliberate unfairness to anyone on racial grounds, was disposed to negotiate with the Tamil leaders on safeguards, and particularly on a definition acceptable to them of what 'the reasonable use of Tamil' should be.

But he was fated never to be able to carry these negotiations far. Strong pressure against which his intelligence revolted was being put on him by those who had, according to their reading of events, been solely responsible for putting him in power. The Prime Minister's tendency to temporize in the face of emotional blackmail led him to believe he could postpone disaster by taking things into his own hands for the time being. But too many strains were being brought to bear upon the organization of law and order in the country for temporizing to have helped. Groups in power were claiming special privileges for themselves, interfering, through permanent secretaries to ministries, with the discipline of the public service and sapping it of any morale it possessed.

The Prime Minister did not, as he had promised, immediately set about making Ceylon a republic, but he honoured that part of his election manifesto which undertook to examine the Defence Agreements with the UK, since the foreign policy of his government was non-alignment with any power bloc. The agreements concluded between D. S. Senanayake and the British Government about the use of Trincomalee and the air base at Katunayake were abrogated. As has been noted earlier, no secret clauses were discovered in these agreements. Changed conceptions of naval and air strategy since the development of nuclear missiles made Trincomalee less valuable to the British as a potential naval base. The RAF found a staging-post in the Maldive Islands not far from the western coast of Ceylon.

In the convulsions of those times it is scarcely credible that anything positive could have been achieved by a government under continual pressure from warring groups in the party. The speech from the throne had stated that 'in pursuance of its socialist policy my government will take early steps, where the best interests of the country so require, to nationalise certain essential services such as transport'.[7] It should be remarked in this context that the word 'socialism' in Ceylon, as used by non-Marxist parties, has never been more than a gesture of hope which calls for charity in interpretation. In a mixed economy like that of Ceylon, where the country's most valuable assets were in foreign hands and where the volume of saving was small, the state was committed to the task of financing development. This fitted in with the traditional attitude of acceptance of the notion of patronage from above. 'Socialism' was neither a political creed nor an economic programme, it was an emotional demand. As such it could quite easily and naturally feature in the programmes of political parties diametrically opposed to each other in their aims. It had something of the flavour given it by Edward, Prince of Wales, when he made the remark in 1895 that 'we are all socialists now'.

Political expediency decided that all private transport should be 'taken over' by the state on 1 July 1958. This was emotionally satisfying to the opponents of the powerful UNP lobby of the bus tycoons and their friends. But it had been so long expected by the operators and their business-like lawyers that the assets of the companies were milked beforehand. Besides the Press was uniformly hostile to nationalization and exaggerated the consequences of the take over. The Ceylon Transport Board, on the nationalization of the private transport companies, took over all their vehicles, depots and the greater part of their personnel. The CTB was the prototype of all such nationalized services, and faced the two difficulties of lack of managerial skill and political interference in the smallest matters of administration. It provided the cheapest transport in the world, since it was a public service which raised fares at its peril. Only after five years was it able to show a profit on its working.

The Port of Colombo Development Project, initiated by the previous government, was completed in 1956. It had been an expensive programme of modernization, giving the island's major port increased warehouse space, more alongside berths and facilities for mechanized handling of cargo. If the modernized port was unable to meet the shipping needs of Colombo and Ceylon, the reason has to be sought not so much in inadequacies of planning but in the vagaries of the political situation, another consequence of the support given to the Prime Minister by political groupings. The Minister of Agriculture and Food was Philip Gunawardena, once a powerful figure among harbour workers as he had organized one of their unions. The personal vendetta carried on by him against the union of his one-time LSSP colleagues led to a series of strikes which held up cargoes to the port and at other times congested warehouses. In August 1958 the government nationalized the handling of cargoes in Colombo, taking over the numerous private operators. But as long as dockers were pawns in the power politics of Cabinet Ministers, Party leaders and Union bosses there could be no improvement in the efficiency of the port of Colombo. The consequence of the long delays in handling cargo was a rise in freight charges and the imposition of surcharges by the Shipping Conference on all cargoes to Ceylon. These, in turn, have meant an increase in the cost of living and a further drain on foreign exchange.

In 1958 Philip Gunawardena introduced his Paddy Lands Bill, intended to give the peasant cultivator the security of tenure without which he could not be encouraged to improve his methods of cultivation. As the bill was sponsored by one of the two Marxist Ministers in the Cabinet, it was looked at with suspicion by the rest and by vested interests in the country (some of them close to the Prime Minister himself). The bill attempted to deal with what had been noted in British times as the major difficulty of the tenant cultivator. The Administration Reports of Government Agents had stressed the importance of security of tenure even over water,[8] if greater productivity was to be ensured. The new bill was intended to be the charter of the peasant, who was to be further helped by a Co-operative Development Bank which would have relieved him of his chronic indebtedness. Personal opposition to these measures by the right wing of the Cabinet was so marked that when the Paddy Lands Bill was passed with its teeth drawn, and the Prime Minister to prevent further dissension took over some of the departments previously controlled by the two Marxist Ministers, they resigned in May 1959.[9]

On two fronts: the industrial, where creeping inflation had intensified workers' agitation for higher wages; and the language, where all attempts to arrive at a negotiated settlement with the Tamils were being actively sabotaged by militant groups in the country, the Prime Minister was more and more involved in struggling on his own and trying to maintain some semblance of order. Infirmity of control was visible everywhere. The administration, weakened by political interference and the consequent frustration of the public service, had reached a low level of efficiency.

In the Tamil areas in the North a campaign of blacking out the Sinhalese letter *Sri* on the number-plates of motor vehicles and nationalized buses set going a campaign in the South to harass and boycott Tamil-owned shops. In this atmosphere of strikes, counter-strikes and the fulmination of fanatical Sinhalese groups against any 'surrender' to the Tamils, the Prime Minister had met the leader of the FP to discuss with him the problem of ironing out Tamil opposition to the Sinhala Only Act. Negotiations between the two had reached the stage of a Pact – the Bandaranaike-Chelvanayakam Pact as it was called – and at the Annual Sessions of the SLFP in March 1958 the Prime Minister expressed his satisfaction that a settlement had been reached.[10] Surmise about the Pact and opposition to any concession to the Tamils set off a further series of incidents of racial hatred in the South. In April a group of fanatical *bhikkhus* forced the Prime Minister by their sit-down strike outside his residence in Colombo to abrogate any arrangements he had made with the leader of the FP. His formal denunciation of the Pact only encouraged the racialists to go further. The FP had called a Convention for the end of May in Vavuniya. Sabotage of trains carrying Tamils to this Convention in the Northern Province and an explosion in which a number of Sinhalese were killed were the prelude to four days of mob law and racial violence as had not been thought possible in Ceylon.

To dwell on the horrors of those four days in which murder, rape, arson and mutilation were commonplaces is only to court disbelief. But cases still being called at sessions of the Supreme Court reduce the hearers of such excesses of racial hatred to tears. Tamils all over the South, the West and Central Ceylon were the victims of savage treatment at the hands of Sinhalese mobs. In the Eastern Province Tamils set upon Sinhalese in grim retaliation for atrocities in the South. In Jaffna there was no loss of life, but a Buddhist shrine was wrecked. From 24 to 27 May, and even later in certain parts of the island, law and order were maintained only by those who had courage to act. The disturbances were larger in scale and fiercer in intensity than any since the Kandyan 'Rebellion' of 1817.

Firmness could have prevented the worst excesses, had it been shown on 24 May when the first wave of general violence engulfed the Tamils in various parts of the island. But the police were paralysed as a force because of contradictory instructions given them and the reluctance of most officers to brave the wrath of politicians. In addition the strikes in Colombo were used by racial elements to add confusion to the disaster already imminent. It has to be said, too, that there were sections in the police force not averse to indulging in racialism themselves.

Despite appeals to the Prime Minister to have a state of emergency declared, nothing happened and chaos reigned. On Tuesday, 2 May the Governor-General, Sir Oliver Goonetilleke, declared a state of emergency, because of, or following upon, the widely publicized statement of the LSSP that their youth leagues and trade unions would try to take over control of the situation. Whether they would have been able to deal with the desperateness of the situation is doubtful. The state of emergency proclaimed on 27 May 1958 lasted until March 1959.

In a situation which called for quick decision and extreme measures Sir Oliver Goonetilleke undoubtedly saved the country from anarchy. His calmness, the dispatch with which he used the wide powers he assumed, such as no Colonial Governor had ever wielded, were in the best colonial tradition. He measured up to his task, being in the first two months of the emergency the administrative and executive head of the country, the Commander-in-Chief of its armed forces and in constant touch with the front line. He was, in addition, chief Press Authority. His action may have been 'without precedent in the recent history of the constitutional government of this country or of the United Kingdom',[11] but the events he had to cope with were without precedent either. The remarks attributed to him, as he greeted pressmen summoned to Queen's House on 27 May: 'When you report the news in future please don't say that I am running the sh-sh-show. I don't want all kinds of jealousies to come up, you know . . .'[12], were typical of his understanding of the situation and his far-sightedness. Had he not taken over, hundreds more would have lost their lives.

The failure of the government at this juncture was a blot on the Prime Minister's reputation. His tolerance of the fanatical pressure groups continually haranguing him had been carried to such lengths that the fools he suffered were encouraged into embarking upon courses of dangerous lunacy.

The army and the navy dealt with the situation as it should have been handled when the mob first took the law into its own hands. Quiet was soon restored, but the state of emergency continued.

The greatest sufferers in the four days of violence were the Tamils. A number of them owed their lives to Sinhalese who risked their own to help and protect them. Numerous deeds of quiet heroism have been recounted, but the events of those four days, when everything is considered, brought no credit to the country's pride in its Buddhist heritage. Nothing is to be gained now by trying to apportion responsibility for the disaster, but a careful investigation into its causes, when passions have died down, is the only office that can be performed in memory of the many hundreds who lost their lives in it. Racial violence had physically divided the two major communities in the island as they had not been divided since the end of the eighteenth century. Refugee Tamils from Colombo and the South had to be transported by sea to the North, because the roads between Colombo and Jaffna were unsafe for them.

The contents of the bulletins broadcast by Radio Ceylon during the disturbances showed a meanness of spirit in keeping with the depths into which the country had sunk. The broadcasting services were a government department; their use by the party in power proved another deplorable result of the incursion of party politics into the administration.

In February 1959 renewed industrial unrest and the desire of the government to invest itself with the widest powers against any future emergency led to the Public Security (Amendment) Act. It was suggested openly in the House (and obliquely in newspapers) that the Governor-General had actively interested himself in preparing the details of the bill.

In September 1959 a government whose accession to power had been celebrated by public demonstrations of joy lost its leader as the result of an act of private vengeance. On 25 September S. W. R. D. Bandaranaike was assassinated by a *bhikkhu*, disappointed in his hopes of becoming a lecturer in the College of Indigenous Medicine. With a revolver concealed in his robes he went to the residence of the Prime Minister and fired at him at close range. In his short and sudden confrontation with death, the many weaknesses the Prime Minister had shown in his political career were forgotten in the admiration of the serenity with which he accepted his fate. To the shocked Buddhist masses the magnanimity with which he referred to those responsible for his death outweighed remembrance of what he had failed to do and what his indecision had brought about.

His lying in state and cremation in the grounds of his ancestral home in Veyangoda became part of a legend which grew up within a few days of his assassination about his plans for the country. By rural folk he came to be regarded as a *Bodhisattva*, or a being destined ultimately to attain enlightenment.

A fresh state of emergency was declared by the Governor-General on 25 September and a period of political confusion followed. The Leader of the House was ill and away from the country. The senior member of the Cabinet, W. Dahanayake, was elected Prime Minister. Rumour, which settled thick on every detail of the events preceding and following the assassination of the Prime Minister, could be stirred only in the House of Representatives. It was impossible to touch it outside those privileged precincts, even if there had been no state of emergency. It had been obvious for some months before the assassination that one of the groups which believed itself responsible for the election victory of the MEP in 1956 had expressed its grave dissatisfaction with the Prime Minister over the failure of one of its nominees to secure a profitable shipping contract. The incumbent of the important *Raja Maha Vihara* in Kelaniya, one of the sacred sites of Buddhism in Ceylon, was one of the disappointed parties. He was one of the accused. Among the others were the *bhikkhu* responsible for the shooting and regarded as only a tool in the conspiracy, and the Minister of Health, the first woman to hold Cabinet rank in Ceylon. She was discharged in the course of non-summary proceedings in the Magistrate's Court.

In November 1959, in a state of growing confusion with accusations and denials flung across benches in the House, the Capital Punishment (Repeal) Act was passed. By it the death penalty which had been suspended in 1958 was not only brought back but also made retroactive. After a long Supreme Court trial the *bhikkhu* who shot the Prime Minister was sentenced to death and hanged. The High Priest of the Kelaniya *Vihara*, regarded as being the major figure in the conspiracy, escaped with life imprisonment, though the mover of the bill, C. P. de Silva, was quite frank that its intention was to 'make special provision for the offenders convicted of conspiracy to murder the late Prime Minister'. As it was framed the Act inadvertently failed to attach the death penalty to the particular offence of 'conspiracy to murder'. A third accused charged with the same offence similarly escaped death by hanging and received a sentence of life imprisonment. It should be noted that the provisions of this bill were strongly criticized in the House by the opposition.

The new Prime Minister, W. Dahanayake, set upon by his critics in the House and the Press, found himself in difficulties with his Cabinet. He was no longer the man he was in his early days in the State Council as the Member for Bibile. He had never taken happily to discipline, but preferred to blaze his own trail, following a rather circuitous route and on occasion whirling a dangerous axe. He soon set about forming his own party, for it was clear that his 'caretaker government', as he himself described it, was not going to last. He had sent too many of its members packing. His 'Political Notebook', put on the air by Radio Ceylon was an unjustifiable use of the state broadcasting services, but it made no difference to the political chances of his new party. He promised that he would ensure a quiet and orderly General Election in March 1960, and this promise he kept. The party he inaugurated failed to justify any of the hopes the Prime Minister built into it, and he and it were swept away in the March election. The ex-Prime Minister bobbed up again in the House, as he was too buoyant a personality to be kept down for long.

The SLFP, led by C. P. de Silva, the former Leader of the House in the Bandaranaike Government, failed to command the support which S. W. R. D. Bandaranaike once rallied. Even the circumstances of his death and the veneration paid to his memory seemed to add little to the appeal of his party until the final stages of the campaign, when Mrs Bandaranaike, who had up to that time never been on a political platform, was persuaded into helping the SLFP.

The campaign was notable chiefly for its vociferousness, the multitude of its promises and the appeal to chauvinistic nationalism by both the SLFP and the UNP, now led by Dudley Senanayake, who had emerged from his retirement from politics in 1959.

The General Election of March 1960 was contested by a number of parties, each for itself and fanatically opposed to all the others. The UNP won the largest number of seats in the House, fifty, but had no absolute majority. It had refused, during the campaign and after to make any concession to Tamil claims. The SLFP gained forty-six seats. The LSSP, tarred by Sinhalese nationalists with the brush of being Indian and Tamil lovers, failed to make any headway, polling about the same number of votes as before but winning only ten seats. Philip Gunawardena, who kept the name MEP for his own mixture of traditional nationalism, contemporary communalism and Marxism, and his group won ten seats too. The FP again secured a bloc of seats in the Tamil areas, fifteen this time.

The UNP Government of Dudley Senanayake was obviously not destined to last long. The one significant change in the policy of a Prime Minister who seven years earlier had refused to alter his decision to cut down the food subsidies, was his immediate reduction of the price of rationed rice. Any possible opponents were apparently to have their guns spiked in advance. With regard to the inflammatory issue of language, the UNP was even more stubborn than the SLFP in its policy of no compromise with the Tamils. The government was defeated within a month of taking office, Parliament was dissolved and a General Election fixed for July.

The election campaign of July 1960 brought Mrs Bandaranaike into the field as the leader of her late husband's party. Her inexperience in politics was no handicap, because she raised no specific political issues, but asked the voter to return her late husband's party to power so that his programme could be carried out. She was subjected to a newspaper campaign of vilification and coarse ridicule, which defeated its own ends by outraging a section of the public which might otherwise have remained neutral. The backlash, in the new journalese, cost the UNP quite a few votes. Its campaign outdid its earlier chauvinism: a map of Ceylon was displayed with regions in the Central Province shaded red – sold by the SLFP to the Tamils and to India. In the mêlée of election campaigns in Ceylon it is impossible to discover who does what. Had the leader of the UNP been consulted about this piece of propaganda, he should have forbidden it; if he was not, he should have dissociated himself from it and had it withdrawn.

Mrs Bandaranaike's strong emotional appeal to the voter was seconded by an electoral agreement between the SLFP and the parties opposed to the UNP in the Sinhalese areas. The result of the General Election was a victory reminiscent of 1956 for Mrs Bandaranaike's party. It won seventy-five seats and could form a government on its own. The UNP lost twenty seats, but its voting strength improved from 829,636 in March to 1,143,290 in July. Once again the combination of an emotional appeal and an electoral agreement had produced a clear result.

Support for the SLFP in July 1960 had come primarily from elements different from those which had put S. W. R. D. Bandaranaike in power in 1956. The *bhikkhus*, after the assassination of the Prime Minister in 1959, had withdrawn from political platforms. The upper levels of the Sinhalese intelligentsia – Ayurvedic physicians and teachers – disappointed at the poor return for the unstinted support they had given the party were not as prominent as before. The younger men in the villages still gave the SLFP their support, though they, too, were tending to be openly critical. The mass vote in rural areas went to it, because by and large the lot of the ordinary villager, in spite of the corruption of middlemen, had improved. Rural voters were further removed than urban workers from the inroads of inflation and housing difficulties. The appeal to national chauvinism was in addition something with which they could sympathize.

The Left and the FP miscalculated the results of the election. The Left underestimated the weight of conservatism in rural areas. Like the FP it had expected to be in a strong bargaining position, but the new government did not need to seek any aid from either.

So, for the first time in the history of any country, a woman held the office of Prime Minister. This remarkable event should not be interpreted as proving anything about the position of women in Ceylon. A woman became Prime Minister of Ceylon because of her late husband's reputation in the country. Mrs Bandaranaike was nominated to the Senate and took the portfolio of External Affairs and Defence. The UNP, as the strongest party in the House, provided the Leader of the Opposition, Dudley Senanayake.

Lack of political apprenticeship had been no handicap to Mrs Bandaranaike in her election campaign. But what she needed, more than her husband had needed it in 1956, was a dependable and efficient Cabinet. As a woman, and particularly as a member of a conservative aristocratic Kandyan family, she could not personally take part in the day-to-day exchanges of political life as a man might have done. By tradition she could not, nor indeed did she wish to, mix freely with her colleagues in the Cabinet or in the party. Most of those on whom she had to depend were unable to handle the tasks assigned to them. Of most of them neither stability nor responsibility could be expected. Prone to mistake desire to be geniuses of political and economic wisdom for possession of the means which alone could have ensured this, they were consumed with a *folie de grandeur* which cost the Prime Minister and the country dear.

Mrs Bandaranaike took office at a time when two crises, the one natural, the other artificially induced, were throwing a severer strain on the country than ever before. The first was incidental to the economic structure and was basically no different from those affecting other countries in the world, in the highly industrialized West and in the underdeveloped backwaters of Asia: difficulties with the balance of payments, of increasing gross productivity and with inflation. Since 1956 the country's external assets had taken a downward turn and kept dropping lower. They stood at Rs. m 1,061·9 in 1956 and were Rs. m 541·3 in 1960, falling in 1964 to Rs. m 423.

The economic structure responded as well as it could to the strain placed on it. Tea production, still providing the country with nearly two-thirds of its revenue from exports, was increased to levels unknown before. Conventional modes of dealing with the crisis through increased taxation, control of imports and of exchange were resorted to.

But these fiscal expedients were not really adequate to cope with one recurring feature of the crisis which, again, is incidental to all countries of the world: 'the population explosion', a cliché which turns into immutable act of God what ought to be a manageable human situation. In Ceylon the population at eight million in 1953 was to rise by two-and-a-half million in ten years. Even if conventional fiscal policies could have coped with these consequences, the storm of resistance to Mrs Bandaranaike's first Finance Minister's attempt to deal with it in 1962 by cutting the ration of rice by a quarter (and his resignation) showed that palliatives or solutions of the difficulty would have to be sought elsewhere.

The government was committed to deficit financing in its budgets, to controls which generated shortages, to an inflationary rise in prices, all of which deepened the effects of crisis, because of a lack of efficient and honest administration and political control without which no financial measures could be effective.

Dependence on foreign aid, which became a more significant item in the country's revenue, was an unreliable prop too. As aid from the Communist bloc and China grew, that from its opponents declined. The political attitudes and interests of the donor countries were almost always involved in the aid they provided. Nationalization and the attempt to cut down the profits made by the private sector upset the USA; the recognition, beyond a certain point, of the East German Government offended the West Germans. Furthermore aid, as it was often linked to specific projects, might be unexpended, mismanaged, or incapable of realizing the expected returns. Before long it became clear that radical changes in the economic structure were called for if the country's needs were going to be met.

But unfortunately the government's response to the crisis was to superimpose on it a crisis of its own making, which developed out of the power politics of rival groups in the Cabinet, and the attitude of some of the government's most influential supporters in the country. They were involved in a cardboard and string project of social engineering by which the religious and political institutions (so far as any blueprints for these could have been resurrected) of the glorious past were going to be restored. In a situation which called for solutions in keeping with the demands of a technological age, there was the unfortunate example of a National Commission on Education in 1962, which proposed to regulate admission to universities and technical colleges on religious and racial quotas. There were members of the Commission who dissented, but the general trend was clear. There were, in addition, business men anxious to cash in on the government's programme of the Ceylonization of trade and to make a quick profit by selling licences to import goods and not trading at all; racialists keen on harrying minorities; public servants dedicated to their duty of forcing government policy in directions they had decided for it. As time went on the government's difficulties assumed the character of a nightmarish football match: players changed their jerseys and attacked their own goal; clamorous groups on the side-lines shouted abuse, interfered with the referee and occasionally swung the area of play into the ranks of the spectators; the game being called off when the centre-forward stabbed the captain and transferred himself to the other side.

The main promise made by the SLFP in its election manifesto was that it would carry out the late S. W. R. D. Bandaranaike's 'socialist' policies. What was specified in this programme, as has been noted, was the nationalization of certain services 'where the best interests of the country so required'. Transport and the handling of cargo in the port of Colombo had already been taken over. In 1958 one of the economists consulted by the MEP Government, N. Kaldor, suggested 'a partial nationalization of insurance and banking in order to obtain public control over the investments of funds in banks and insurance companies'.[13] These were objectives within reach of any well-organized administration, but the way in which Kaldor's proposals for taxation were sampled by the unmethodical Finance Ministry in 1958 was not a hopeful augury that advice would, or could, be taken. The result of the new tax proposals was confusion, not only to the tax payer but also to the taxing authorities.

Nor was the government helped by the poor publicity gained by some of the State Corporations. Most of them, having struggled against the twin difficulties of persuading the mass of their workers that they were not entitled, either on the strength of having voted for the government or as members of a union, to living at the expense of the community, and of persistent political interference, were beginning to provide a range of import substitutes.[14]

But there were others, the story of whose operations, if it had not been a grave indictment of the managerial skill available to the country and of deplorable laxity in public control, would be high comedy. The National Salt Corporation was buying derelict buses in order to produce a harbour at Hambantota by dumping them into the sea; the Chemicals Corporation at Paranthan, where the temperature throughout the year is over 80° F, spent a large sum reinforcing its roof in order that it should bear the weight of a load of snow.[15]

Industrial unrest was once again causing chaos at the port of Colombo. Delays there had forced exporters of tea to use Trincomalee in order to speed shipments abroad. On a scale undreamt of in its history Trincomalee had become a commercial port. By 1963 the bulk of the island's tea was being shipped from there, not even the disastrous cyclone of 1964 could for long affect its use.

The permanent crisis in which the government found itself could be measured in the frequency of changes in the Ministry of Finance – there were no less than five in four years – and of the declaration of states of emergency and the prorogation of Parliament.

The government's programme, inadequately planned and imperfectly executed, confirmed its opponents in their hostility to it and won it no new friends. In 1961 the Language of the Courts Act vexatiously refused to allow Courts records to be kept in Tamil in Tamil-speaking areas. This provoked a *satyagraha* campaign in the north which was unnecessarily handled by the army, and the declaration of a state of emergency.

Since 1944 education in all schools but those privately owned was free. Assisted schools – those in receipt of government grants – charged no fees, but were still under the management of various religious bodies, the majority of them being Christian. In 1961 all Grade III schools were taken over, and secondary schools, of Grades I and II, were to be allowed to claim grant only in respect of those pupils who were of the same religious denomination as the management of the school. (This had been a demand made by the Buddhist Commission five years earlier.) This meant the end of all secondary schools run by the Christian missions, except the few which were already private schools. The take-over of all schools with their buildings and equipment roused very dangerous feelings of indignation, particularly among Roman Catholics. The government was saved from the grave situation it had on its hands by the personal intervention of Nehru with the leader of the Catholic hierarchy in India.[16] The take-over was followed by no attempt at a rationalization of the system or any diversification of the curriculum, which might have been some justification of the measure.

The plan to put an end to the monopoly of the Press and to vest its control in a public corporation – a measure aimed specifically at the Associated Newspapers of Ceylon – had been mentioned during the Prime Ministership of S. W. R. D. Bandaranaike. It became a constant preoccupation of his widow's government. Of course she could not hope for any quarter from the Press, and particularly not from the Associated Newspapers of Ceylon. Indeed there was no reason why any efficient newspaper organization should not have used all its weapons against a political opponent.

Certain features of the structure of ownership of the Press, attacked in Ceylon, have been under fire in other parts of the world too. Douglas Jay, President of the Board of Trade, recently described these as 'potentially an insidious threat to real democracy in this country'.[17] Bills for controlling the Press were continually before the House in Ceylon and were withdrawn. The Government's suggested modes of control through Press Councils and Press Tribunals did not dispel the justifiable feeling that one kind of misrepresentation was going to be substituted for another.

In 1962 a clear sign of the divisions in the country was provided by the discovery of a *coup* planned by high-ranking army and police officers. They intended to take over the government and also to incarcerate certain Left politicians. But, except for the arrest of an M.P., the rest of the conspiracy did not go beyond the stage of instructions in writing by a group of officers who, uncertain of success, shelved their plans. The government was informed and those concerned – all of them upper-class *élite*, some of them Aldershot trained – underwent a long trial of three years which ended in the sentencing of ten of the principals to a term of imprisonment and to forfeiture of their property. This penalty was devised in advance by the passing of the Criminal Law (Special Provisions) Act of 1962. The judges who tried the case made the following reference to the Act:

But we must draw attention to the fact that the Act of 1962 radically altered *ex post facto* the punishment to which the Defendants are rendered liable. The act removed the discretion of the Court as to the period of sentence to be imposed and compels the Court to impose a term of ten years' imprisonment, although we would have wished to differentiate in the matter of sentence between those who organised the conspiracy and those who were induced to join it. It also imposes a compulsory forfeiture of property. These amendments were not merely retroactive; they were also *ad hoc*, applicable only to the conspiracy which was the subject of the charges we have tried. We are unable to understand this discrimination. To the Courts, which must be free of political bias, treasonable offences are equally heinous, whatever be the complexion of the Government in power or whoever be the offender.

Coups had been topics of gossip before 1962, but the prospect of military rule had never been seriously regarded. Since then, however, the political loyalty of both army and police have been the subject of interested speculation and calculation by politicians.

Another state of emergency followed the discovery of this conspiracy. Rumours arising out of it were used by elements in the government unfriendly to the Governor-General to force him out of his office, though he had no connection with the attempted coup. Sir Oliver paid the penalty for superior powers of mind which cast a continual reproach on the self-esteem of small persons. Throughout his long public career – a career of great distinction – highly regarded and popular as he was, he was always viewed with cautious respect because of his cleverness. Something of this feeling comes through the comments made by Sir Henry Moore who knew him well.[18] Sir Oliver had been the outstandingly successful public servant of his time and during the chaotic times of 1958 had brought order back into the country. He was succeeded by W. Gopallawa, a Kandyan lawyer who had been Municipal Commissioner of Colombo and later ambassador to the USA. He belonged to the family circle of the Prime Minister.

The government had been two years in office and was losing the support of its most loyal following in the country: the young Sinhalese-educated voters in rural constituencies who expected to find work and a place in the community awaiting them after their years of schooling. They had been given the vote and were likely to be an imponderable factor in future elections. The schoolgoing population was increasing; so were unemployment and under-employment, both of them difficult to assess in a country where statistics were not carefully kept and where hardship was masked by the family system and traditional acceptance of low standards of living. The effect of population growth on future planning made Professor Joan Robinson, who paid a brief visit to Ceylon in 1958 and prepared a memorandum for the government on planning, revise her earlier optimism: 'New estimates of future population show larger growth.'[19] Between 1931 and 1953 the population rose from 6·7 million to 8·1 million and it was continuing to grow at not less than 2·6 per cent per annum. In 1963 the population stood at 10,664,809 – an increase of 31 per cent since the 1953 census.

Foreign aid, some of which was being drained away by current financial difficulties and not being expended on development programmes, was jeopardized by the take-over of the oil installations and assets in Ceylon of the American and British commercial oil companies. The Ceylon Petroleum Corporation had been set up in 1961 and began in 1962 by working some of the retail outlets of the oil companies. In 1964 it took over all the internal distribution of petrol and oil products. Oil was purchased at prices lower than the Western companies were ready to sell it. It came from Soviet, Eastern European and Middle Eastern sources. It certainly saved the government some valuable foreign exchange, but American aid to the country was stopped until adequate compensation was paid to the oil companies. Negotiations between the companies and the Ceylon Government resulted in deadlock.

The Bank of Ceylon was taken over in 1961, and the last of the government's forays into the sector previously dominated by private enterprise came in 1964, when the Insurance Corporation of Ceylon, set up earlier, extended its activities to include non-life insurance. Since 1 January 1964 every type of insurance but marine has been handled by the Corporation.

Control of imports, consequent shortages, the activities of hoarders and the rise in prices increased opposition to the government. The UNP, not content to wait hopefully in the wings for its turn on the stage, had entered the trade union front and was organizing youth leagues to which school-leavers discontented with the government's failure to tackle unemployment were attracted. In 1963 the Left opposition endeavoured to organize a United Left Front, composed of the LSSP, the MEP (really Philip Gunawardena and a few others) and the CP. But it was never cordially supported by all the parties to it. One section of the LSSP was suspicious of any 'Popular Frontism'; the CP leadership was suffering from the internal strains caused by the growing tension of the ideological dispute between the Soviets and China, and could not speak with one voice; Philip Guna-wardena of the MEP was always too much of an individualist to remain for long member of a group which he did not lead.

The deteriorating political situation had not prevented the Prime Minister from taking up the role of mediator between India and China in the border dispute which led to war between the two countries. Ceylon's policy of non-alignment and its close ties of culture and trade with both disputants made the choice of Mrs Bandaranaike as negotiator understandable. But little came of these worthy activities.

In March 1964, the government, unwilling to risk open defeat in the House, took the step of proroguing Parliament. Before 1 July when Parliament was due to reassemble, some accession of strength to its ranks had to be found. The UNP could feel strong enough to provide an alternative government. The United Left Front seemed to be the only possible ally. The Minister of Finance, T. B. Ilangaratne, was believed to be sounding opinion on the Left. The first approach was apparently made to Philip Gunawardena. Later, when negotiations opened with the United Left Front, this *ad hoc* grouping crumbled away. Another result of the *pourparlers* was the threat of a split in the SLFP itself – the group round C. P. de Silva, the Leader of the House and one of the founder members of the Party, threatening to carry its opposition to any alliance with the Left to the extent of walking out of the government.

In the end, after two months of talks, only one section of the original United Left Front – the group in the LSSP led by Dr N. M. Perera – was ready to consider the government offer of a coalition with it. Another section of the LSSP left it to organize itself as the LSSP (Revolutionary), affiliated with the Fourth International. Yet another group in it was ready to support a coalition between the LSSP and SLFP, but not to hold office in it.

Why did a party which prided itself on its loyalty to its Marxist principles depart from them on such an occasion? If it had spent too much time on the arid heights of theoretical speculation before, it seemed now to have come down to the noisome bogs of the corruption and racialism of the government it joined. Philip Gunawardena had accused the SLFP in 1959 of being no different from the UNP in the matter of corruption.[20] If his remark was justifiable then, things had not improved since.

As leader of a new coalition government Mrs Bandaranaike began the fifth year of her term of office in 1964, becoming the first Prime Minister of Ceylon to have continued so long. The new Finance Minister, Dr N. M. Perera – the fifth since 1960 – could do little in the three weeks before he presented his budget but acknowledge the gravity of the financial situation and impose greater stringency. He placed a moratorium of one year on all remittances of profits, dividends, interest and investment income from Ceylon. Attempts to deal with shortages and corruption had an immediate effect as a result of the threat of special courts to deal with hoarders and Vigilance Committees. A flood of textiles, previously in short supply, swamped the market. But attempts to put an end to the illicit brewing and distillation of dangerous alcohol offended Buddhist opinion, which read into the proposal to license the tapping of coconut trees for toddy an affront to the Buddhist prohibition of intoxicants. This was subsequently withdrawn, but the government's days were already numbered.

There was hardly time for the new coalition to touch any of the problems with which Mrs Bandaranaike's Government had been beset, when it was defeated in early December. The Leader of the House, C. P. de Silva, with no notice to anyone in the Cabinet, crossed over to the opposition with some of his supporters. Mrs Bandaranaike accurately described it as 'a stab in the back'. There was no alternative but to dissolve Parliament.

The General Election was fixed for 22 March 1965. The campaign was conducted on a level of hatred and vituperation not exceeded before. The SLFP–LSSP coalition presented two targets in one and was subjected to concentrated fire by both the Press and the groups opposed to the government. Personal hostilities between the leaders of opposing groups and irrelevancies of rumour masked the real issues of the campaign, which was the failures of the government to deal with inflation and unemployment.

The involvement of the SLFP with a Marxist party did not improve its chances with the Sinhalese Buddhist intelligentsia who had once supported S. W. R. D. Bandaranaike's party whole-heartedly. On the issue of coalition with a Marxist group, cleavage was to be noticed between all sections and groups, even in the *sangha*. The hierarchy tended towards the UNP, the rest being on the whole sympathetic to the SLFP. But there was one significant sign of the times: a few of the political *bhikkhus* of the old *Eksath Bhikkshu Peramuna* had gravitated to the UNP. The splinter group from the SLFP under the leadership of C. P. de Silva organized itself into the Sri Lanka Freedom Socialist Party, the label 'Socialist' proving the freshness of its complexion and the sound-ness of its anti-Marxist constitution. It could count on support from the caste group to which its leader belonged and had an understanding with the UNP.

The UNP had some agreement with Philip Gunawardena's MEP. It could take the field with confidence, but the result was never a foregone conclusion. The Left was disunited. Two groups in the LSSP supported the government; the third which left the original LSSP was subjected to bitter attack. The CP was on the government side, but two sections in it contested the elections: a Russian and a Chinese wing. It was obvious that most of the seats in the north would go to the FP which was already looking ahead. Its manifesto hinted at securing as a result of the election 'a different fate for our people'.[21]

The sacred liberty of the Press, of which much was made in newspaper propaganda, was hardly likely to enthuse the majority of voters, who were not subscribers to newspapers. But Press propaganda, taken up on political platforms by opponents of the coalition, undoubtedly helped to alienate Buddhist sympathy from the SLFP in towns.

Those plantation workers who did have the vote used it against the government, because in October 1964 Mrs Bandaranaike had succeeded in pressing the Indian Government to accept 525,000 plantation workers as Indian citizens. These were to be repatriated from Ceylon over a period of fifteen years, on conditions to be determined by agreement between the two parties. This came as a consequence of the plight of the Shastri Government which had to accept the forcible deportation of Indians from Burma in July. This agreement was accepted by the LSSP element in the coali-tion.

The faulty propaganda of the latter finally drove the hesitant from Mrs Bandaranaike's camp. There had been all party agreement that no private transport should be provided voters to the polling booths. LSSP talk of violence and of the stoning of cars lost the coalition a number of votes.

The election – on 22 March 1965 – gave the UNP the largest number of seats (sixty-six), but no absolute majority. The SLFP with forty-one were its nearest rivals. The LSSP, with ten seats and the CP, with four, were ready to support Mrs Bandaranaike. C. P. de Silva's new party won five seats; the MEP two; the FP fourteen and the Tamil Congress three.

The defeat of Mrs Bandaranaike's Government was received with jubilation which seemed to echo the joy at the rout of the UNP in 1956. The support given by the voter in 1965 to the opponents of the government was much more a protest vote than it had been in 1956. Mrs Bandaranaike's Government had failed to deal with the real problems of the country, and the arrogance and corruption of certain elements in it had evoked passionate hostility. There may have been – as she claimed during her election campaign – foreign interests in the field against her. But a similar attack was made by her opponents on the help allegedly given her by the Chinese. No foreign elements, however, had anything to do with the result. Had the record of the SLFP been cleaner, it might have saved itself a General Election in March 1965.

The SLFP lost most of its support in the urban Sinhalese educated masses in the first years of her administration, because the government had been unable to cope with inflation and shortages which bedevilled the lot of the urban population. The rural masses began to drift away when they too began to be affected by the results of the government's incompetence. The coalition in the six months in which it functioned did little indeed to stem the tide.

After two days of delay, in the hopeless and misguided attempt to rally support for her government from other groups, Mrs Bandaranaike resigned and the Governor-General called on Dudley Senanayake to form a government. He could count on the support of various groups, practically all of them in the recent past redoubtable opponents of the UNP – the FP, the two-member MEP, the C. P. de Silva group, and a one-member 'group' of a strongly racialist character. The Tamil Congress, though not holding office in the new government, supported it. The new coalition could command eighty-five seats in the House, which with six nominated members would give it an absolute majority in an assembly of 151.

Dudley Senanayake called his government a National Government, but the title is misleading. A government from which a strong element in the country is absent is, of course, not truly national. The present situation must be regarded as being fluid and uncertain, until the new government begins to work out its programme.

Mrs Bandaranaike's tenure of office showed that whatever she lacked she possessed personal courage and determination. She was tenacious of power, over-solicitous of her friends and not without a trace of vindictiveness towards her opponents. But these have been the traditional weaknesses of most political leaders in Ceylon. Her lack of experience prevented her from being either a good party leader, or a good judge of a political situation. It is possible that had she gone to the country in March 1964, instead of seeking a coalition with the United Left Front, she might have secured a fresh mandate from it. Her deficiencies were to some extent offset by the spirit with which she faced difficulties such as no party leader in Ceylon has had to encounter.

With the return to power of a Coalition Government in which the UNP forms the main element, it may seem that the wheel has come full circle and that the country is back where it was in 1947, when D. S. Senanayake formed his government, itself a coalition with the UNP as the senior partner. Outside the country, newspaper opinion likely to notice events like a change of government in an island of no great importance, described it as a swing to the right. Inside, the *élite* sighed with relief, and, with strong conviction in the magical potency of their wishes and the certainty that J. R. Jayawardena in the ambiguous position of Minister of State could be depended upon to be ruthless when occasion demanded, felt that they could somehow hope for a return to the happier days of 1947.

But the wheel has not come full circle. The force that moved it has placed no one among the old contestants quite where he wants to be. The old UNP is not back in power. Associated with it now, and more than generously rewarded for his support, is one of its doughtiest opponents of old: the one-time Trotskyist, Philip Gunawardena, dressed up by the press as 'the Father of the Revolution' – a Santa Claus in whose get-up the red shows only in the bag stuffed with presents for the kids who believe in him. Others in high places in the UNP Coalition Government are still more recent opponents – communalist lions of yore, now prepared to coo like any sucking dove. To the *élite* these are awkward *mouches volantes* which impair the vision of the pleasing prospect without obscuring its most reassuring feature: the return to power of the party which best represented them.

Nor are the present opponents of the UNP quite where they want to be either. The SLFP is still a major party, but it is discredited and an important section of its support is gone. It still claims to be wedded to the principles it espoused in 1956, but it is now in alliance with *soi-disant* Marxists, as much a burden to it in the General Election as a boon. These recent allies of theirs – the remains of the LSSP – can claim to be associated with a people's movement, but for the time being they have little in their hands but a few grimy cards from the pack of communalism and religion – odd suits for Marxists to lead.

The force which pushed the wheel round was a shift in the balance of electoral forces. No high moral grounds or political principles provided the impulse. Personal animosities, the minority vote in the Central Province which made marginal seats of what were once SLFP strongholds, and the disappointment of those just over eighteen, using the vote for the first time, with a government which had done little for them, changed things. As these new voters were not a radical political element, they merely registered their protest against the party in power. What they were voting for was perhaps not clear to them, but they were certain that they wanted some change, since all they could perceive in the government in power was inefficiency and corruption. The present alignment of forces in the country is therefore only temporary. Regrouping, as a result of the sharpening of economic tensions, must inevitably follow.

Whatever criticism there may be of the changes since 1947, their direction cannot now be reversed. Much less can the slate be wiped clean and a new set of diagrams chalked on it. These changes since 1947 have been given various names: Communism or totalitarianism by their opponents; socialism by their friends. Whatever they are called, they have been the working out of a process observable since 1931, its direction not at all clear and its movement erratic. Its unevenness has been due both to the slowness with which the masses have perceived the extent of the political power they commanded, and to the determination of the *élite* to keep their grip on controls which seemed to be slipping out of their hands and to 'fix' things in such a way that, whatever may have been conceded, the new beneficiaries could ultimately be lined up in their ranks.

To this determination as much as to traditional hostilities and suspicions of long standing is owed the present-day accentuation of communal feeling in Ceylon. It was not the mass movement which produced communal hostilities in 1956; its leaders deflected its political and social energies into racialism. It was the misfortune of the country that the *élite* who led this movement had nothing to offer their followers but the satisfaction of the lowest levels of primitive aggressiveness. The Left Opposition at the time – also *élite*-led – which could have risen to something better, was not strong enough to rally support for itself. It is probable that economic insecurity, the scramble for state employment, the determination of the party in power to use power to help its friends and to harass its foes, the consequences of inflation and the ever increasing growth of population would in any case have embittered communal feeling. But attention diverted from economic grievances, together with repeated injections of racial hatred, helped to drive politically inexperienced masses into excesses of blind communal rage. To say that the country has now, as a result of the protest vote cast in the General Election of March 1965 against the erstwhile leaders of the mass movement and the apparent change of heart of the new Coalition Government of Dudley Senanayake, awakened to the futility of this expense of energy is an exaggeration.

Two possibilities have to be taken into account in any survey of the future of Ceylon. Both of them are incidental to underdeveloped countries and transitional societies in Asia. There can be seizure of power by a group determined to oppose political trends distasteful to them. Though Ceylon has no large regular army, navy and air force – its police force outnumbers these three units – the present strength of all of them, including the police, would be sufficient to ensure the success of such a move if it were resolutely planned. The attempted *coup d'état* of 1962, the use of army units to terrorize the population before 1962 and after, indicate that these unintentional dress rehearsals could guarantee a successful public performance. Of course there are politicians in Ceylon hankering after the satisfaction of autocratic power concentrated in their hands. But, on the other hand, where are they not?

The other possibility is that of the development of the trend towards state capitalism observed earlier. The new Coalition Government of Dudley Senanayake has accepted all the nationalization measures of the previous government. It has agreed to compensate the nationalized foreign oil companies on their own terms and will receive credit from the foreign commercial banks operating in Ceylon to enable it to do so. Whether this will greatly relieve the economic crisis in the country, except temporarily by allowing American aid to be resumed, is doubtful.

The economy may receive a boost, temporarily again, as it did during the Korean War, but the future cannot be described as anything but cheerless. As the economic crisis deepens, there is likely to be stronger polarization of the old forces of the *élite* and the new mass forces which are as yet *élite*-led, with the likelihood of further domestic upheavals.

Into calculations of the future must enter, too, consideration of more than the domestic situation in Ceylon. Its people, like those of other countries in Asia, are engaged in the struggle to free themselves from the encumbrances of the traditional past, from the old political and economic forms imposed on them by the imperialist powers of Europe, and from the newer involvements of power politics. The attempts of these people to rehabilitate themselves in a world of technological change belong to the colonial revolution as it can be observed in Asia. Its portents are the wars now being waged on that continent: in South Arabia; on the frontiers of India and Pakistan; in Malaysia; and in Vietnam. The imperiousness of the demand of this part of the world for change can be thwarted by the intervention of external forces resolved to stay a process ultimately inimical to their interests; but it will eventually have to be conceded.

Whatever the immediate future may bring, it is clear that the old structure in Ceylon, even with the modifications made in the last eighteen years, can no longer satisfy the strains put upon it. There can in reality be no great freedom of choice in the building of the new. Those who will reconstruct it on the model of an ancient Buddhist fane will be more quickly disappointed than the rest. Others, who believe in the viability of schemes promoted by private enterprise and financed by uncertain foreign aid, will have a slightly longer period in which to discover that their confidence has been misplaced. To expect much of foreign aid, to depend on it to work out the details of a new master plan is to disregard the experience of the recent past not only in Ceylon but elsewhere in the world. A man can as surely set up high-jump records by pulling himself by his shoe-straps over the bar, as an industrially undeveloped country, without capital and dependent on the political vagaries of the Cold War, can set its house in order and plan for the future on contributions made in the name of foreign aid.

The kind of structure built up in Ceylon will depend on what has already been achieved, on the changing world situation and, most of all, on the will of the people of the country. Ultimately the people of Ceylon will have to fall back on their own determination in building a structure which can acommodate their hopes and desires. This task will outlast the span of life of both the old and the very young now. Those who undertake it will perhaps have profited from their assessment of the deficiencies and the mistakes of their predecessors.

NOTES

CHAPTER 1: A FAVOURED AREA

1. CO 55/63, No. 19 of 10 May 1815.

2. Henry Marshall, *Ceylon*, London, 1846, p. 157.

3. P. E. Pieris, *Sinhale and the Patriots*, 1815–1818, Colombo, 1950, p.1.

4. The phrase is taken from Bhikkhu W. Rahula's *History of Buddhism in Ceylon*, Colombo, 1956, p. 72. The whole of the paragraph on the relations between 'church' and state is very much indebted to Bhikkhu Rahula's extremely interesting chapter on 'Buddhism as State Religion'.

5. G. C. Mendis in *Ceylon Today and Yesterday*, Colombo, 1957, p. 54 holds that the changes made by the Portuguese in Ceylon 'were not very considerable and it cannot be concluded that Portuguese rule was a turning point in the internal history of the Island.' He goes on to remark, however, that 'as far as external influences were concerned it certainly was a turning point'.

6. Fr Fernao de Queyroz in *The Temporal and Spiritual Conquest of Ceylon*, tr. Fr S. G. Perera, Colombo, 1930, p. 1008, gives a very different account of how the laws and customs of the Sinhalese were observed by the Portuguese captains and *foreyros* (lease-holders of land).

7. C. R. Boxer in *Four Centuries of Portuguese Expansion*, Johannesburg, 1961, thinks that the argument that the Portuguese were peculiarly fitted to inaugurate the series of maritime and geographical discoveries which changed the course of world history in the fifteenth and sixteenth centuries' because (among other things) 'they dispensed with the colour bar', must not be pushed too far. See pp. 3–4, 42, 82–3.

8. Queyroz, *op. cit.*, p. 174.

9. J. B. Tavernier, *Travels in India*, ed. V. Ball, Vol. II, p. 188.

10. Queyroz, *op. cit.*, p. 295 quotes this letter of the Portuguese king to Don Afonco de Noronha on 20 March 1552.

11. Johan Wolffgang Heydt, *Allerneuester Geographisch-und-Topographischer Schau-Platz von Afrika und Ost-Indien.* 1744, tr. Raven Hart, Colombo, 1952, G90/1, p. 91.

12. H. A. Colgate, *Trincomalee and the East Indies Squadron*, unpublished. M.A. thesis, University of London, 1959: 'The American War had shown that the British, whilst still relying on Bombay for docking and major refits, could not afford to see Trincomalee in French hands.' In an

article in *CJHSS*, Vol, 7, No. 1, January–June 1964, Colgate traces the history of the Royal Navy and Trincomalee.

CHAPTER 2: THE AGENTS AND THE DEVELOPERS

1. P. E. Pieris, *Ceylon and the Hollanders*, Colombo, 1918, p. 168.
2. H. A. Colgate, *Trincomalee and the East Indies Squadron*, unpublished thesis for the degree of M.A. London University, 1959.
3. North MSS, (Muniments of the Waldeshare Estate of the Furnese and North Families 1334–1922), County Archives, Maidstone.
4. Fr S. G. Perera, ed. *The Douglas Papers*, Colombo, 1933, p. 32. Sylvester Douglas's notes of 19 September 1800.
5. Fr S. G. Perera, *op. cit.*, p. 23. Douglas's notes of 17 September 1800.
6. For this I am indebted to U. Wickremeratne's unpublished Ph.D. thesis, London University, 1964: *The British Administration of the Maritime Provinces of Ceylon* – 1796–1802.
7. Fr S. G. Perera, *op. cit.*, p. 26. Douglas's notes of 17 September 1800.
8. CO 54/74, Barnes to Bathurst, 31 July 1819.
9. Fr S. G. Perera, *op. cit.*, p. 27.
10. *Ibid.*
11. North MSS – North to Glenbervie, 6 March 1804.
12. Fr S. G. Perera, *op. cit.*, p. 37. Henry Dundas's note on Douglas's dispatch of 19 September 1800.
13. The Rev. James Cordiner, *Description of Ceylon*, London, 1807, p. 161.
14. North MSS., Considerations on the Cinnamon of Ceylon.
15. *Ibid.*
16. T. A. Anderson, *Poems written chiefly in India*, London, 1809, p. 63.
17. Government Gazette Extraordinary of 18 July 1805, Colombo.

CHAPTER 3: CLEARING THE GROUND

1. CO 55/63, Bathurst to Brownrigg, 30 August 1815.
2. S. M. Hardy, *William Huskisson 1770–1830*, unpublished Ph.D. thesis, University of London, 1943, makes a strong plea for the recognition of Huskisson as a man whose vision influenced imperial policy.
3. North MSS, Glenbervie to North, 21 April 1804.
4. *Op. cit.*, Glenbervie to Minto, 10 March 1804.
5. C. J. Napier, *The Colonies*, London, 1833, p. 51.
6. *Op. cit.*, p. 154.
7. *The Life of the Rt. Hon. Sir James Mackintosh*, ed. by his son R. J. Mackintosh, London 1835, Vol. 2, p. 8.
8. CO 54/22, Maitland to Castlereagh, 21 May 1806.
9. CO 54/22, Castlereagh to Maitland, 11 June 1807.
10. CO 54/38, Liverpool to Maitland, 5 June 1810.
11. North MSS, North to Glenbervie, 15 October 1802.

12. Lennox Mills, *Britain and Ceylon*, London, 1945, p. 24.
13. P. E. Pieris, *Tri Sinhala*, Colombo, 1939, examining the evidence in Appendix H. holds 'that the story was fabricated as a piece of political propaganda of the type so familiar today and was intended not merely to estrange the minds of the Sinhalese from their king, but also to counter the declared policy of Downing Street against territorial expansion'.
14. T. Skinner, *Fifty Years in Ceylon*, London 1891, p. 7.
15. Mackintosh, *op. cit.*, p. 6.
16. CO 55/63, Bathurst to Brownrigg, 30 August 1815.
17. Henry Marshall, *Ceylon*, London, 1846, p. 163.
18. Jawaharlal Nehru, *The Discovery of India*, Calcutta, 1946, p. 383.
19. CO 54/77, Barnes to Bathurst, 19 May, 1820.
20. Lt.-Col. J. Forbes, *Recent Disturbances and Military Executions in Ceylon*, London, 1850.
21. CO 54/74, Barnes to Bathurst, 31 July 1819.
22. Quoted by F. A. Stockdale, T. Petch and H. F. Macmillan, *The Royal Botanic Gardens, Peradeniya, Ceylon*, Colombo, 1922, p. 6.
23. CO 54/112, Barnes to L. H. Hay, 22 January 1831.
24. G. C. Mendis, *The Colebrooke–Cameron Papers*, London, 1956, Vol. I, p. lv. The author goes on: 'In fact some of their proposals had been anticipated much earlier by others like North, Johnston and Brownrigg.'
25. *Op. cit.*, p. 374.
26. *Op. cit.*, p. 182
27. G. C. Mendis, *op. cit.*, Vol. II, p. 41.
28. G. C. Mendis, *op. cit.*, Vol. I, p. 251.
29. CO 54/118, undated.

CHAPTER 4: RAISING THE STRUCTURE

1. I. Vanden Driesen, '*Coffee Cultivation in Ceylon*', *CHJ*, Vol. III, No. 1, July 1953, p. 34.
2. A. M. and J. Ferguson, *Planting Directory for India and Ceylon*, Colombo, 1875, p. 5.
3. Vanden Driesen, *op. cit.*, p. 40.
4. Major J. Forbes, *Eleven Years in Ceylon*, London, 1849, Vol. II, p. 16.
5. I. Vanden Driesen, 'Plantation Agriculture and Land Sales Policy in Ceylon – The First Phase 1836–1886, Part I' *UCR*, Vol. XIV, Nos. 1 and 2, January–April 1956, p. 10.
6. Quoted by A. M. and J. Ferguson, *op. cit.*, p. 7.
7. Sir Samuel Baker, *Eight Years in Ceylon*, 2nd Ed., London, 1847, p. 87.
8. T. Skinner, *Fifty Years in Ceylon*. London, 1891, p. 215. This was part of Skinner's Memorandum to the Select Committee of the House of Commons, July 1849.
9. Sir J. Emerson Tennent, *Ceylon*, London, 1859, Vol. I, p. 11, n. 1.
10. CO 54/171. Stewart Mackenzie to Normanby, 16 July 1893.

11. I. Vanden Driesen, 'Land Sales Policy and Some Aspects of the Problem of Tenure – 1836–1886, Part II', *UCR*, Vol. XV, Nos. 1 and 2, January–April 1957, p. 41.

12. K. M. de Silva, 'Studies in British Land Policy in Ceylon, Part I', *CJHSS*, Vol. 7, No. 1, January–June, 1964, p. 39.

13. CO 54/210, Murdoch's Memorandum at Stephen's request on Campbell's Dispatch to Stanley, 15 of 24 January 1844.

14. Quoted by E. Trevor Williams, 'The Colonial Office in the Thirties', Historical Studies (Australia and New Zealand) Vol. II, Melbourne, 1942–3.

15. CO 54/345. Ward to Newcastle, 29 August 1859.

16. James Steuart, *Notes on the Monetary System and Cinnamon Revenue of Ceylon*, Colombo, 1850. Essay on 'The Government of Ceylon' p. 7.

17. CO 54/235. Tennent's minute of 19 April 1847 to Grey. Tennent's memory was much more convenient than reliable, but since he is quoting from reports sent him their evidence can be accepted.

18. Edward Sullivan, *The Bungalow and the Tent*, London, 1854, p. 48.

19. See Maria Graham, *Journal of a Residence in India*, 2nd ed., Edinburgh, 1813, p. 94, for an account of her visit to the vegetable gardens of some Chinese immigrants in Galle brought to Ceylon by the government for the purpose of growing vegetables.

20. W. J. Clutterbuck, *About Ceylon and Borneo*, London, 1891, p. 41.

21. CO 54/190 Stephen's Minute of 16 October 1841 on Campbell's dispatch of the Annual Blue Book.

22. CO 54/235. Tennent's Minute of 19 April 1847.

23. CO 54/185. P. E. Anstruther's Minute of 23 November 1840.

24. Lennox A. Mills, *Ceylon Under British Rule*, London, 1933, p. 77.

25. *The Private Life of a Coffee Planter by Himself*, Colombo, n.d. The writer was Alfred H. Duncan.

26. See note 23.

CHAPTER 5: THE STRUCTURE COMPLETED

1. W. Austin, in Appendix VIII of J. Ribeiro's *History of Ceylon*, retranslated by G. L., Colombo, 1847.

2. The date of David Wilson's *Facts Connected with the present Condition of Wants of Ceylon* is probably 1847.

3. See I. H. Vanden Driesen, *Some Aspects of the History of the Coffee Industry in Ceylon*, Ph.D. thesis, University of London, for a discussion of the probable sum invested in coffee. He writes: 'If the total capital invested in the plantations was something like £12–£13 m . . . then the total profit earned on the entire coffee period was no more than £4–£5½ m.'

4. See Ronald P. Doig, 'Lord Torrington's Government of Ceylon 1847–1850,' *Durham University Journal*, March 1962, Vol. LIV, No. 2, p. 49.

5. The fullest contemporary account is that of Capt. J. Macdonald Hender-

son, *The History of the Rebellion in Ceylon during Lord Torrington's Government*, London, 1868. He gives a useful account of what took place at Matale. Henderson was, with good reason, hostile to Tennent.

6. T. Skinner, *Fifty Years in Ceylon*, London, 1891, p. 225.
7. Maria Graham, *Journal of a Residence in India*, Edinburgh, 1813 (2nd ed.), p. 90.
8. Henderson, *op. cit.*, p. 35.
9. Knox relates how the other English captives and himself decided to complain at the court to the Adigar of their grievances – Robert Knox, *An Historical Relation of Ceylon*, ed. Ryan, Glasgow, 1911, pp. 235–6.
10. PPHC, 106 of 1850, Vol. XII, p. 47.
11. CO 54/493 A. W. Birch to Cox, 3 August 1874.
12. Minute by R. L. W. Herbert on Gregory's dispatch of 15 February 1874. CO 54/492.
13. North MSS. Bertolacci to North of 10 January 1811.
14. Lytton to Ward, 17 August 1859. CO 54/344.
15. R. W. Jenkins, *Ceylon in the Fifties and the Eighties*, London, 1886.
16. F. A. Stockdale, T. Petch and H. F. Macmillan, *The Royal Botanic Gardens, Peradeniya, Ceylon*, Colombo, 1922, p. 44.
17. Alec Waugh, *The Lipton Story*, London, 1951, p. 58.
18. S. Rajaratnam, 'The Growth of Plantation Agriculture in Ceylon, 1886–1931,' *CJHSS*, Vol. 4, No. 1, provides figures of the planting acreages under coffee and tea. J. Ferguson, *Rise of the Planting Enterprise and Trade in Ceylon Tea*, New Zealand, n.d., p. 2, writes: 'The maximum area ever under coffee was 272,000 acres in 1877 ... thirty years later we have only about 1,000 acres of coffee left in the island; but we have 380,000 acres yielding 170 million lbs of tea.'
19. S. A. Pakeman, *Ceylon*, London 1964, p. 75, doubts the authenticity of Wickham's story, but despite his reference to Rutherford's *Planter's Handbook*, Colombo, 1931, there is nothing to contravene Wickham's account.
20. Lennox Mills, *Ceylon under British Rule*, London, 1933, p. 122 fn. 4, quotes an extreme example: 'Torrington inquired how he should assess the land-tax on a raiyat whose holding was 1/22,000 part of a coco-nut tree.'
21. The myth (though the point of association is not the palm but tea) is beautifully rendered by Joyce in *Ulysses*: 'So warm. His right hand once more slowly went over again: choice blend, made of the finest Ceylon brands. The far east. Lovely spot it must be: the garden of the world, big lazy leaves to float about on, cactuses, flowery meads, snaky lianas they call them. Wonder is it like that. Those Cinghalese lobbing around in the sun, in *dolce far niente*. Not doing a hand's turn all day.' See James Joyce, *Ulysses*, London, 1936, pp. 64–4.
22. Joan Robinson, *Economic Philosophy*, Penguin Books, London, 1964, p. 46.
23. Philalethes, *Letters on Colonial Policy*, Colombo, 1833, p. 1, 'Political

Economy' was described as 'common sense and experience directed to the promotion of private and public wealth'.

24. *Op. cit.*, p. 17.

CHAPTER 6: TENANTS OF THE HOUSE

1. Colonialism – from the German which Karl Marx frequently used in the nineteenth century – was a word which the English language took some time in digesting. Its present-day senses and popularity are due to English translators of Lenin.
2. CO 54/178: James Stephen's minute of 22 April 1840 on Stewart Mackenzie's memo of 12 February 1840.
3. B. R. Blaze, *The Life of Lorenz*, Colombo, 1948, p. 76.
4. PPHC., 106 of 1850, Vol. XII, p. 344. Anstruther knew Sinhalese and Tamil and was glad to snipe at civilians who did not know either. Whether he knew the people whose language he understood is another matter.
5. William Knighton, *Forest Life in Ceylon*, London, 1854, p. 7.
6. For more recent accounts of this see P. R. Smythe, *A Ceylon Commentary*, London, 1932, and S. A. Pakeman, *Ceylon*, London, 1964, pp. 106 ff.
7. North MSS: North to Lady Glenbervie, 23 April 1801.
8. Speculum (George Wall), *Ceylon, Her Present Condition*, Colombo, 1868, p. 172. Wall wrote during the political agitation of the sixties and was disposed to regard the Governor as an unconstitutional anomaly.
9. Frederick Lewis, *Sixty-Four Years in Ceylon*, Colombo, 1926, p. 217.
10. C. Drieberg, *Looking Back*, Colombo, 1933, p. 66.
11. From a letter by Sir Hugh Clifford (in the London Library copy of his English Association lecture on Joseph Conrad in 1927.
12. Leonard Woolf, *Growing*, London, 1961, p. 16.
13. *Op. cit.*, p. 35.
14. Joseph Grenier, *Leaves from my Life*, Colombo, 1923, p. 6.
15. Leonard Woolf. *op. cit.*, p. 120, on his month in Mannar as AGA.
16. The Army had little to do after the 'Rebellion'; all its active service was outside Ceylon: in India during the Mutiny; in New Zealand during the Maori War in 1863; in Natal in 1879, etc. See John Ferguson, *Ceylon in 1893*, pp. 164–5.
17. J. G. Wall, *Britain's Folly*, London, 1924, p. 209.
18. *Ceylon and Its People*, Colombo, 1945, p. 21.
19. W. Digby, *Forty Years in a Crown Colony*, London, 1879, Vol. 2, p. 97.
20. CO 54/203: Stephen's minute of 15 May 1843 on Campbell's dispatch of 16 March 1843.
21. For the intensity of these feuds see K. M. de Silva, *Some Aspects of the Development of Social Policies in Ceylon*, Ph.D. thesis University of London, 1961.
22. Bryce Ryan, *Caste in Modern Ceylon*, New Brunswick, N. J. 1953, p. 6. Not until the Prevention of Social Disabilities Act, No. 21 of 1957, was legislation passed imposing penalties on such extreme forms of caste dis-

crimination as not allowing *Rodiya* women to cover the upper parts of their bodies. Taboos against the lower castes are still rigid in Jaffna and some parts of the south.

23. Wilfred Jayasuriya. 'Some Aspects of Colonisation in Gal Oya Valley', *CJHSS*, Vol. 6, No. 2. (July–December) 1963, p. 185.

24. I am indebted to Mrs Yasmin Gunaratne for this reference to the records of the Wesleyan Missionary Society, 1830–31.

25. W. Skeen, quoting the *Ceylon Observer* of 13 June 1853 and 23 April 1870 in *Adam's Peak*, Colombo, 1870.

26. The centenary of Dharmapala's birth was celebrated in Ceylon with a great deal of official ceremony, a special stamp being issued in honour of his work.

27. PPHC., 106 of 1850, Vol. XII – see the evidence of Skinner (17 July 1849), F. Saunders (5 July 1948) and H. L. Layard (10 July 1849).

28. A.R., North Central Province, 1878. On the subject of the villager in the dry zone see Speculum, *op. cit*. p. 51.

29. C. S. Salmon, *The Ceylon Starvation Question*, London, 1890, p. 9.

CHAPTER 7: REPAIRS AND RENEWALS

1. *Examiner*, 23 April 1870.

2. CO 54/299, 25 April 1853.

3. The Rev. S. O. Glenie, 'Hints towards the promotion of Education in Ceylon', *Ceylon Magazine*, Vol. 2, No. XVII, January, 1842.

4. 'Henry Candidus', *Young Ceylon*, Christmas 1853.

5. CO 54/301, Merivale's minute of 26 September 1853.

6. H. A. J. Hulugalle, *The Life and Times of D. R. Wijewardene*, Colombo, 1960, p. 63.

7. CO 54/709, on dispatch No. 408 from Ceylon. Churchill's minute, with which the Secretary of State did not agree, was on 11 July 1907.

8. See PPHC 106 of 1850 Vol. XII for the evidence of Layard and Saunders, 5 July 1849.

9. CO 54/301, Blackwood's minute of 26 September 1853.

10. *Ibid*., Anderson's dispatch.

11. CO 54/702, Churchill's minute of 19 October 1906 on Blake's dispatch of 15 September 1906. His further minute is in CO 54/703.

12. Quoted by H. A. J. Hulugalle, *op. cit*., pp. 15–6.

13. CO 54/702, Blake's dispatch of 16 August 1906.

14. In fact with the declaration of the state of war between the United Kingdom and Germany in August 1914, military law had been declared in Ceylon. As the Gazette Proclamation that Ceylon was at war with Germany was made on 5 August 1914, it made the necessary proclamation bringing into operation an Order in Council of 1896 to deal with any emergency. This by Article III (i) placed every person in Ceylon under military law. Everyone in Ceylon therefore was under Martial Law from 5 August 1914. In 1915 the Executive and the Army began to operate various provisions contained in Article III. The Proclamation

which brought into operation the Order-in-Council of 1896 by Gazette notification of 5 August 1914 was never revoked. This was how in 1937 Sir Reginald Stubbs, the Governor, used one of the Sub-sections of Article III to order the deportation of M. A. L. Bracegirdle.

15. Professor W. T. Stace in a personal communication to the present writer on certain remarks on the riots in *The Story of Ceylon*, London, 1962. A. S. Pagden was one of the Commissioners. The Rev. A. G. Fraser was the Principal of Trinity College Kandy.

16. See Sir Henry Moore's account of his experiences as a junior officer in the Ceylon Civil Service during the riots in H. A. J. Hulugalle, *British Governors of Ceylon*, Colombo, 1963, p. 213.

17. Sir Hugh Clifford, *Encyclopaedia Britannica*, 14th ed., 1929.

18. Hector Bolitho, *The Reign of Queen Victoria*, London, 1949, p. 353.

19. *Handbook of the Ceylon National Congress*, ed. S. W. R. D. Bandaranaike, Colombo 1928, p. 110.

20. *Op. cit.*, p. 228.

21. *Op. cit.*, p. 231.

22. *Op. cit.*, pp. 228–9.

23. For the text of the decisions made by the governor after he had received the Congress deputation, see *op. cit.*, pp. 245–6.

CHAPTER 8: THE FIRST CRACKS

1. *Handbook of the Ceylon National Congress* 1919–1928, ed. S. W. R. D. Bandaranaike, Colombo, 1928, pp. 734–5.

2. Quoted by Mrs Kumari Jayawardena from Ceylon Government Archives Confidential File P. (5) 3, Vol. 1.

3. I am indebted for this reference too to Mrs Jayawardena's Ph.D. thesis, University of London, 1964: *The Urban Labour Movement in Ceylon, with reference to political factors*, 1893–1947.

4. *Handbook of the C.N.C.*, p. 495. The name of Martinus C. Perera, a pioneer in many technical processes in Ceylon, should be mentioned here. He worked in the labour movement organizing workers and deriving a great deal of his energy from the literature of the Rationalist Press Association, of which he was a member. Dr Cassius Pereira, in an article recalling these early days, remembers how those who forgathered at Martinus Perera's house used to sing 'atheistic hymns'!

5. Mrs Jayawardena makes this point in her thesis.

6. See DLCC 1928, Vol. 3, p. 1418 for A. Mahadeva's remark: 'There will come a time, as I hope, when there will be real parties in Ceylon. But at the present moment as far as I can see there are no parties in Ceylon.' There was, in 1928, a group of people calling themselves the Unionist Party, but this was a conglomeration of persons momentarily associated for some semipolitical aims.

7. Sir Henry Blake, *Progress of the Colony of Ceylon* 1904–7, Colombo 1907, p. 29.

8. CO 54/666, Dispatch No. 20271. The 2nd Baron Ampthill served as Under-secretary under Joseph Chamberlain.
9. *Encyclopaedia Britannica* (14th ed.), 1929.
10. *Handbook of the C.N.C.*, p. 842.
11. Cmd. 2062, 1924, p. 26.
12. *Handbook of the C.N.C.*, p. 709.
13. *Encyclopaedia Britannica* (14th ed.), 1929.
14. *Handbook of the C.N.C.*, p. 785.
15. S. Arasaratnam, *Ceylon*, New Jersey, 1964, p. 168.
16. Sir Anton Bertram, *The Colonial Service*, London, 1930, had this comment to make on the recommendations of the Donoughmore Commission: 'In Ceylon the axe has already been laid at the root of the tree.' Sir Anton had been Chief Justice of the colony.
17. S. Namasivayam, *The Legislatures of Ceylon*, London, 1951, p. 34.
18. *Op. cit.*, p. 41.
19. For a contrary opinion: that this power was not that of legislating by decree, see Namasivayam, *op. cit.*, p. 43.
20. *Handbook of the C.N.C.*, pp. 829–30.
21. See DLCC, 1928, Vol. 3., p. 1912.
22. *Op. cit.*, p. 1626.
23. *Op. cit.*, p. 1724.
24. *Op. cit.*, p. 1797.
25. *Op. cit.*, p. 1800.
26. Sir Charles Jeffries, *Ceylon, The Path to Independence*, London, 1962, p. 60.

CHAPTER 9: REDECORATION

1. Cmd. 3419 (1929), p. 17.
2. DSCC, 1932, p. 1816.
3. Cmd. 3131 (1928) p. 83.
4. DSCC, 1933, p. 1844.
5. Ralph Pieris, 'Universities, Politics and Public Opinion in Ceylon', *Minerva*, summer 1964.
6. In conversation with the present writer in 1934.
7. H. A. de S. Gunasekara, *From Dependent Currency to Central Banking*, London, 1962, p. 200.
8. *Op. cit.*, p. 205.
9. Dr L. Nicholls, quoted by the Commissioner for the Relief of Distress in SP. V of 1936, p. 5.
10. Cmd. 3131 (1928), p. 121.
11. SP. V of 1936, p. 12.
12. Leslie Goonewardene, *A Short History of the Lanka Sama Samaja Party*, Colombo, 1961, p. 24.
13. Cmd. 3419 (1929) p. 35.
14. SP XI of 1937, p. 7. In a debate in the House of Representatives in 1959, C. Suntharalingam acknowledged that 'for the actual working of the formula there were two parties responsible, my Assistants, Lecturers in

the University College, and myself'. He went on to say that, when the formula was worked out, the European minority in the Council supported the Sinhalese and that one European nominated member was promised a seat on the Board of Ministers. This did not, however, work out because of manœuvres in the Committee concerned. See HRD., Vol. 33, 5 January 1959, Col. 2522.

15. The member for Point Pedro (G. G. Ponnambalam) described the Ministers' proposals as 'conceived in darkness and hatched in secrecy'. DSCC, 1937, p. 824.
16. Sir Ivor Jennings and H. W. Thambiah, *The Constitution of Ceylon*, London, 1952, p. 39.
17. *Op. cit.*, p. 40.
18. See A. J. Wilson, Ph.D thesis, University of London, 1956, 'The Manning Constitution of Ceylon'.
19. CO 54/709: Stubbs' minute of 15 July 1907.
20. SP XVIII of 1938, para 197.
21. Quoted by Mrs Kumari Jayawardena, *The Urban Labour Movement in Ceylon with reference to political factors*, 1893–1947, Ph.D. thesis, University of London, 1964.
22. Cmd. 5910 (1938), para 15 and 41.
23. DSCC, 1940, p. 491.
24. *Op. cit.*, p. 614.
25. DLCC, 1928, Vol. III. 'Caucus', a word of Algonquin origin, went into North American political slang. Sir Ponnambalam Ramanathan obviously used *Indian* which occurs first in this context to mean North American Indian.
26. DSCC, 1939, p. 3474.
27. *Op. cit.*, p. 3481.
28. DSCC, 1942, pp. 56 f.
29. DSCC, 1940, p. 714.
30. Sir John Kotelawala, *An Asian Prime Minister's Story*, London, 1956, p. 54.
31. DSCC, 1943, p. 965.
32. *Ibid.*
33. *Op. cit.*, p. 4.
34. *Op. cit.*, pp. 831. ff.
35. *Op. cit.*, p. 1021.
36. Sir Ivor Jennings, 'D. S. Senanayake and Independence', *CHJ*, Vol. V, 1955–6, p. 19.
37. 401. H. C. Deb. 5s, Col. 1143.
38. Sir Ivor Jennings, *op. cit.*, p. 19.
39. Sir Ivor Jennings and H. W. Thambiah, *op. cit.*, pp. 45–6. (My emphasis.)
40. DSCC, 1945, p. 311.
41. Sir Charles Jeffries, *Ceylon, The Path to Independence*, London, 1962.
42. *Op. cit.*, p. 100. See also Sir Ivor Jennings, *op. cit.*, p. 21.
43. Cmd. 6690, p. 7, para. 10.
44. DSCC, 1945, p. 6293.

45. This was implicit in the various declarations made by His Majesty's Government. See also Sir Frederick Rees, one of the Soulbury Commissioners. He stated 'The appreciation at the Colonial Office of the position in Ceylon was more alarming than was justified by the facts.' 'The Soulbury Commission', *CHJ*, Vol. V, p. 23. In other words the Colonial Office thought that much more had to be conceded to the Ceylonese leaders than was actually necessary.

46. Sir Ivor Jennings, *op. cit.*, p. 18.

47. Cmd. 6767, p. 110.

48. Sir Frederick Rees, *op. cit.*, p. 45.

49. DSCC, 1945, p. 6970.

50. H. A. J. Hulugalle, *British Governors of Ceylon*, Colombo, 1963, p. 232.

51. SP. VI of 1947.

52. Leslie Goonewardene, *op. cit.*, p. 31.

53. Beatrice Webb, *Diaries 1924–32*, London, 1956, p. 215. (My emphasis.)

CHAPTER 10: THE NEW FAÇADE

1. H. A. J. Hulugalle, *The Life and Times of D. R. Wijewardene*, Colombo, 1960, pp. 186–7.

2. HRD, Vol. X, Col. 1399.

3. *Free Ceylon Rejoices*, Associated Newspapers of Ceylon, Colombo, 1948, p. 4.

4. DSCC, 1945, Col. 3034.

5. Sir Ivor Jennings, 'The Ceylon General Election of 1947', *UCR*, Vol. VI, No. 3.

6. Sir Ivor Jennings, *The Constitution of Ceylon*, 3rd ed., Bombay, 1953, p. 29.

7. Cmd. 5910, 1938, p. 35.

8. Sir Ivor Jennings, 'The Ceylon General Election of 1947', *UCR*, Vol. VI, No. 3.

9. Cmd. 5910, 1938, p. 10.

10. Sir Charles Jeffries, *The Path to Independence*, London, 1962, Ch. XV.

11. Sir Ivor Jennings, *The Constitution of Ceylon*, 1st ed., Bombay, 1949, Preface.

12. DSCC, 1947, Col. 1544–6.

13. SP XIX of 1953 – addendum of the Director of Industries. I owe this reference to Dr V. Kanapathy.

14. HRD, Vol. X, Col. 1402.

15. The Ceylon Chamber of Commerce, 125 *Years of Service*, Colombo, 1964, p. 34.

16. HRD, Vol. I, Col. 3599.

17. S. A. Pakeman, *Ceylon*, London, 1964, p. 160.

18. *Op. cit.*, p. 157.

19. Cmd. 3131, 1928, pp. 42–3.

20. S. A. Pakeman, *op. cit.*, pp. 160–61.

21. L. C. A. Knowles, *The Economic Development of the British Empire*, London, 1924, Vol. I, p. viii.
22. SP III of 1938, p. 26.
23. DSCC, 1937, Col. 2368.
24. *Op. cit.*, Col. 2380.
25. DSCC, 1943, Col. 263.
26. I. D. S. Weerawardana, 'The General Elections in Ceylon 1952', *CHJ*, Vol. II, Nos 1 & 2, July and October 1952, p. 158. For the opposite point of view on the effect of the plantation workers' vote see Nimalsiri Silva, 'The Problem of Indian Immigration to Ceylon', *St. Anthony's Papers*, No. 8, London, 1960, pp. 149–52.
27. W. Howard Wriggins, *Ceylon: Dilemmas of a New Nation*, Princeton, 1960, p. 115.
28. HRD, Vol. X, Col. 3602–3.
29. See Hamza Alavi in 'Imperialism Old and New', *The Socialist Register* 1964, London, 1964, pp. 121–3.
30. HRD, Vol. X., Col. 701.
31. *Op. cit.*, Col. 700.
32. Sir John Kotelawala, *An Asian Prime Minister's Story*, London, 1956, Ch. 9.
33. I. D. S. Weerawardana, *op. cit.*, p. 135.
34. DSCC, 1943, Col. 2600.
35. HRD, Vol. XII, Col. 800. In the House when this was quoted against him by Dr N. M. Perera, Dudley Senanayake stressed his use of the word 'sole'.
36. *The Economic Development of Ceylon*, Report of the Mission of the IBRD, Baltimore, 1953, p. 186.
37. *CHJ, D. S. Senanayake Memorial Number*, Vol. V, Nos. 1–4, p. 11.
38. The Ceylon Chamber of Commerce, *op. cit.*, p. 43.
39. Cmd. 8080, 1950, p. 32.
40. See W. Howard Wriggins, *op. cit.*, for a sympathetic account of the 1954 Conference in Colombo.
41. In these popular plays Lanerolle, with a sensitive ear for the nuances of the English spoken in Ceylon and his broad comic and satiric effects, produced an amusing sketch of *la dolce vita* of the Kotelawala régime. The success of his plays was due as much to his talents as to the verve and gusto of the actor responsible for the interpretation of the leading role – E. C. B. Wijesinghe.

CHAPTER 11: A RECENT CONVERSION

1. G. C. Mendis, *Ceylon, Today and Yesterday*, 2nd ed. Colombo, 1963, p. 188.
2. I. D. S. Weerawardana, *Ceylon – General Election 1956*, Colombo, 1960, pp. 94 ff.
3. Doric de Souza, 'Parliamentary Democracy in Ceylon', *The Young Socialist*, October–December 1961, p. 133.
4. Weerawardana, *op. cit.*, p. 12.

5. *Op. cit.*, p. 103.
6. This figure leaves out the Tamil-speaking plantation workers.
7. HRD, Vol. 24, Col. 26.
8. See AR of GA, NCP; and Indaratne, 'An Analysis of Agricultural Credit in Under-developed Countries with special reference to Ceylon', *CJHSS*, Vol. 2, July 1959, pp. 193 ff.
9. HRD, Vol. 35, Col. 50 and 51.
10. T. Vittachi, *Emergency '58*, London, 1958, pp. 27–8.
11. A. J. Wilson, 'The Governor General and the State of Emergency, May 1958–March 1959', *CJHSS*, Vol. 2, No. 2, July 1959, p. 167.
12. T. Vittachi, *op. cit.*, p. 72.
13. N. Kaldor, *Papers by Visiting Economists*, Colombo, 1959, p. 32.
14. Joan Robinson in *Papers by Visiting Economists*, Colombo, 1959, p. 41, noted that 'Ceylon has tasted the fruits before she has planted the tree. Her trade unions are anxious to share in profits, but the energetic, enterprising and thrifty capitalists for them to share with have not as yet appeared.' Whatever the system one has to agree that the worker owes his legitimate share of work to his employer.
15. I am indebted to V. Kanapathy, 'A Study of Current Trends in the Industrial Development of Ceylon', Ph.D. thesis, University of London, 1964, and to the work of S. Hewavitarne on industrial planning in Ceylon for information here.
16. The Deputy Speaker of the House of Representatives at the time made this statement in an interview with the BBC in London.
17. 709. H. C. Deb. 5s, Col. 1217.
18. Sir Henry Moore in *British Governors of Ceylon* by H. A. J. Hulugalle, Colombo, 1963, made the following comment on Sir Oliver: 'He was in many ways indispensable in keeping me informed of the gyrations of the political wheel, as he had a foot in most camps.'
19. Joan Robinson, *op. cit.*, p. 37.
20. See note 9 above.
21. From the Federal Party Manifesto as quoted in *The Weekly Times of Ceylon*, 6 March 1965.

A SELECT BIBLIOGRAPHY OF
BOOKS IN ENGLISH

The Ancient Background

The two most important source books are the Pali chronicles, translated into English originally under the auspices of the Pali Text Society and since reissued by the Government of Ceylon Information Department:

The Mahavamsa or the Great Chronicle of Ceylon, translated by Wilhelm Geiger, assisted by Mabel H. Bode, with an addendum by G. C. Mendis, Colombo, 1950.

The Culavamsa, being the more recent part of the *Mahavamsa*, translated by Wilhelm Geiger, and from the German into English by Mrs C. Mabel Rickmers, Colombo, 1953.

An important study of the establishment of Buddhism in Ceylon and the place of the religion in the earliest period of the Sinhalese kingdom will be found in Bhikkhu W. Rahula, *History of Buddhism in Ceylon : The Anuradhapura Period*, Colombo, 1956.

There have been several histories of ancient Ceylon by antiquarians and scholars. The first serious study of the material from the standpoint of modern scientific scholarship was that of G. C. Mendis, *The Early History of Ceylon*, Calcutta, 1932, subsequently revised and reprinted. The most recent edition is that of 1948.

More recently the University of Ceylon, Peradeniya, began publication of a *History of Ceylon*, of which Vol. 1, Part 1, ed. S. Paranavitane appeared in 1959, and Vol. 1, Part 2, under the same editor, in 1960. The two parts survey the history of the island from the earliest times till the arrival of the Portuguese in 1505. This authoritative work undertaken by the History Department of the University of Ceylon and incorporating the researches of scholars in the university and outside it, is chiefly interesting for its survey of the archaeological material and conclusions based upon it. A shorter version: *A Concise History of Ceylon*, by C. W. Nicholas and S. Paranavitane appeared in 1961.

Ceylon From *1505-1795*

The continuation of the University of Ceylon's *History of Ceylon*, soon to be published, will certainly place knowledge of the history of this period on a new footing. Most of the numerous accounts of Ceylon by Europeans during these years are not easily available. Father S. G. Perera's scholarly edition of Queyroz's *The Temporal and Spiritual Conquest of Ceylon*, Colombo, 1930, 3 vols., is the best source book for the Portuguese connection with Ceylon. Queyroz in the seventeenth century examined, with much heart-searching and diligence, the reasons for the failure of his countrymen to conquer Ceylon and to win the island for Christianity.

There is nothing comparable with Queyroz on the years of Dutch rule of the maritime areas of Ceylon. Memoirs of successive Dutch Governors have been translated into English by the Ceylon Government's archivists and others. On Kandyan Ceylon in the late seventeenth century there is an extraordinarily interesting record by an Englishman who spent eighteen years in the Kandyan country as a detenu of the Kandyan king: Robert Knox, *An Historical Relation of the Island Ceylon*. It was first published under the aegis of the newly formed Royal Society in London in 1681. The most recent edition, which includes Knox's later *Autobiography* is that of James Ryan, Glasgow, 1911. This was reprinted, without Ryan's introduction but with another by S. D. Saparamadu, for the *Ceylon Historical Journal*, at Maharagama, 1958.

A selection of some passages of Knox's *Relation* and his *Autobiography* was made by the present writer: *Robert Knox in the Kandyan Kingdom*, Bombay, 1948. The recent discovery in the British Museum of an interleaved copy of *An Historical Relation*, in which Knox made numerous additions to his printed reminiscences, gives special interest to the forthcoming Hakluyt Society's edition of Knox's work by J.H.O. Paulusz.

The best study so far of the social structure of the Kandyan

kingdom and its system of land tenure – a subject of great import-
ance in the nineteenth century when the country was opened up – is
Ralph Pieris, *Sinhalese Social Organization in the Kandyan Period*,
Peradeniya, 1956.

Ceylon in Early British Times

A large number of books of reminiscences of the years they spent
in Ceylon by early British officials, army men and missionaries was
published in the early nineteenth century. Most of them are
focused on the burning questions of the times: arguments for and
against the waging of war on the king of Kandy, and the way in
which the new territories were being administered. Those who
sometimes endeavour to place current events in Ceylon in a
broader frame provide interesting information on the country and
its people. The best of these is John Davy, *Account of the Interior of
Ceylon and of its Inhabitants, With Travels in that Island*, London,
1821. Davy was the brother of Sir Humphry Davy and served in
the army as surgeon immediately after the fall of the Kandyan
kingdom.

Pioneer work in assembling and examining the early British
records is to be found in L. J. B. Turner, *Collected Papers on the
History of the Maritime Provinces of Ceylon, 1795–1805*, Colombo,
1923. Lennox A. Mills, *Ceylon Under British Rule 1795–1932*,
London, 1933, concentrates on the administration during the
early years of British rule, when the chief problems were the
Kandyan kingdom, the form of rule to be adopted in Ceylon and
how it was to be organized, the cinnamon trade and the disturbances of 1848. A single chapter hurries over events after 1850.
The book was reprinted in 1965.

P. E. Pieris, *Tri Sinhala*, Colombo, 1939, and *Sinhale and the
Patriots*, Colombo, 1950, are useful correctives to the effect of
most work on the conquest of the Kandyan kingdom by British
writers, besides being by the way an eclectic assemblage of much
lore and tradition about Kandyan custom as it survived in the
recollection of the older chieftains.

Colvin R. de Silva, *Ceylon Under the British Occupation, 1795–1833*,
Vol. 1, Colombo, 1941, Vol. 2, Colombo, 1942, analyses the
political and administrative development of the island in early

British times and the island's cinnamon trade. Vol. 1 was reprinted in 1953.

G. C. Mendis, *Ceylon Under the British*, Colombo, 1944, studies the whole British period and contains – on this as on later phases of British rule in the island – a well-planned general study. Its sub-sections on education and administrative reforms are most useful. A revised third edition appeared in 1952.

The Development of the Plantation Industry

Unfortunately no single book studies the economics of the growth of the plantation industry. Some of the old pioneers contributed to the flood of reminiscences of the coffee days. In the same way a number of tea planters described their sojourn in Ceylon. A. M. and J. Ferguson compiled gazetteers and records of the planting industry, but their work was more in the nature of journalists' surveys, dependent on personal memory and excellent contacts. A small part of the work of I. H. Vanden Driesen who made the first serious study of some aspects of coffee cultivation in Ceylon and of S. Rajaratnam who similarly studied the tea industry, has appeared in the *CJHSS*. Very valuable investigation into the social and administrative background of the years when coffee established itself as the major product of Ceylon will be found in K. M. de Silva, *Social Policy and Missionary Organisations in Ceylon*, London, 1965. His chapter on the immigrant coolies who came to Ceylon to work on the plantations is invaluable.

The lack of a modern study of the shaping of Ceylon's economic structure is a serious drawback. On this, as on other topics linked with it, the forthcoming Ceylon University *History of Ceylon* Vol. 2 must be awaited with interest.

Education in English and the Rise of the English-speaking Élite

On this subject, too, little is available in the way of special studies. T. R. Ruberu, *Education in Colonial Ceylon*, Ceylon, 1962, surveys the opening of various schools by the state and by missionary organizations between 1796 and 1834. On this subject and on the increasing prosperity of the English educated, G. C. Mendis, *Ceylon Under the British*, already referred to has useful subsections.

The same author's *The Colebrooke-Cameron Papers*, London, 1956, 2 Vols. reprints the report by the two Commissioners as well as a number of relevant documents. The long introductory essay examines attitudes current in the 1830s in both England and official circles in Ceylon to Colonial development and education.

H. A. J. Hulugalle, *British Governors of Ceylon*, Colombo, 1963, deals with the personalities and interests of the men who had the biggest influence on British rule in Ceylon.

The subject of the growth of a class of Ceylonese educated in English can be viewed by reflection in the prominence given to the study of the movement for constitutional reform in Ceylon. The stress laid on this tends to move the attention of the reader away from the condition and interests of the majority of people in the island.

Constitutional Developments

The most interesting and succinct historical reviews are necessarily those produced by the two Commissions empowered by His Majesty's Government to investigate this very subject. The reports of the Donoughmore Commission (Cm. 3131, 1928) and of the Soulbury Commission (Cmd. 6767, 1945) entitled *Ceylon: Report of the Special Commission on the Constitution* should be consulted. As the matter of constitutional reform was the prime interest of the *élite*, it produced a fair literature ranging from the scholarly academic to personal reminiscence. The first edition of Sir Ivor Jennings' *The Constitution of Ceylon* appeared in Bombay in 1949; the most recent edition is the third of 1953. It is an authoritative record of recent constitutional changes. S. Namasivayam, *The Legislatures of Ceylon*, London, 1951, examines the history of earlier constitutional development and concentrates on twentieth-century changes with a sober air of detachment. Sir Ivor Jennings and H. W. Thambiah, *The Dominion of Ceylon*, London, 1952, cover the same ground as Namasivayam much more cursorily in order to clear the decks for an examination of the legal aspects of the constitution given the new Dominion.

The story of the events leading to self-government is the subject of Sir Ivor Jennings, *The Approach to Self-government*, Cambridge, 1956, and Sir Charles Jeffries, *Ceylon – The Path to Independence*, London, 1962.

Unwieldly and poorly edited, but none the less interesting as a record of the agitation carried on by the *élite* in the 1920s and immediately before, is *Handbook of the Ceylon National Congress*, ed. S. W. R. D. Bandaranaike, Colombo, 1928. Of more interest as a study of the immediate background (in *élite* circles) of the movement for constitutional change is H. A. J. Hulugalle, *The Life and Times of D. R. Wijewardene*, Colombo, 1960.

I. D. S. Weerawardana, *Government and Politics in Ceylon, 1931–1946*, Colombo, 1951, based chiefly on debates in the Legislative and the State Councils, is worth consulting on reactions to the Donoughmore Constitution and its working.

Ceylon Since Independence

An interpretation of the major political and social problems of Ceylon since independence, with reference to the main currents of Ceylon's history, is the subject of G. C. Mendis, *Ceylon Today and Yesterday*, revised ed., Colombo, 1963.

Most recent studies of Ceylon, whether they have attempted to survey the whole of its historical development or have contented themselves with recounting the major events of the story, have necessarily dealt with Ceylon since independence. The most recent of these, S. Arasaratnam, *Ceylon*, New Jersey, 1964, is the most rewarding, because the historian's easy familiarity with his material enables him to link the current problems of racial disharmony and political stresses with the history of the peoples who now inhabit the island. S. A. Pakeman, *Ceylon*, London, 1964, gives a personal and kindly rendering of more recent events, as seen by a historian who sat in the House of Representatives as a Nominated Member for a few years. B. H. Farmer, *Ceylon A Divided Nation*, London, 1963, takes up the worsening of relations between the majority Sinhalese and the minority Tamil communities and subjects it to close scrutiny in its historical aspects. The present author's *The Story of Ceylon*, London, 1962, examines the political struggles of the last twenty-five years in its concluding chapters. W. Howard Wriggins, *Ceylon: Dilemmas of a New Nation*, Princeton, 1960, conscientiously covers the ground, providing a surface impression of the political, economic and social difficulties besetting politicians in power. Its bibliography is most useful. Tarzie

Vittachi, *Emergency '58*, London, 1958, contains valuable first hand evidence of government reactions to the communal disturbances of 1958 by a high-ranking Ceylonese journalist. B. H. Farmer, *Pioneer Peasant Colonization in Ceylon*, London, 1957, is a critique of the colonization schemes of the first UNP government of 1947–51.

Bryce Ryan, *Caste in Modern Ceylon: The Sinhalese System in Transition*, New Brunswick, N.J., Rutgers Univ. Press, 1953, examines the nature of Sinhalese caste institutions. Part Four contains an interesting discussion of caste in present-day Ceylon. Marshall R. Singer, *The Emerging Elite: A Study of Political Leadership in Ceylon*, Cambridge, Mass., 1964, need be mentioned only because it is the first full-length study of the subject.

The special subject of monetary policy in Ceylon, was treated by H. A. de S. Gunasekara, *From Dependent Currency to Central Banking in Ceylon*, London, 1962. It contains an authoritative history of the development of banking in Ceylon with some reference to the economic problems of the country's small wealthy class. It is to be regretted that apart from Henry M. Oliver, *Economic Opinion and Policy in Ceylon*, Durham, N.C., Duke Univ. Press, Cambridge, 1957, there are no serious studies of the economic structure of Ceylon. Oliver's is a cautious rendering of trends in post-Independence years. An analysis in depth is badly needed. *The Economic Development of Ceylon*, Baltimore, John Hopkins, 1953, the Report of the special mission of the International Bank for Reconstruction and development, surveys the ground, but it hardly fills the breach.

The Culture of Ceylon

The most impressive study of the ancient art of Ceylon is to be found in W. G. Archer and S. Paranavitane, *Ceylon, Paintings from Temple, Shrine and Rock*, Paris, 1957, published under the auspices of UNESCO. The text and the plates are of a high standard. S. Paranavitane, *Art and Architecture of Ceylon. Polonnaruwa Period*, Colombo 1954, is an Arts Council of Ceylon publication. It contains an illuminating assessment of the art of this period. The plates unfortunately are not of high quality. W. Geiger, *Culture of Ceylon in Medieval Times*, ed. by Henry Bechert, Wiesbaden, 1960, is a collection of chips from a notable scholar's workshop on the Pali chronicles of Ceylon. D. T. Devendra, *Classical Sinhalese Sculpture*, London, 1958, develops an interesting thesis and has a number of well-produced illustrations. The present writer's *The Footprint of the Buddha*, London, 1958, describes the chief archaeological sites in Ceylon.

On the later traditional arts which developed out of the ancient the best record is undoubtedly that of Ananda K. Coomaraswamy, *Medieval Sinhalese Art*, originally published by the Kelmscott Press in 1908 and reissued in N.Y., Pantheon Books 1956. It throws light both on traditional Sinhalese art as it survived in the Kandyan country, and also on late nineteenth-century attitudes to traditional arts in Ceylon.

Beryl de Zoete wrote with much feeling and perception on the Kandyan and Low country dance forms in *Dance and Magic Drama in Ceylon*, London, 1957. Her account of the South Indian dance forms, which are well known in Tamil art circles, in *The Other Mind*, London, 1953, should also be consulted.

Sinhalese Literature has been the subject of several monographs, the most interesting being Martin Wickramasinghe *Sinhalese Literature*, translated by E. R. Sarathchandra, Colombo, 1950, and C. E. Godakumbura, *Sinhalese Literature*, Colombo, 1955, much more an academic study than that of Wickramasinghe who writes as a craftsman interested in his technique. E. R. Sarathchandra's, *The Sinhalese Novel*, Colombo, 1950, examines a form developed in Sinhalese in the last hundred years and now extremely popular. The same author's *The Sinhalese Folk Play and the Modern Stage*, Colombo, 1953, is a fascinating study of traditional drama and its role in the community. It is scholarly but popular in its approach.

The report of a symposium in Peradeniya on Traditional culture will be found in *Some Aspects of Traditional Sinhalese Culture*, ed. Ralph Pieris, Peradeniya, 1956. The best of the essays contributed to it on Kandyan dancing. M. D. Raghavan, *Ceylon: A Pictorial Survey of the Peoples and Arts*, Colombo, 1961, is unexciting, but it is a fuller record than most.

The new Department of Cultural Affairs, Colombo, has in recent years been producing brochures on various aspects of Sinhalese culture.

Leonard Woolf, *The Village in the Jungle*, London, 1961, remains the most sensitive imaginative record of village life in

Ceylon – the setting is the untypical Southern Province jungle in the early years of the century. The same writer's *Growing*, London, 1961, is an excellent record of colonial English outstation society and the preoccupations of an English civil servant who spent the years 1904–11 in Ceylon.

Numerous periodicals published in Ceylon, most of them unfortunately both irregular and short-lived, contain articles of value on the history, the archaeology and the culture of Ceylon. Among those which still continue in existence are *The Journal of the Ceylon Branch of the Royal Asiatic Society*, published in Colombo, and *The Ceylon Journal of Historical and Social Studies*, published in Peradeniya.

CEYLON 1796

The Maritime Provinces
and the Kandyan Kingdom

Key:
P – Puttalam
W – Walapone

Jaffna

Mannar

Vanni

Jaffna

Kommandement

Trincomalee

Nuwarakalawiya

Kalpitiya

P

Puttalam

Tamankaduwa

Seven

Chilaw

Colombo

Korales

Matale

Batticaloa

Bintenna

Kandy

Negombo

Four
Korales

Wellassa

W

Three
Korales

Udapalata

Colombo

Sabaragamuwa

Uva

Kalutara

Galle Kommandement

Galle

Matara

CEYLON 1966

Key:
CP – Central Province
WP – Western Province
SP – Southern Province

Jaffna

Jaffna

NORTHERN

PROVINCE

Mannar

Mannar

Vavuniya

Trincomalee

Trincomalee

Anuradhapura

Anuradhapura

Kala River

NORTHERN CENTRAL PROVINCE

Puttalam

Puttalam

Polonnaruwa

EASTERN PROVINCE

NORTH WESTERN

PROVINCE

CP

Mahaweli River

Batticaloa

Chilaw

Kurunegala

Matale

Batticaloa

Chilaw

Kurunegala

Matale

Kandy

Negombo

Kegalla

Kandy

CP

PROVINCE

OF UVA

Galoya Dam

Colombo

Kegalla

Nuwara

Colombo

Eliya

SABARAGAMUWA

Badulla

Kumbukkan River

WP

Kalutara

Ratnapura

Monaragala

Kalutara

Galle

SP

SP

Hambantota

Matara

Hambantota

Matara

296

INDEX